Fighting for Kate

The Inspirational Story of a Family's Battle and Victory over Cancer

L. Erin Miller

5 Fold Media
Visit us at www.5foldmedia.com

Fighting for Kate: The Inspirational Story of a Family's Battle and Victory over Cancer
Copyright 2017 by L. Erin Miller
Published by 5 Fold Media, LLC
www.5foldmedia.com

ISBN: 978-1-942056-57-7

Library of Congress Control Number: 2017956235

Printed in the USA.

To Nonna and, of course, Kate

Acknowledgments

To my husband: Brandon, when we first married, I never could have pictured how beautiful our marriage would become. Not perfect, but still beautiful. Our journey with Kate revealed what a godly man you are and how much I admire you. You keep me grounded. You remind me of what is most important in life and make me a better person. I am so thankful our paths crossed on that Fourth of July so many years ago.

To Kate, Jenna, and Elijah: You have brought such joy to my life, each in your own unique way. I pray that in spite of my flaws and mistakes as a mom, you will continue blooming in your love for God and desire to serve others. I thank God every day for the blessing of being your mom.

To my parents and in-laws: Your support over the years has been invaluable. When our lives stopped to battle cancer, you took our battle on as well. Thank you for being a solid rock to lean upon during our weakest times.

To our extended family, friends, and brothers and sisters in Christ: We could not have made it through this journey without you. Your prayers and generosity brought us to our knees. Our journey was by no means a short one and you saw us through the years with great grace and longsuffering. We pray that when it is our time to encourage, we will possess the same qualities.

To the nurses, doctors, and staff at St. Jude Children's Research Hospital and Affiliate Clinic: We are forever indebted to you for the life of our child. The time, attention, care, and love you gave to our family will never be forgotten. While we would never have chosen this journey for our family, we count it a blessing and privilege to have you in our lives.

To 5 Fold Media: Choosing a publishing company for this book was a huge decision. Within a few days of signing with you, I knew we had made the right choice. I have the utmost appreciation for the guidance and information you have provided along the way and, most importantly, for keeping God as your number one priority.

Contents

Foreword

*I*t was a typical evening with the "young marrieds." As minister for the Church of Christ on Hughes Road and Gooch Lane in Madison, Alabama, I, along with my wife, Pam, enjoyed hosting these dedicated parents in our home, hoping to help and encourage them in their spiritual growth. Our monthly Bible study followed its normal course with the adults downstairs for a study, while brave and dutiful Pam entertained the horde of children upstairs so that their parents could have uninterrupted time in biblical pursuits. Kate was her usual three-year-old self that evening. After her normal stop to move the mouth of a low-standing nutcracker soldier, she was off to join the other kids.

The abnormal bruising on her legs, however, was of concern to her parents. Her mother, Erin, planned a doctor's visit just to make sure they were nothing of major significance. Little did she know that in a matter of three days their world would be turned upside down.

Leukemia is a frightening word for anyone. When used to describe the medical condition of a child, it is horrifying. Parents faced with this diagnosis for a son or daughter are immediately placed in a situation that will forever change not only their lives but their view of life itself. This is the situation in which Erin Miller found herself upon hearing the grim words of Kate's doctor. Along with her husband Brandon, she began a journey to save Kate's life from this terrible disease. Their world now consisted of doctors, infusions, lumbar punctures, and countless hours of prayer for the help of their heavenly Father through the odyssey of the months and years that would follow.

Faith is a necessary cornerstone of Christianity, yet its strength is known only when tests come. The New Testament writer James stated,

"Count it all joy, my brothers, when you meet trials of various kinds" (James 1:2). He does not teach that trials bring joy; rather, the rich fruit of active faith produced by these trials brings joy to the follower of Christ. Faith was born in the Miller household as the uncertainty of Kate's illness tested her young parents and as they met and faced these "trials of various kinds."

In *Fighting for Kate*, Erin selflessly lifts the curtain to allow readers to know what was happening in these years. To those who watched from a distance, she demonstrated strength, determination, and strong faith. In her writings, Erin reveals not only times of spiritual strength but also the lonely hours of doubt and fear that she, along with Brandon, faced as they watched the suffering of their precious daughter. Her story is highlighted with illustrations of support received from strong and godly grandparents, dedicated friends, and encouraging fellow Christians. Interspersed in the anguished account of Kate's illness are lighthearted anecdotes from her vivacious little sister, Jenna, and the joys and challenges of adding to their family during this grievous time.

Readers of *Fighting for Kate* will find a blessing within its pages. Whether a parent facing similar struggles with a child, a Christian in a time of challenge, or simply someone interested in the story, this book provides encouragement and strength. It reminds and equips us with strength to trust in God when the storms of life prevail. It strengthens our faith.

The life of a child is a precious jewel. In it flourishes hopes, dreams, and optimism for the future. *Fighting for Kate* reveals how the life of a child can influence parents and countless others to a closer walk with God. Erin's story will also help you in your trek to higher ground.

— Minister Greg Chandler
Church of Christ on Hughes Road at Gooch Lane
Madison, Alabama

Letter from the Author

Fighting for Kate began just as each chapter opens and closes—as a letter. From the day I found out I was pregnant with each of our babies, I began writing letters to them and have continued to do so every few months since. The letters' topics range from foods they liked and hated, new physical feats achieved, funny things they said or did, and accounts of whatever was going on in our lives at the time.

Needless to say, my letters to Kate became quite lengthy and frequent after she was diagnosed with cancer. These letters, however, proved invaluable when I sat down to turn our journey into a book. My husband Brandon traveled often for work, so after the kids went to bed at night, I wrote. Sometimes I wrote for five minutes; sometimes I wrote late into the night.

Journaling the ups and downs of our journey was therapeutic. The pain and stress and joys and triumphs poured out of me and collected in a pool of words on the computer screen. But sometimes the story was too hard to tell. The turn of events at the end of Kate's treatment was such a shock that it was months before I was able to write about it. It was too emotionally raw to dwell upon and put into words. Even after allowing time for the wound to heal, I still wept as I wrote and recounted the end of treatment. The anguish and fear and worry of those weeks was just too deep and perhaps always will be.

Two years after beginning, I typed the final words of our story. I felt a sense of closure and peace. That chapter of our lives was over and our new chapter of life after cancer had begun.

From the very day Kate was diagnosed, we prayed that God would be glorified in our journey. This novel is an extension of that prayer. I pray that you as the reader can find hope and encouragement within the pages of this book. I pray that your faith in our gracious God will be strengthened. And I pray for steadfastness as you battle your way through whatever trial you may face in life, always remembering that the mighty God is fighting for you every step of the way.

May God bless you!

L Erin Miller

P.S. I have included a "Definition of Terms" and a chart listing Kate's treatment plan at the back of the book. It took us weeks to learn the names of these chemotherapies and medications. Hopefully, the definition of terms will help you navigate through the medical jargon in the book and the chart showing Kate's treatment plan will give you a big picture of what Kate endured.

> *"Count it all joy, my brothers, when you meet trials of various kinds, for you know that the testing of your faith produces steadfastness"*
> (James 1:2-3).

Chapter 1: For the Good

March 26, 2013

Dear Kate,

There are moments in our lives we will never forget—the day we graduated from high school, the day your daddy got down on one knee and asked me to be his wife, the day we said, "I do," the birth of our sweet babies. The memories of these days fill our hearts with joy and bring smiles to our faces.

But then there are days we remember for other reasons—days when we knew our lives would be changed forever, days when every detail and every moment was seared into our memories as if with a branding iron, days when the world stopped turning for the briefest of seconds.

Today, March 26 of 2013, is a day we will never forget. Today, you were diagnosed with cancer.

*P*ump it! Pump it up!" shouted the peppy aerobics instructor on the television as she bounced across the screen, leaping with boundless amounts of energy. I dodged two pairs of tiny feet as I bounced across the living room, mimicking the instructor's movements. Kate's and Jenna's little feet skipped around the room, blonde hair flying behind them as they exercised with me.

"Pump it! Pump it! Pump some milk for Jenna!" yelled my three-year-old Kate.

I briefly paused from my workout, bent double with laughter, but also amazed at what her young mind remembered. Jenna was now eighteen months old and my nursing days were months behind me. We finished the last few minutes of our workout and I glanced at the wooden clock on the mantle. *Almost noon*, I noted.

"All right, girls," I said, turning off the television. "We need to go ahead and eat a quick lunch and then take naps. Your doctor's appointment is in a couple of hours, Kate."

"But I'm not sick!" Kate whined as she stomped to the kitchen table for lunch. Inwardly, I sighed.

"I know," I replied as I headed into the kitchen. "We're just going to get those bruises on your legs checked out." *I hate taking a kid to the doctor for bruises,* I thought to myself. *I mean, she's a kid! She's going to have bruises!*

Over the past two weeks, bruises had begun rapidly accumulating on Kate's legs, and we even found a few stray ones on her torso. She had been taking a gymnastics class for the past month, so at first, I had dismissed them. But after her last class, I had been helping her change clothes and when I took off her pants, I'd gasped in shock. The bruises on her legs were glaring and ghastly. I snapped a picture of the bruises with my phone and showed it to friends over the weekend, asking if their kids' legs ever looked like that.

"Never that bad," the moms had murmured.

Kate had also been more whiny the past couple of weeks and often complained of feeling tired, but we'd been really busy the past month and I guessed that maybe she was also going through a growth spurt. However, when red dots appeared on her torso over the weekend, I took another picture and e-mailed the pictures to my mom. Mom had called that morning and joined my husband Brandon in urging me to take her to the doctor.

It is rare that I actually listen to my mom. If Mom has a tendency to overreact to things, I definitely have a tendency to underreact. But the urgency in her voice reluctantly caused me to telephone Kate's doctor and schedule an appointment for that afternoon.

"Mom," Kate's voice brought me out of my daydream, "I'm hungry and I'm really sleepy."

"Hung-ee!" Jenna squealed, echoing her sister.

"Coming," I replied, quickly spreading some peanut butter and jelly onto bread and making plates of sandwiches, fruit, and chips for the girls and myself.

We ate lunch, cleaned up, and then the girls and I piled onto Kate's bed to read our Bible story and a book before naptime. After our stories, I carried my chubby Jenna to her crib, sang to her for a minute and laid her down. Then I headed back to Kate's room to sing to her, but she was already fast asleep.

She was worn out, I thought as I quietly closed her door. I headed for the shower, knowing I had less than an hour before I needed to wake the girls up to leave for the doctor. Forty-five minutes later, I gently shook each girl awake, slipped on their shoes, ran a quick brush through their hair as they rubbed their bleary blue eyes, and loaded them into the car.

Little did I know then that neither Kate nor I would be returning home that evening.

We drove the short drive to the pediatricians' office where we were scheduled to see Dr. Laue. Kate's regular pediatrician, Dr. Klemm, was out of town for spring break, so Dr. Laue was filling in for him. We had seen him a time or two before and Kate always called him Dr. Loud, which was quite appropriate as he tended to burst into the exam room and was very enthusiastic.

We waited only a few minutes in the empty waiting room before Kate's name was called and we headed back to a room. The nurse with curly black hair began clicking away on the computer in the room as I settled onto the bench with both girls nestled in my lap.

"Reason for visit?" she asked, briefly glancing in my direction.

I pulled my cell phone out of my pocket and found the pictures of Kate's bruised legs and tiny red dots covering her torso. "Well, she's just had some bad bruises lately and then these red dots appeared a few days ago. My mom instructed me to get her to a doctor right away, but she's a grandmother, so she worries a lot," I laughed and rolled my eyes. The nurse's eyes widened at the picture of Kate's battered legs so I quickly explained, "She's been taking a gymnastics class this month so she probably just has extra bruises from that. Her last class was last week and her legs already look better."

Pursing her lips together, she continued clicking away on the screen, took Kate's vitals, and then bustled out of the room to get Dr. Laue. I pulled a few books out of a brown wooden basket in the room and began reading one of them to the girls. A few pages into the book, the door suddenly flung open and Dr. Laue briskly entered the room.

"Hello, Mrs. Miller! What seems to be going on today with Miss Kate?" he asked as he settled himself on the rolling stool in the room.

I showed him the same pictures I had shown the nurse, offered the same explanation, and Dr. Laue's eyes widened, just as the nurse's eyes had.

"Well, let's get some bloodwork and go from there," he decided, hopping up from the stool and quickly heading out the door.

Kate found a book about trains in the basket and, being an avid train fan, wanted to read it right away. The book made different sounds with each button that she pushed, and the girls quickly became absorbed in pushing the buttons. Sounds of piercing train whistles and whooshing engines filled the room.

A few minutes later, a young lab technician entered the room carrying the infamous basket that terrifies any kid who knows what lies inside. Kate glanced up as he entered and immediately became concerned with what was about to happen when she noticed the vial-filled basket.

"What's he doing, Mommy?" Kate asked as he gently took off her tennis shoe and began pulling off her sock.

"He's just trying to help you get feeling better," I explained and I tightened my arms around her in preparation for the wrestling match that was about to ensue.

Kate's eyes grew wide as she saw what was coming toward her big toe. "No," she began screaming. "Don't poke me! Don't poke me!" I tightened my arms even more, trying to hold her still.

After a quick jab, bright red blood began to bead on the end of her toe and Kate's wails escalated. She sobbed as he firmly squeezed drop after drop of her blood into a tiny vial. He quickly covered her toe with a bandage and I slipped on her sock and shoe. I gave her reassuring pats on the back, whispering to her that everything was going to be okay. Jenna, who had been watching the scene unfold with wide eyes, joined in comforting her sister.

"It otay," she murmured, nuzzling Kate's side.

"All done? All done?" Kate whimpered.

"Yes, he's all done," I confirmed and quickly redirected her attention to her book. One whoosh of the engine and clickety-clack of the wheels and the drama was momentarily forgotten.

A few minutes later, however, the lab technician came back into the room. "The machine didn't work. I need to check her again," he mumbled as he shut the door. He kept his eyes lowered as he approached us.

The return of the lab tech sent poor Kate into another fit of terror and we struggled to hold her down to get her shoe and sock off again. He peeled the bandage back and muttered, "That's what I thought," as blood still oozed from her toe. He was able to squeeze another vial of blood and Kate was even more traumatized that she was being made to suffer again in such a short period of time. As soon as he collected what he needed, he headed out the door again.

In the back of my mind, a red flag was waving as I considered the curiosity of needing to draw more blood and the technician's seeming discomfort. I quickly pushed aside the fear creeping up inside me and focused on reading some more pages of the book to the girls.

When the door opened again, Kate panicked, but then relaxed when she saw it was Dr. Laue.

I smiled and looked expectantly at him as he sat down on the rolling stool again and faced me. "All right," he began without a moment's hesitation. "We've run her blood twice and it looks like what we're dealing with here is leukemia."

The smile on my face froze as his words sank in. The room became absolutely still and for the briefest of moments, the world stopped spinning on its axis. "Leukemia?" I questioned, confused. *As in cancer?* I thought. *Aren't you supposed to tell me to go home and you'll call me with the results in a few days while I wait anxiously by the phone?*

"Yes. We want you at the emergency room at the hospital *immediately*. As far as making the decision about where Kate needs to be treated, we have the choice of sending you to Birmingham or to St. Jude in Memphis. I want you in the best care possible, so I am going to contact the Affiliate Clinic for St. Jude here in Huntsville and the St. Jude doctor will meet you at the emergency room." Dr. Laue was not wasting a single second in unloading this news to me. "Do you have someone to keep her?" he continued, nodding at Jenna.

"I...I...we can find someone." I stumbled over my words, still trying to wrap my mind around what he was telling me. This was all happening so fast. "When you say immediately, are you talking about right now? Or this weekend?" My voice faded away as I still tried to grasp what was happening.

"I want you there *right now*," he urged. "I can get one of my nurses to sit with the girls while you make whatever phone calls you need." His eyes softened momentarily as he noticed the stricken look in my eyes. "In terms of cancer, leukemia has a survival rate of over ninety percent. I had a patient many years back who was diagnosed with it and he's a teenager now and doing wonderfully."

Cancer. Survival rate. Were we really using these terms in reference to *my* daughter? My Kate? The little girl who had been running around so full of life a few hours ago? People who had cancer were hooked up to IVs and in hospital beds, clinging to life. Not my Kate.

I took a deep breath as I grabbed my phone and stood up. Dr. Laue stuck his head out the door and asked one of the nurses to come sit with Kate and Jenna. I followed him out of the room and as he went to call the St. Jude doctor, wandered into the back of the building until I found a quiet office.

Taking a deep breath, I dialed Brandon's work number, which I only call when I need to get in touch with him immediately. The last time I had called it was when I was in labor with Jenna.

"Hey," he answered and I felt my heart constrict, the first feelings of panic rising in my chest.

"Hey," I replied in a shaky voice. "Brandon, we're at the doctor and they've run some bloodwork on Kate. Her doctor thinks...he thinks she has..." I couldn't even say the word. If I said it, it made it real. I took a deep breath and forced out the words. "He thinks she has leukemia."

Brandon was quiet for a moment. I knew he was trying to wrap his mind around what I was telling him, just as I had done only minutes before.

"Are you serious?" he finally asked in disbelief.

"Dr. Laue says we need to go to the emergency room immediately and that you'll need to meet us there. We also need to call someone to get Jenna."

"I am on my way right now," Brandon replied, his voice calm. "Who do we know that works at or near the hospital who can get Jenna?"

"Well, Jana works at the pharmacy in the hospital, but she gets off around three. She's long gone by now."

"Erin, it's just now three o'clock. I'd try calling her."

Three o'clock? It felt as though hours had passed. *Has it really only been half an hour?*

"Okay, I'll call her. Can you call my parents to tell them what's going on and ask them to come? We're going to need someone to keep Jenna, but I don't know for how long."

"I'll call them right now," Brandon answered and then he paused. "Everything is going to be okay. I love you."

"I know. I love you, too." I tried to sound strong and confident, but felt my insides beginning to crumble. As I hung up the phone, I fell to my knees, clutching the blue plastic chair in the room, gasping for air. In long, shuddering breaths, I cried out to God to please help us be strong. I pleaded with Him to watch over Kate.

Once I caught my breath, I called Jana's phone. In a thick fog, I briefly explained to her that Kate's pediatrician was sending us to the emergency room and asked if she could meet us there to get Jenna. Jana was on the tram headed to her car, but readily agreed, no questions asked, to turn around and meet us.

I headed back toward the exam room where the girls were waiting and caught a glimpse of Dr. Laue behind the desk talking earnestly to someone on the phone. I stuck my head back into the room where the girls were and asked the nurse if it was time for us to leave.

"Wait just a minute for Dr. Laue to get back. He's on the phone with the St. Jude doctor right now."

The girls were completely oblivious to my exit and my return. They were fully absorbed in the train book. I leaned against the exam table next to them, my mind blank and my eyes focused somewhere in the distance.

Dr. Laue came in, snapping me out of my daze, and told us Dr. Jennifer Cox, a doctor at the St. Jude Affiliate Clinic in Huntsville, would be waiting for us at the emergency room. I offered a small smile to Dr. Laue and the nurse and thanked them both. After taking a deep breath, the girls and I headed to our car.

Once buckled, Kate asked if we were going home. "Well, Dr. Laue wants you to see another doctor so we're going to head up the road here to visit her."

Kate began crying, "I don't need to see another doctor. I don't want another needle! I'm all better, Mommy! I'm all better!"

I tried to smile and reassure her, although all I wanted to do was turn the car around, head for home, and pretend that the doctor's appointment had never happened. "Dr. Laue just wants to make sure you are all well and this doctor is going to help you get all better." But my smile faltered as I spoke.

We pulled into the parking lot of the emergency room just a couple of minutes later and my heart jumped at the sight of Brandon, already waiting beside his silver truck. We climbed out of the car and I tried to smile bravely for him as he hugged the girls. He hugged me too, his brown hair brushing against my face, and whispered in my ear, "She's watching us. We have to be strong for her."

"I know," I agreed, looking determinedly into his startling blue-green eyes. Taking a deep breath, I scooped Jenna up in my arms while he hoisted Kate into his.

The four of us headed inside. As we came through the doors, a team of nurses and doctors were waiting for us on the left and Jana was waiting on the right. One of the doctors, a petite woman with chin-length strawberry-blonde hair, walked forward. I assumed she was Dr. Cox.

"I'll go on with Kate," Brandon offered as Dr. Cox and the nurses escorted him and Kate immediately through the doors into the back.

"Hey," Jana greeted with a look of concern in her eyes.

I couldn't even offer any explanation to her of what was going on. I gave her a quick hug and then passed Jenna over to her, tears falling as I did so. I was scared to let go of my baby girl with the pretty blue eyes, soft round cheeks, and full pink lips, already knowing that in this moment our lives were changing forever. I handed Jana my keys, telling her where my car was parked, and gave her a quick rundown of Jenna's evening routine. I told her that Mom and Dad were supposed to be on their way up, but I had not talked to them so I had no idea when that would be.

"We'll be fine," Jana reassured me. With one final hug and kiss for Jenna, I rushed through the doors Brandon and Kate had gone through moments earlier. A nurse motioned for me to come into the room to the right and I walked in to find two more nurses bustling about the room.

"Hi, Mom," one of the nurses called. She offered a quick explanation that they were going to need to get some blood from Kate and how they were going to go about doing it. Brandon was already on the other side of the bed, holding Kate's hand and attempting to comfort her as she watched everyone with terror-filled eyes.

I began answering a hundred different questions for another nurse who was manning the computer while the first nurse tended to Kate. After I'd answered the final question, the two nurses worked together to get an IV started in Kate's little arm. Brandon struggled to hold her down as the nurses pushed the needle into the tiny vein on her left arm, but finally the deed was done and they wrapped a board under her arm to keep her from moving it.

The first half hour or so was filled with the hustle and bustle of nurses in and out of the room—getting blood, monitoring Kate, and asking questions. A sweet child life specialist entertained Kate with toys, coloring books, and a movie. Before long, Dr. Cox entered the room. She introduced herself to me, having already met Brandon when he and Kate first got there, and then motioned for us to follow her down the hall to a room labeled "Counsel Room." As soon as I saw the box of tissues sitting on the table in the middle of the room, I knew this was not a room where we were to receive good news.

Dr. Cox didn't waste a single second. "We've been looking at the numbers sent to us from Dr. Laue, but we are running our own tests as well to verify what he sent and gather additional information too."

She briefly explained to us how Kate's white blood cell count was very high, while her platelets and hemoglobin levels were critically low—all of which indicated the presence of leukemia cells in her blood.

I dug deep to try and recall whatever I could from my science classes in high school. I remembered that hemoglobin were red blood cells that carried oxygen, while white blood cells were responsible for fighting infection. It was still hard to follow everything Dr. Cox was telling us, especially in regard to our daughter.

Dr. Cox continued to explain that Kate would need some fluids and would need a platelet transfusion to help stabilize her little body before we could leave for Memphis. She said we would either be med-flighted there or travel by ambulance. One of us would ride with Kate and the other would need to drive separately. Kate would also need a blood transfusion, but because her counts were so skewed, giving her blood at this point would shock her system and cause her to have a stroke. The blood transfusion would have to wait until her body was more stable.

Around this time, a nurse entered the room bearing a piece of paper with some numbers jotted down on it and handed it to Dr. Cox. Dr. Cox's eyes widened as she looked at the numbers. "These are Kate's lab results. We want her in Memphis *now*. We will give her the fluids and platelet transfusion, and I hope to have you on the road by eight o'clock."

Brandon began to address the logistics of our trip and stay in Memphis. How long did we need to pack for? Did Dr. Cox have information on hotels so we could make reservations for our time there?

"I would pack to stay for one to two weeks," she instructed. With a small smile, she added, "And don't worry about anything. I think you will find that St. Jude will take *very* good care of you." She handed Brandon a booklet about St. Jude and said we could read through it whenever we got a chance. It would answer a lot of our questions about what to expect.

Brandon turned toward me. "Do you want to ride with Kate, and I'll go home and pack for us?"

During the past few minutes tears had suddenly begun to fill my eyes as the reality of what was happening sank in. I reached for a tissue to dab them away, cleared my throat, and nodded my head. "May I have a piece of paper and a pen?" I asked Dr. Cox.

"Sure," Dr. Cox readily agreed, handing me a pad of paper and the pen that she'd been holding. She hesitated for a moment and then she and the nurse stood up. "I'll give you two a few minutes alone. You can go back down to Kate's room whenever you are ready." With that, they left, the door closing solidly behind them.

I began making a list of things that Kate and I would need over the next couple of weeks so that Brandon could pack our bags, but it was impossible to do so as the tears I had been holding back began spilling over onto the paper. Brandon reached to take my hand and, suddenly, we both jumped up from the table, wrapped our arms fiercely around each other, and cried onto each other's shoulders. After a few moments, Brandon clutched me to him and whispered in my ear, "She's going to be okay. God will take care of her. This is just a bump in the road. It's just a bump in the road."

I buried my face in his chest. "God will. I'm just scared." I pulled away and looked at him. "All I could think while Dr. Cox was talking was what if Kate dies while we're not with her? All I want to do right now is get back in that room with her. I don't want to be away from her."

We both took some deep breaths to calm ourselves and then sat back down at the table to finish our list. After jotting down a few more items, I read over the list once more and then we headed back to our daughter.

The nurse intercepted us along the way and showed us to the new room where Kate had been taken. She was propped up on a pillow, hooked up to an IV, and was watching a movie and eating a grape popsicle. She had been begging to eat a snack, but solid food had been put on hold for the time being. She would have to be satisfied with popsicles—lots and lots of popsicles.

We stood in the door of Kate's room, watching her for a moment, taking it all in. After a minute, Kate spotted us and grinned.

How is it she is so sick? I wondered. *She is smiling at us and eating a popsicle. She looks so content! How can it be?*

The nurse came in behind us and informed us that they needed to take Kate for a chest scan.

"I'll go with her. Do you want to call your parents?" I asked Brandon as I helped Kate up from the bed.

"Yes, now that we know better what's going on, I'll go give them a call." Grabbing his phone, he left the room.

Kate was not a huge fan of having to sit on a little stool away from her mommy, but cooperated long enough for them to get the scans that they needed. Brandon arrived back in her room just shortly after we did.

L. Erin Miller

Right behind him was Kate's nurse, carrying a bag of what she identified as platelets. She hooked the bag up to Kate's line.

"This will take about an hour to run," she explained. "And then we'll get you on the road to St. Jude."

A few minutes after Kate's bag of platelets finished, I noticed that a child-sized stretcher had been rolled outside the sliding glass door of her room. A team of paramedics was talking with the nurses outside and came in to introduce themselves. One paramedic explained that I would not be able to ride in the back with Kate, but would have to ride up front with the driver.

"You'll be able to see her," he explained, "but she won't be able to see you. If I could give you any advice, it would be to try and get some sleep on the way over because it's going to be a really long night after you arrive in Memphis."

I smiled feebly at the thought of sleeping on our drive and he smiled back in understanding. "I know," he said, "but maybe just close your eyes or something. We're going to finish up a few things here and hope to be on the road in about fifteen minutes."

I helped Kate up and down the hall to use the bathroom before we left. When we emerged, the paramedics stood smiling, waiting on us. "Ready?" asked one.

"Ready," I nodded and turned to Kate, forcing a big smile on my face. "We're going for a ride, okay?" I told her and hoisted her onto the stretcher.

As I tried to step away from Kate, she began screaming. A couple of the paramedics tried to hold her down while another strapped her to the stretcher. This only sent Kate into further hysteria.

"Mommy, don't leave me! Mommy, don't leave me!" she wailed, straining with all her might against the straps that held her from me. Over and over she cried for me, and over and over she reached for me, trying her best to wrap her little arms around me and never let go.

My heart breaking, I smiled as best as I could and spoke to her reassuringly. "It's okay, baby. I'm not leaving you. I'm going with you.

25

I'll be riding up front." I continued to repeat these words over and over. As she clutched my hand, I felt the sobs rising in my throat. *Don't cry, I told myself. Be strong.* I followed the stretcher out to the ambulance, holding on to her hand the entire time. She begged me again and again not to leave her and I kept repeating those words until her little stretcher was pushed into the back of the ambulance. Brandon climbed in for a quick hug and kiss, climbed back out, and the doors were shut.

As soon as the doors thumped closed, I stepped to the side of the ambulance where she couldn't see me and let the sobs erupt from my chest. Brandon grabbed me into a bear hug.

"I just hate to see her so afraid," I sobbed. "I don't want her to be scared."

We stood there for a minute. Then, as became the story of our grieving over the upcoming days, it was time to move on. The paramedics sat in the ambulance, waiting. I gave Brandon a final hug and last minute packing instructions and jumped into the passenger seat.

Kate had already calmed down and was actually chatting with the three paramedics sitting in the back with her. I called out to her from the front seat, "Hey, baby girl!"

She squealed, "Mommy!" and tried to turn her head to see me. "I can't see you, Mommy!"

"I know," I replied, "but I can see you!"

One paramedic called out from the back, "We usually find that the kids are out within the first fifteen minutes of the ride, so it should get quiet back here pretty soon." With that, the driver pulled out of the hospital parking lot, and we were on the road to Memphis.

Kate, however, did not fall asleep in the first fifteen minutes of the ride. Nor did she in the next fifteen minutes or even in the next two hours. I could hear her talking off and on with her new buddies in the back, and occasionally they would share what she was saying with me. She kept on asking who "That Man" was sitting behind her. At one point when they tried to turn the light off to get her to go to sleep, she told them to turn it back on so "That Man" could see how cute she was!

I chatted with the driver some, but spent most of the trip staring out the window. My mind was blank as I watched the dark silhouettes of trees blur into the past. The current state of my mind was a stark contrast to the shock and scrambling it had gone through over the past few hours. Now, I felt lost. My world had just crumbled around me and I had absolutely no idea what lay ahead around the next curve in the road. A single tear slid down my cheek. I did try to close my eyes for a little bit, but sleep did not come.

We entered the outskirts of Memphis, Tennessee just after midnight. Kate had been asleep for about forty-five minutes and I was glad she was able to get some rest. We finally pulled up at the black, wrought iron gates of St. Jude Children's Research Hospital.

The guard checked for Kate's name on his list, checked the driver's licenses of everyone in the ambulance, and then opened the gates to let us through. I leaned forward to catch my first glimpse of the hospital—tan stucco with red trim, only a few stories tall and sprawling, with large windows that allowed a glimpse into the main entrance of the hospital.

A tall stone statue of St. Jude, the patron saint of hopeless cases, stood to greet us. *Hopeless cases?* My heart lurched in my chest as I looked back at my precious daughter in the stretcher behind me.

A nurse was waiting for us just inside the front door of the hospital and came out to greet us as we pulled up front. I took a deep breath as the paramedics unloaded Kate's stretcher from the ambulance. She was wide awake now and wide-eyed. I tried to smile at her reassuringly, but it was hard to calm the fear that was creeping in my heart. I took her little hand in mine and we headed toward the door of St. Jude, ready to take on whatever lay on the other side of those doors—together.

Before you were born, your daddy and I prayed that God would bless us with a healthy baby. After you arrived, we petitioned God to guide us as new parents. We prayed that we would teach you above all to love Him and to point you on the road to heaven.

Never, in all our rose-colored fantasies, did we ever imagine this dark day of March 26. Never could we have fathomed the strength of the fear that assaulted our hearts or the feelings of utter helplessness and loss of control.

One truth that rang clear on this day, however, is that God is good. And on that we can rely. We may not understand today why this is happening to our family. We may never understand.

But God will work this for good. With His all-powerful, all-knowing, mysterious and loving ways, He will work this for good.

And so today, we begin a new prayer. Today, we pray that we will let His light shine through us even when things seem dark, that we will show our children the true meaning of faith, and that we will give praise to Him as we face the most difficult time of our lives.

God will work this for good, Kate, if we trust in Him.

Love,

Mommy

"And we know that God causes all things to work together for good to those who love God, to those who are called according to His purpose" (Romans 8:28 NASB).

" 'For I know the plans I have for you,' declares the Lord, 'plans for welfare and not for evil, to give you a future and a hope'" (Jeremiah 29:11).

Chapter 2: Fighting for Kate

March 29, 2013

Dear Kate,

The Intensive Care Unit (ICU) has the word "intensive" in it for a reason. From the moment we were whisked upstairs and into your room in ICU in the wee hours of Wednesday morning, our days and nights have been non-stop! We are not sure that there is such a word as "rest" in ICU, or frankly even the word "mealtime" in ICU. This past week has been the most difficult week of our lives—mentally, emotionally, and physically. However, even through the most trying week of our lives, God has still given us a ray of light, has given us hope, and has reminded us that He, in all things, is watching over our little family each and every moment of the day.

*A*s Kate's stretcher was wheeled through the doors of her room in the ICU, our team of paramedics from Huntsville began handing over paperwork to Kate's new team of doctors and nurses. Kate was frightened and clutched my hand so tightly that her knuckles were white. She refused to let go of me as the nurses attempted to move her from her stretcher into her bed, only agreeing to be moved as long as she could sit in my lap. She clung to me as we sat on her bed, and honestly,

I clung to her as well. Fear gripped my heart and a nervous anticipation settled in my stomach.

Once again, I began answering a million questions as they were fired at me one after another by a nurse while a child life specialist tried to set Kate up with some entertainment—movies, coloring books, stickers, and a few toy cars. Kate's eyes lit up at the toy cars and her hand immediately held on to a tiny blue one.

Dr. Nora, the doctor on call for the night shift, came in to sit with me after I finished answering the nurse's questions. Tall and thin with her brown hair pulled back into a ponytail and a soft smile on her face, she helped ease a little of my nervousness.

Dr. Nora sat on a rolling stool opposite me and asked very kindly, "What do you know about why you're here?"

I took a deep breath and slowly replied, "I know that they think Kate has leukemia. And I know that leukemia is cancer of the blood." I paused, thinking. "And I know Dr. Cox said to expect to be here for a week or two. And then we're done?" I asked hesitantly.

Dr. Nora gave a small smile. "Well, you're correct on most of that. However, you should expect to be here for the next six to eight weeks, and the treatment plan for leukemia lasts two and a half to three years."

I felt as if I'd been punched in the stomach and sat in stunned silence as the news sunk in. *Six to eight weeks in Memphis? Three years of treatment?* Three years seemed unthinkable. Insurmountable. Impossible.

A few of the upcoming events on our calendar were going to need to be cancelled, but the thought that stung the most was mine and Brandon's recent plan to begin trying for a third baby. That hope crumbled away as we sat in the ICU. Immediately, I felt guilty that the thought had even crossed my mind when my daughter just had been diagnosed with cancer. It seemed petty and selfish.

Dr. Nora respected my silence for a moment and then answered my random jumbled questions as they began pouring from my mouth. "What happens next? How long until she is cured? Will we be in the hospital the entire two months?"

Dr. Nora answered these questions briefly, but then explained we would just take this one step at a time. Kate would be placed in the care of Dr. Ching-Hon Pui, who would be by to meet us first thing in the morning. She encouraged us to get some sleep because the rest of the day would be a long one. And then she was gone.

During Dr. Nora's visit, nurses continued bustling in and out of the room, hooking Kate up to numerous machines as well as to a bag of fluids, taking her blood pressure, drawing blood from the line in her arm, and checking her temperature. Every touch, every procedure, even a mere glance from a nurse elicited cries and screams from Kate. She was petrified, and so was I.

Soon after the doctor left, Brandon appeared outside Kate's sliding glass door with a couple of bags slung over his shoulder. I was relieved to see his face and he gave me a tired smile. The night nurse assigned to Kate followed Brandon into the room.

"My name is Jaq," she said with a smile. "I need to go over some rules with you that you'll need to follow while you're in the ICU." She proceeded to review a myriad of rules and regulations about procedures in the ICU ranging from washing our hands every time we left and returned to Kate's room, to keeping a record of Kate's urine output, to making sure Kate's blankie that Brandon had just delivered to her was washed daily, and much more—all designed to keep Kate as healthy as possible during her stay. While Kate sat in a daze watching a movie and holding her blue car, the nurse showed us the family room that attached to her room. It had a window looking into her room so she was never out of our sight if we needed a break. The family room had a small bathroom and a pull-out couch to sleep on, as well as a tall wooden cabinet for personal belongings.

"One of you can sleep in the room with Kate and the other can sleep on the couch in the family room for tonight. When the hospital opens in the morning, we can get you registered and checked in at the Grizzlies, the on-campus housing for short term stays. Later on, you'll be moved to the Ronald McDonald House," she explained as we walked back into Kate's room. She glanced at the clock on the wall, which showed it was already four in the morning. "I suggest you go ahead and try and get some sleep. Things will be busy in the morning and you'll need your rest."

Brandon and I glanced at each other. "I'll sleep in the room with Kate," he offered, "and you can get some rest on the couch."

"Okay," I agreed. I turned off the movie Kate was watching, leaned down and gave her a soft kiss on the forehead. "Mommy's going to go sleep in the next room and Daddy will sleep in here with you."

Kate jolted out of her daze and began crying, clinging to my hand. "Don't leave me, Mommy!"

I pointed through the window just behind her. "Mommy is going to be right there. You'll be able to see me and I'll be able to see you." I calmed her down enough to where she let me run into the family room. I peeked through the window and made a silly face at her and Brandon. She gave me a small smile and I waved good night to both of them as Brandon climbed into the stiff reclining chair next to her bed.

Kate took a few minutes to settle down though. Unfortunately, we had not had the presence of mind to ask the nurses at the emergency room to put the IV in her right arm rather than her left. Kate sucked her left thumb, and the board taped at her elbow prevented that thumb from reaching her mouth, try as she might. Brandon urged her to suck her right thumb instead, but she protested, "It doesn't taste the same!" When he asked what her left thumb tasted like, she replied, "Like strawberries." Finally though, with a few sucks of her right thumb and her little blue car clutched tightly in her fist, she fell fast asleep.

I unfolded a blanket, pulled it over me, and lay down in exhaustion. *How in the world am I going to fall asleep after a day like today?* Tears briefly filled my eyes as I considered everything that had happened in the past thirteen hours, but I closed my eyes and tried to erase the horrific images that were flashing through my mind. I finally dozed off a little after four.

The next thing I knew, I was awakened by the sound of Kate screaming. It was five thirty in the morning. I jumped up from the couch, threw on my shoes, and ran from the family room into her room, pausing only to squirt some hand sanitizer on my hands.

Brandon and Jaq were standing beside Kate's bed, trying to console her. Jaq had merely attempted to get vital signs and this alone had jolted Kate out of her sleep and sent her into a frenzy. Kate's cries reverberated off the walls in the room and she cowered in fear next to the rail of the hospital bed. We eventually got her calmed down and Jaq was able to take her blood pressure and temperature.

Before leaving, Jaq helped us take Kate to the bathroom. Taking Kate to the bathroom was very involved and took almost fifteen minutes from start to finish. She had to be unhooked from several different machines, all attached to her in various ways. Then we had to open a cabinet door in her room where her toilet was concealed, pull the toilet out, unplug her IV pole, lower her bedrails, and help her walk to the toilet, pushing her pole as we went. After Kate went to the bathroom, we had to measure her output in a little "hat" that sat in the toilet and then record it on a sheet. Once measured, we could dump the contents of the hat into the toilet, flush, rinse the hat in the sink to be ready for Kate's next trip, and close the toilet back into the cabinet. Once back in bed, Kate had to be reconnected to all the machines. She had a continuous drip of fluids, so we could be sure that we would be making bathroom trips frequently.

After Jaq left the room and Kate was settled in bed, Brandon and I looked wearily at each other. "Why don't you go get some sleep on the couch in the family room, and I'll sleep in the chair in here with Kate?" I offered to him.

"Are you sure?" he asked, scanning my tired eyes.

"Yes," I said and without further protest, he shuffled out of the room.

I lay down in the reclining chair, but after being awakened so abruptly, adrenaline still coursed through my veins. There was no way I could go back to sleep now. I checked my phone, charging on the floor, and began reading through hundreds of e-mails and notifications from family and friends far and wide, letting us know that they were praying for Kate. Overwhelmed by the love and support, I turned my phone off and sat in silence, staring at the wall.

A little before seven that morning, Jaq and a new nurse walked into the room. Jaq explained that it was time for a shift change and that the other nurse would be taking care of us during the day today.

The new nurse offered a smile and introduced herself as Phoebe. Phoebe appeared to be in her fifties. Her light brown hair just reached her shoulders and her face was careworn. She was very businesslike, but had a softness to her eyes that drew us to her. She explained that the night nurse would spend the next half hour or so briefing her on how Kate's night went and then she would return and go over what to expect that day with me. Meanwhile, however, a lady from registration was waiting in the hall to get us officially checked in to the hospital.

I followed the lady to the lower floor of the hospital, sneaking brief peeks at the other patients and their families around me as they filed in for a day of appointments. I tried not to stare at the array of little bald heads shining around me and at some children whose faces were covered with masks. I knew that soon enough that would be our little girl too.

The lady from registration sat with me as I provided her with the needed information. As I handed her my driver's license, I noticed that it had expired three days ago. Tears suddenly filled my eyes and she subtly nudged a box of tissues in front of me as she left the room to go make a few copies and print out our paperwork.

Now that I was out of sight of my daughter, I sat in the chair with tears streaming down my face. I wasn't really upset that my driver's license had expired; it was just the trigger for an avalanche of emotion that I had been holding back. Now, though, I didn't have to be brave; I didn't have to put on a smile and act as if everything was okay. I was finally free to grieve.

The tears couldn't last long though. The registrar came back with a few forms for me to sign and to give me our meal cards. These cards would also serve as keys to our room at the Grizzlies, the short-term housing provided by St. Jude, which we would be able to check into later that afternoon. This housing was sponsored by the professional basketball team the Grizzlies. She took me on a brief tour of the hospital and pointed out A Clinic (the leukemia clinic), the cafeteria, pharmacy, and a few other places our family would visit on a regular basis. We finished our tour in front of the elevators, and I headed back up to the third floor where the ICU was located.

It was a little after eight in the morning when I slipped back into the ICU. I peeked first into Kate's room and saw that she was still asleep. Then, slipping down the side hall, I quietly opened the door to the family room to find Brandon lying on the couch already awake. Tears were streaming down his face.

"I just can't stop crying," he whispered, wiping the tears from his eyes. "What if we lose our daughter?"

I took his hand in mine to reassure him, just as he had reassured me in the emergency room back in Huntsville. "We're not," I said firmly. "She's going to be okay."

Suddenly, we heard a small cry from the adjoining room. Kate was just beginning to wake up to start her first full day as a patient of St. Jude Children's Research Hospital. It was time to dry our tears and move on.

The day started at a sprint. Phoebe stayed busy, administering medications for Kate, drawing blood from the IV in Kate's arm, and taking her vital signs. Brandon and I spent the day unhooking Kate from numerous lines to go to the bathroom every forty-five minutes and hooking her back up, recording urine and stool output, and attempting to entertain Kate. Keeping a three-year-old confined to a hospital bed was no small task, although her not feeling well and being exhausted made our job a little easier than normal.

In between these routines, we sat down with an array of people multiple times that day. We met the social worker assigned to us, the chaplain for the hospital, the child life specialist in the ICU, more specialists, a few more specialists after that, and finally the team of doctors who would be caring for Kate.

Dr. Ching-Hon Pui, Kate's primary doctor, was a small gray-headed man in his early seventies. Brandon commented later that he thought Dr. Pui looked like a Chinese version of his dad. He was very businesslike with us, but had a subtle sparkle about him that drew our hearts to him. We had to pay very close attention when he spoke, as he was difficult to understand with his heavy accent. He was also using many terms with which we were unfamiliar. The nurses and doctors in the room hung on his every word and scurried to perform each task he assigned. We were impressed with him, but slightly afraid of him as well as we observed the reactions of the nurses and doctors!

Dr. Pui explained they had taken a sample of Kate's blood that morning and the lab would be examining it to confirm and specify Kate's diagnosis. He explained that there were two types of Leukemia—Acute Myeloid Leukemia (AML) and Acute Lymphoblastic Leukemia (ALL). ALL had the highest survival rate at over ninety percent. Then there were two subtypes of ALL, depending on when the white blood cells converted to a leukemia cell. There was ALL B-cell and ALL T-cell. ALL T-cell was the less desirable of the two. He was fairly certain that Kate had Acute Lymphoblastic Leukemia, but that it was T-cell. However, he would wait for confirmation from the lab before giving her official diagnosis.

After our brief meeting, Dr. Pui informed us that he would be back later that day to sit down with us and discuss Kate's diagnosis and treatment plan. He left the room after giving a few brief orders to Phoebe for medications he wanted Kate started on. Phoebe and another doctor remaining in the room commented that Brandon and I probably had no idea that we had just been in the room with a world-renowned doctor! Dr. Pui, apparently, was the rock star of all pediatric leukemia doctors!

The next few hours were occupied with another myriad of bathroom trips, medications, and mounds of paperwork to sign and pamphlets to read. Brandon and I attempted to take turns to go downstairs and get something to eat from the café, but as soon as one doctor left, in would walk another. Kate was finally permitted to eat again at lunch and Brandon and I hungrily ate the scraps of her unfinished food.

Shortly after lunch, Dr. Pui reappeared to meet with us, true to his word. Kate was getting very sleepy and fell asleep as we began talking, her right thumb hanging loosely in her mouth and the blue car clutched tightly in the other.

Dr. Pui began by discussing Kate's diagnosis. The lab confirmed his tentative diagnosis of Acute Lymphoblastic Leukemia, T-cell. How scary it was to find out just how sick Kate was on the inside! The average person's white blood cell count is around 5,000. Kate's registered at 539,000 back home, over one hundred times that of a normal individual! The lab work also showed that ninety-five percent of Kate's blood was leukemia cells. Also, Kate's platelets and hemoglobin had reached critical levels, which explained the bruises and petechiae (the multitude of tiny red dots covering her little frame) and the extreme fatigue she'd been experiencing the past couple of weeks.

Brandon asked the dreaded question of what would have happened if we had not caught this when we did. Dr. Pui said it was hard to say, but with her hemoglobin as low as it was, Kate was not getting enough oxygen to her brain. He speculated she more than likely would have had a stroke in a matter of days if we had not taken her to the doctor. He also commended Dr. Cox for stabilizing Kate with fluids and a platelet transfusion, saying that Kate might not have made the trip to Memphis without incident if she had not done so.

"So what happens now?" Brandon asked.

Dr. Pui explained his plans to us in his choppy English. "Normally, leukemia patients would have surgery to have port placed and begin chemotherapy right away. However, Kate's body is not stable enough yet to do so. If we attempted chemotherapy right now, the drastic plunge of white blood cells would shock system and cause seizures or stroke. Instead, I want to spend few days slowly raising platelet and hemoglobin levels by transfusions and slowly lowering white blood cell count through steroids. Once white blood cell count reaches satisfactory level, Kate will be put to sleep to have port placed. We will then also do bone marrow aspiration to determine if there are leukemia cells present in spinal fluid. Judging by percentage of leukemia cells in her blood, I am fairly confident they are present in spinal fluid too. We will also do lumbar puncture with intrathecal chemotherapy, otherwise known as LPIT. The purpose of LPIT is to send triple doses of chemotherapy through spine into Kate's brain to destroy any leukemia cells present there. Brain is so well protected, only way to get chemotherapy to it is through spine."

Dr. Pui planned to do the surgery in two days, but, of course, all of this would be determined by how well Kate responded to the steroids.

Dr. Pui also discussed the numerous chemotherapies Kate would be receiving over the next two to three years and, while I couldn't recall a single name of these drugs at that moment, their side effects were emblazoned in my memory. Words like "hair loss," "potential infertility," and "weakened heart" were the most difficult to hear. These were considered mild side effects, with "death" being the less likely side effect for each and every chemo Kate would be receiving. That "side effect" had to be pushed immediately from our minds.

Dr. Pui mentioned that one side effect of a particular chemo might cause her skin to have a yellowish tint. "But don't worry," he reassured. "She will not turn Chinese." He didn't skip a beat and plowed on into describing more side effects of other specific chemos.

Brandon and I smiled hesitantly. *Did Dr. Pui just make a joke?* We wondered. Were we allowed to laugh at his jokes? Dr. Pui was intimidating and we were too scared to laugh! After about an hour or so of going over Kate's treatment plan and answering our questions, Dr. Pui got up to leave the room.

"I think she's going to be okay," he commented, looking back and forth between us and Kate. And with that, he was gone.

All day our phones had almost continuously vibrated with messages and texts. The buzzing was occasionally interrupted by phone calls from friends and extended family members. We decided right away that we would not reply to any texts or messages individually nor would we answer our phones unless it was one of our parents. The only calls we made each day were to our parents to give them updates and to check in on Jenna who was at our house in Huntsville with my parents. We wanted all of our focus to be on Kate and the information we were trying to process from her doctors, and then we would attempt to meet our needs as well. We learned very quickly that if either of us had the desire to eat, one of us had better follow on the heels of the doctor, nurse, or specialist leaving the room because it would be about thirty seconds before someone else would walk in needing something. In fact, that first day, we only had time to eat one partial meal each.

As the sun began to set, extreme fatigue set in and we began to discuss our sleeping arrangements for the night. I offered to stay with Kate that night while Brandon went to get us settled in at the Grizzlies and to sleep there for the night. Before he left though, he gave both Kate and me a kiss good night and told us he loved us.

I began to get Kate ready for bed. I brushed her teeth and, with the help of the same night nurse Jaq, unplugged her plethora of lines to help her to the toilet. By nine o'clock, Kate and I were worn out and ready for bed. I tucked her in and sang a few songs to her as she clutched her blue car in her hand and settled for sucking her right thumb. I lay in the recliner listening to Kate tossing restlessly in her bed. Finally, she was still and I drifted off as well.

I was awakened abruptly to the sound of Kate screaming an hour later. A nurse had come in to get Kate's vitals and I arose immediately and began trying to soothe Kate. As she screamed and kicked the sheets back, I noticed she had soaked through her panties during her fit. After the nurse checked Kate's blood pressure and temperature, she helped me get Kate cleaned up and changed and then replaced the pad lining Kate's bed. After the nurse left, it took us both a little while to fall asleep again.

Not even an hour later, I was awakened to the sound of someone forcefully saying, "Mom!" I am pretty sure my mouth had been wide open and I snapped it shut as I sat up, rubbing my eyes and trying to take in my surroundings.

Jaq was standing in front of me, holding a bottle of medicine. "Kate's potassium levels are spiking. She needs to drink this immediately to help

39

stabilize her levels. It's a lot to drink and the medicine tastes terrible," she offered apologetically.

I climbed out of the chair and followed Jaq to Kate's bedside. "Kate, honey, wake up. We need you to drink this. Wake up," I urged, shaking Kate gently.

Kate took a minute to wake up and immediately started crying. Jaq poured a little of the medicine into a medicine cup and held it to Kate's lips. Kate took a tiny sip, gagged on the foul tasting medicine, and began crying more. Jaq held the medicine cup out to Kate to try again, but Kate refused.

Jaq asked if we could try a straw and I agreed. Once the straw was in place, I took the bottle from her to see if I would have better luck getting Kate to drink it.

"Come on, Kate," I coaxed her. "You have to drink this. You can do it. I know you can!" I urged her over and over again, my words coming forcefully at times when I saw that she responded to the encouragement. Each minute of encouraging words was rewarded by a tiny sip from the bottle and then Kate would continue with her wailing. In all, it took over twenty minutes to get her to drink the bottle of medicine. At last, we heard the slurping sound of the yucky medicine being drained.

Having just experienced my first tiny victory in the world of cancer, I breathed a sigh of relief and handed the bottle back to Jaq. Another nurse walked into the room and asked Jaq incredulously, "You got her to drink it all?"

"That was all Mom," Jaq replied.

I asked Kate if she needed to go to the bathroom while we were up and, pulling back the covers, noticed she'd had another accident. Sighing in dismay, I asked Jaq if they had any pull-ups that we could put on Kate for the night.

"Of course," she answered, returning momentarily with a pack of pull-ups for Kate.

Kate cried as I stripped off her panties and shimmied her into the pull-up. "No, Mommy!" she protested. "I'm a big girl!"

L. Erin Miller

My heart ached for my little girl. She had only been potty-trained for a couple of months and had been so proud to finally wear her big girl panties. I hated to disappoint her, but I knew this setback was very small in the grand scheme of things.

I explained to her that she was hooked up to a bag of fluids so it made it harder for her to stay dry at night. "The pull-ups are just to wear at night. First thing in the morning, we'll put you right back into your panties," I reassured her.

Brandon arrived in Kate's hospital room the next morning to find two tired and hungry girls. He had already eaten breakfast at the Grizzlies and I got ready to run to the café downstairs to eat breakfast.

"Mommy, will you read a book to me?" Kate begged.

My stomach growled, but I obligingly lowered the side rail of Kate's bed to sit down next to her and read the book. I sat down next to Kate and jumped up immediately, trying to control my terror. Pooled all on the side of the bed and all over Kate was blood. Kate's blood.

I ran for the door of her room and yelled into the hall for Phoebe, who was sitting at the nurses' station just outside the room. She immediately came and stood for a second by Kate's bed, surveying the scene before her.

"In all my twenty years of being a nurse, this has never happened," she began, shaking her head. "The IV in her arm broke," Phoebe determined.

"What does that mean?" I asked in alarm.

"It means that we are going to have to take that IV out and put another one in," she answered.

I sighed that Kate was going to have to be stuck again, but immediately brightened at one thought.

"Can you move it to her other arm so she can have her sucking thumb back?" I called out as Phoebe headed out of the room for supplies and reinforcement.

Phoebe smiled and called over her shoulder. "We sure can." Brandon and I smiled at each other, recognizing a blessing in disguise.

41

Phoebe reappeared a minute later with a new IV for Kate and a nurse to help hold Kate down. She rubbed some numbing cream into the crook of Kate's right arm and we waited a minute for it to take effect.

Once Phoebe was ready, I laid down on top of Kate's lower half and Brandon held her hand, while Phoebe held Kate's upper body. Kate knew right away that something awful was about to happen and started wailing and thrashing. We tightened our grip on her. The other nurse quickly removed the broken IV from her arm and after cleaning up the left arm, prepared to put her new IV in her right arm. For several minutes, the nurse struggled to find a vein in Kate's arm, while Kate screamed. After several unsuccessful attempts, the nurse announced that the vein had blown in Kate's arm and determined that they were going to have to try to find a vein on Kate's hand, but without numbing cream this time.

My heart sank. I knew Kate couldn't wait for this to be over and neither could I. All I wanted to do was to scoop my baby up in my arms and soothe her little soul. All I wanted to do was to make all of this go away. To make the tears go away. To make the needles go away. To make the cancer go away.

Phoebe and I tightened our grips again as the nurse moved down to work on Kate's hand. Kate's screams escalated even more, feeling every ounce of pain this time as the needle poked and prodded around in her hand. The nurse dug for a few minutes, desperately seeking a vein. I began praying, "Please God. Please God, let her find a vein. Please." And suddenly, we saw a rush of bright red blood flood into the IV and we all breathed a sigh of relief. Another small victory had been achieved in the world of cancer.

It was nearing lunchtime by this point and I still had not even had breakfast yet. I was starting to feel lightheaded from hunger and lack of sleep and Brandon urged me to eat. While he got Kate wound down for a nap, I was able to run and get a couple of sandwiches from the cafeteria.

After Kate fell asleep, we met with a team of surgeons who would be performing Kate's surgery the next day if her counts were stabilized. One surgeon showed us the port that would be placed in her chest. It was a round disk that would be slipped under her skin. A tube hung from the disk and would be threaded into an artery in her heart. The center of the disk was a rubberlike material and a needle with an access line attached would be pushed through her skin into the center of her port. All infusions—chemo, blood, platelets, and medications—would run through the line and into her heart, which would send the infusion to the rest of her body.

Dr. Pui came by again that day to check on Kate. I began to wonder if he ever went home. I had seen him checking on Kate at six that morning and it was now after six in the evening. He took a look at Kate's bloodwork from the morning and discussed the results with Phoebe who had followed him into the room.

"It looks like Kate will be ready for surgery in the morning," he told us. "White blood cell count is significantly lower and transfusions have helped raise hemoglobin and platelets. It will be safe to go forward with procedures tomorrow. She will have bone marrow aspiration, an LPIT, and port placed." Then with a nod of his head, he and Phoebe left the room. Brandon and I tentatively smiled at each other.

The day was drawing to a close by this point so we ordered Kate some dinner from the cafeteria. After she'd finished eating, I said my goodbyes and walked over to the Grizzlies. A hot shower never felt so good and sheer exhaustion set in as I climbed into bed. I tried to recall if I had ever been this tired before in my life. Only the exhaustion of Kate's newborn days rivaled what I felt right then. Before lying down, however, I called my parents to check in with them and Jenna. I then called my sister Haley in Denver and talked to her for the first time since Kate had been diagnosed.

After chatting briefly with both, I said good night and lay down, letting sleep carry me far away from the nightmare in which our family was living.

Friday morning, I awoke with the sun and quickly got out of bed. It was surgery day. I showered and headed downstairs to eat a quick breakfast. As I sat eating my bagel with cream cheese, I overheard a grandmother at the table next to me on the phone with her granddaughter.

"Today is a big day," the lady said. "It's your last day of chemo!" She paused as the granddaughter responded. "I am so happy for you, sweet girl! You've come so far! I can't wait to see you in a little bit!"

My tears started to flow. Here we were standing at day one, facing a long road ahead of us, and sitting across from me was someone who was finishing her journey. The emotion was overwhelming. I continually wiped the tears trickling down my face as I finished my breakfast and headed back upstairs to get my things for the day.

Kate and Brandon were awake by the time I reached the ICU. Brandon ran to go get a quick shower and breakfast while I sat with Kate and waited.

Dr. Pui stopped by again to check Kate's results from her bloodwork drawn a few hours earlier and determined that she was ready to go for surgery that day. He left the room to find Phoebe. Phoebe discussed a few things in the hall with Dr. Pui, and when she returned she said, "Dr. Pui is thrilled with the way Kate's body is responding to the steroids. Her white blood cell count is down from 539,000 to 86,000. In all my years of working with Dr. Pui, I have never seen him this ecstatic."

Ecstatic? Yes, that is a word I never would have chosen to describe Dr. Pui!

"Mommy, I'm hungry!" Kate's voice spoke up and I gave her a sad smile.

"You can eat in just a little bit. It won't be long now," I promised her.

Patients who were scheduled for anesthesia were considered NPO— *nil per os*, or nothing by mouth. Kate could have nothing to eat eight hours before a scheduled procedure and could only drink clear liquids up to two hours before. I distracted her by reading some books while we waited for Brandon to get back and for the team to call her for surgery.

It happened almost simultaneously. Brandon returned from his shower and breakfast and a minute later, the surgery team called that they were ready for Kate.

We were now ready to begin induction, Kate's first phase of treatment that would last approximately eight weeks. Today marked day one!

Phoebe and another nurse worked to get Kate's hospital bed ready to travel down the hall to pre-op. Kate realized that something big was going on and began to whimper in fear. Both nurses encouraged me to hop on the bed beside her and ride along. I loved the chance to get to snuggle with my baby, and Kate loved the chance to get to snuggle with her mommy as well! The nurses unhooked her lines from the wall and one pushed her pole, holding her bag of fluids, while the other wheeled her out of the ICU toward pre-op. Kate and I pretended we were princesses and waved at everyone we passed on the way out the door, while Brandon followed by our side down the hall.

We headed into a single room where Kate was assessed and deemed ready for surgery. One parent was allowed in the operating room, so I suited up from head to toe in surgical attire. The three of us prayed together and then Kate and I said goodbye to Brandon. He headed to the waiting room as we rolled down the hall into the operating room where a team of surgeons was waiting for us.

Kate had been given some loopy medicine in pre-op and was already starting to get a little silly. They transferred her onto the operating table and began reviewing her operation with me as nurses worked to hook Kate up to different lines and monitors. Suddenly, Kate began singing "Twinkle, Twinkle, Little Star" at the top of her lungs and used the breathing tube dangling above her as a microphone. The team laughed and the anesthesiology nurse declared, "That's it! I'm in love!" As the anesthesia coursed into her little body, she fell asleep mid-verse. The team moved aside and told me I could kiss her.

I leaned forward, stroked her soft cheek, and gently kissed her on the forehead. I savored the feel of her skin against mine. I could have stayed in that moment forever, but I knew it was time to go. I whispered, "I love you, baby girl," before slipping out of the room. I stripped my suit off, threw it in the trash can outside the door, and headed off to find Brandon.

Brandon was sitting in the waiting room talking with another parent. Her son had been diagnosed with cancer over a year ago and had had one of his legs amputated. She and her son had been living in the Target House, a residence for long-term patients, for the past year when they found out his cancer had spread to his lungs. Today he was in surgery to have a portion of his lung removed. Brandon and I glanced at each other and it was as if we could read each other's minds: *We are very fortunate that all we were dealing with is leukemia.*

About forty-five minutes had passed since Kate's operation had begun. It seemed like an eternity. Suddenly, the door to the waiting room opened. A surgeon who had assisted in placing Kate's port came in and we stood to meet him.

He greeted us with a smile. "Well, my part is over and she did great. Her port is now in place! Next, she will have her bone marrow aspiration and lumbar puncture with intrathecal chemotherapy. She should be in recovery in the next hour."

We thanked him for taking good care of our daughter and sat down to wait once again.

Before long, we received a phone call that Kate was out of surgery and was waiting for us in recovery. A nurse came to show us the way and we could hear Kate crying as we approached.

"Well, she's awake," Brandon commented smiling.

The doors opened and we saw Kate sitting up in bed. A tall nurse had his arms wrapped around her, consoling her as she cried.

"Mommy! Daddy!" Kate yelled as we walked in, a smile breaking through her tears.

The nurse holding her moved aside so we could have room beside our little girl. As we were asking Kate how she felt and stroking her long blonde hair, another nurse walked up and said, "We learned three things about Kate as soon as she woke up. She wanted her car, her blanket, and her mommy!"

That about summed it up!

We stayed in recovery for about an hour as the nurses monitored Kate to make sure she was stable. Then we rolled our way out of recovery and back to the ICU. Phoebe was waiting.

"Everything went well, I see," she observed with a smile. We nodded in assent. "Good," she continued briskly. "Because I need to check Kate's vitals, administer her chemo medication (Vincristine), and then she has a CT scan scheduled as soon as we get done."

It was after lunch by this point and we called the cafeteria quickly to try and order Kate some lunch before her next appointment. Brandon ran down to the cafeteria and picked up a sandwich for us to split. Kate had just enough time to eat her lunch before Phoebe was ready to take her for the scan. We moved Kate into a wheelchair to take her over to the Chili's Care Center, where patients had their scans. Brandon and I took a bite of our sandwiches and left the rest to be finished whenever we returned. Another nurse walked us over there so Phoebe could record Kate's data.

The CT scan went fantastic because Kate was surprisingly perfectly content to have a lead vest draped over her body. She was also perfectly content to be put into a tunnel that made a loud whirring noise to check the density of her bones. Sometimes that girl surprised us! She was also pretty amused by the lead vest covered with hot pink lips that her daddy had to wear during the scan.

I sat in the wheelchair with Kate in my lap on the way back. A nurse pushed us and Brandon pushed the IV pole. We entered her room and prepared to move her back into her bed. The nurse warned us that picking her up under her arms would be painful because of the surgery she'd just had. We checked to make sure her lines weren't wrapped around anything before we moved her, and Brandon gingerly picked Kate up to transfer her back to her hospital bed.

Just as he moved her from the wheelchair to her bed, I saw the line from her port curl around the edge of the wheelchair at the very last second. I shouted out to stop, but it was too late. The tube tugged and Kate cried out. Whether her pain was from being moved or from the line pulling from her chest, we did not know.

I held my breath as the nurse carefully checked Kate's dressing. She said she was pretty sure everything was still in place and we breathed a sigh of relief. Brandon and I sat momentarily to finish our almost forgotten sandwiches and after I was done, I went to sit with Kate on her bed.

As soon as I sat down, I felt wetness underneath me. I felt the sheets around Kate and they were soaked. I pulled back the covers and checked her panties, thinking maybe she'd had an accident, but she was completely dry. We summoned Phoebe back to the room, explained what was going on, and she began to search for the source of the leak.

A look of realization dawned in Brandon's eyes as Phoebe began her search and he quickly explained to her what had happened when we'd transferred Kate from the wheelchair to the bed. Phoebe closed her eyes for a second and then, taking a deep breath, she carefully examined under Kate's gown to see if her suspicions were correct.

"Her needle was pulled from her port when the tube caught on the wheelchair," Phoebe affirmed, her face grim. "The wetness you felt is from her IV fluids leaking out. We're going to have to take the needle out and re-access her port immediately. I think I might cry," she added as she left the room.

Brandon and I both felt our stomachs sink to the floor. Our poor baby had just had surgery, was terribly sore where her incision was, and was about to have a needle pushed back into her chest without numbing cream.

Phoebe returned with a new needle for Kate's port and another nurse for reinforcements. Because Kate's incision was about to be exposed, it was mandatory for all of us to wear masks to prevent infection at the surgical site. We put on the masks and I held Kate's over her face as she cried at this new intrusion. One nurse pinned Kate's right side down and I curled up next to her in bed, holding her down on her left side. Brandon stood at the foot of the bed, holding Kate's legs and offering reassuring words to our distressed child.

Phoebe worked quickly, removing the dressing that covered Kate's port and swiftly pulled the needle from Kate's chest. Kate screamed in pain with every touch and I buried my head in her hair as my tears flowed. "It's okay," I whispered over and over again in her ear, trying to control the grief building in my chest. My tears were soaking my mask and Kate's hair as they flowed freely now. There was no holding them back.

Phoebe was poised, ready with the new needle and access line in her hand. "Ready?" she asked. *Ready? Were we ready to hurt our child more?* My heart was absolutely not ready, but my mind knew it had to be done and we nodded. Phoebe firmly pushed the needle into Kate's chest and Kate screamed in agony, trying to wrench herself from our grasp. And then, it was over. Phoebe quickly covered Kate's port with a dressing, smoothing its edges flat. We all sat up and the others sighed that the trauma was over.

"I need a minute," I choked and ran from the room, barely able to hold back my tears before the door to Kate's room closed behind me. I ran into the family room and into the bathroom, shutting the door behind me where I collapsed on the cold tile floor, sobbing uncontrollably. I sat against the wall for a few minutes, letting my pent-up grief and all the emotions of the past few days out in my tears. It felt good to cry. It had been exhausting to hold back my sorrow for so long and this release was cathartic for my soul.

And then, it was time to move on. I dried my eyes and washed my face with a wet paper towel. The cold water felt refreshing to my red puffy eyes. Taking a few deep breaths, I headed back to Kate's room calmed down, but still trembling uncontrollably.

The day was drawing to a close once again and as we glanced at the clock, we realized that we had completely missed dinner with everything that had gone on in the past few hours. The cafeteria had closed and none of us had eaten anything. Phoebe had switched out with the night nurse, and when we explained what had happened she told us she would be back in just a little bit and not to worry. She reappeared about fifteen minutes later, her arms laden with various snacks for us and Kate.

"We don't really keep food in the ICU, so I went to every floor and raided their cabinets. I think I found enough of a variety so that Kate might find something she likes," she said, laying an assortment of crackers, cereals, and fruit cups on Kate's bedside table. We smiled in appreciation of the effort she had put forth into finding something for Kate's dinner.

Brandon and I settled on a pack of crackers and Kate eagerly ate a bowl of cereal and fruit. After we'd all finished eating, we got Kate ready for bed and then Brandon headed to the Grizzlies for the night while I settled down to spend the night with Kate. We had heard a rumor that the doctors were hoping to move Kate out of the ICU the next day and onto the second floor into a regular hospital room. We also knew that our families were coming to visit, so Saturday was shaping up to be an exciting day!

All I knew, though, as I pushed the squeaky chair back into reclining position, was that I was so glad the day was over. And the next one was just a sunrise away.

While you were in surgery today, Kate, and your daddy and I were in the waiting room, I pulled my Bible out to read. I had been reading through the Bible this year and found my marker in Deuteronomy where I'd left off the week before. I paused for a moment and considered skipping ahead to Psalms where I might find some more uplifting verses, but decided I would resume where I'd left off in Deuteronomy 20.

I read the first few verses of the chapter and then froze, tears springing to my eyes. I pointed the verse out to your daddy.

"Hear, O Israel, you are approaching the battle against your enemies today. Do not be fainthearted. Do not be afraid, or panic, or tremble before them, for the Lord your God is the one who goes with you, to fight for you against your enemies, to save you" *(Deuteronomy 20:3-4 NASB).*

Never in my life had the Lord spoken so clearly to me as He did in that moment through His Word. Today, we were facing our enemy. Today, we were beginning our battle. But we needn't be afraid or weak-hearted because God was with us. He was going with us into battle against our enemy—against cancer.

Right then and there, I knew everything was going to be okay.

God was fighting for you, Kate.

And He was going to save you.

Love,

Mommy

> *"The Lord will fight for you"*
> (Exodus 14:14a).

Chapter 3: A Rainbow

April 5, 2013

Dear Kate,

Grief has an unexpected way of creeping up on you when you least expect it. It can be triggered by an event, a song, a change in routine, and maybe just by seeing the bandage covering the toe prick that diagnosed you with leukemia.

In the ICU, there was very little time to grieve and we were still most assuredly in shock. As the news of the diagnosis sunk in, the changes in our lives hit us like a ton of bricks. My tears were triggered by one thing after another as I watched our happy, normal life crumble before my very eyes.

God was watching. Even though there were times when we couldn't see for all the rain, He was watching—watching and waiting to send us a rainbow.

We hit the floor running Saturday morning, just as we'd done every morning in the ICU. Kate was scheduled for another round of chemo called daunorubicin that she would receive just before being relocated from the ICU to the second floor, the regular hospital floor. We had received confirmation from her bone marrow aspiration that leukemia cells were indeed found in her spinal fluid. However, in just three days, her white blood cell count had gone from 539,000 to 13,000 and from 95 percent leukemia cells to 76 percent leukemia cells. We were beyond thankful to see such dramatic improvement!

Kate had to have two more platelet transfusions and a blood transfusion since we'd been in Memphis as well. While the chemo certainly did its job in killing the leukemia cells, it also wiped out Kate's good cells such as her platelets and hemoglobin. These platelet and blood transfusions were essential in saving her life.

After her chemo was finished, we packed up our room, which was overflowing with coloring books, crayons, and activities that Kate's child life specialist had been hoarding away for her. We filled up a cart, moved Kate into her wheelchair, and bid farewell to the nursing staff in the ICU. Phoebe would forever have a special place in our hearts. She had helped guide us through the most difficult days of our lives. We thanked God for putting such a capable and caring nurse in charge of our Kate.

Kate's new nurse in the ICU transferred downstairs with us because the second floor was busier than the ICU that day and she helped us get settled in our room. It wasn't long before we were trained on the rules of the second floor, which were a little less strict than those in the ICU. However, during our stay on the second floor, we would transition to taking care of Kate a little more ourselves because her nurse would also be assigned to several other patients.

Not even an hour after moving to the second floor, our visitors for the day began to arrive. Jana, the friend who had met us at the emergency room to get Jenna, and her husband Josh were the first to arrive, bearing an armload of cards from all of Kate's buddies from church. Tears sprang to my eyes as I saw the name of each little friend written inside a giant red card that read on its cover, "Little Kate—Big God!" Josh also told Brandon that they had a few other things for us in their car that they would unload later.

Kate perked up at the first sight of her visitors, but soon slumped back over into her hospital bed, sucking her thumb and staring at the wall. Twenty minutes later, Papa Don and Grammy, Brandon's parents, appeared. Once again, for a moment Kate's eyes lit up at the sight of her visitors. Then, almost as soon as it had appeared, the light was gone from her eyes and she slipped her thumb quietly back into her mouth.

How she must have longed to be a normal three-year-old—running, playing, giggling, and enjoying her company! Instead, Kate was feeling the full effects of a crazily unbalanced blood chemistry as well as the full effects of her steroids and chemotherapy.

After a quick lunch in the hospital cafeteria, my excitement mounted as I headed back to the second floor. My parents and Jenna were due to visit any time. Sure enough, when I peeked through Kate's window, there sat my parents and my baby girl. Oh, how I'd missed her! Had she already grown a foot? Was that an extra pound or two around that sweet chubby waist of hers? For days, I had envisioned the moment I would be reunited with her, and I couldn't wait to get my hands on that sweet baby.

I swung open the door to Kate's room and Jenna's eyes lit up at the sight of me. Squealing, she ran and jumped into my arms. I hugged her tight and fought back the tears that were threatening to spill down my cheeks. I carried her over to Kate's bed and sat down on the edge. That was a mistake. Kate, who'd had Mommy to herself all week, did not want to share Mommy with anyone else, especially her little sister. And poor Jenna, who had been away from her Mommy all week, did not want to share Mommy either. Shrieking fits ensued as each girl vied to climb in my lap and push the other off. Kate became increasingly out of control so I passed Jenna back to my parents who took Jenna out of the room. She cried for me the whole way out.

Disappointment filled my heart as all the images of a happy reunion vanished. Kate was very irritable for the next few minutes, snapping angrily at anyone who tried to talk to her and bursting into tears in between, so I cleared everybody out of the room and got her ready for a nap. I read a book to her, sang to her, and then quietly left the room. Everyone else had crowded into the adjoining family room. Jenna reached for me, and after taking her in my arms we decided to head to a common area near the elevators to have some more room. Brandon and Grammy went to sit with Kate in her room while she slept and the rest of us headed down the hall.

The common area had a jukebox, a small stage for puppet shows, and a few tables with chairs. My parents, Josh and Jana, and I visited at a table for a while and Papa Don devoted himself to chasing Jenna around. Someone had set up a television in the common area that was playing the Disney movie *Tangled*, a favorite of both girls. I talked with my parents and friends until the song "I See the Light," one of the songs in the movie, began playing. My heartstrings tugged within me as the golden glowing lanterns were released into the darkened night sky on the screen. I suddenly began stumbling over my words.

"I don't need to watch this part," I excused myself as I tried to scoot my chair around so I couldn't see the screen. "It's going to make me..." I smiled trying to suppress my building emotions and then I burst into tears. I cried for a long time as my friends and parents huddled around me, rubbing my back, their eyes filled with tears too.

All the feelings and fatigue from the past few days had caught up with me. I was tired of smiling like everything was okay. I missed my home. I missed my Jenna. I missed being a family. I missed the feeling of being in control. I missed the feeling of innocence. I missed our life before cancer had crashed into us like a giant wrecking ball.

It wasn't much longer before Brandon texted that Kate was awake. While Grammy sat with her, Brandon and Josh went to unload some things he and Jana had brought to us from our friends back home. Jenna was exhausted as it was nearing late afternoon and she'd not had a nap. We took her back to Kate's room so that they could say goodbye to one another, but it ended in a screaming match and my parents had to rush Jenna out of Kate's room. I didn't even get to say goodbye to her. After they left, Brandon and his parents also left to go out to dinner while Josh and Jana said their farewells to me.

And then it was just Kate and me.

We read books and watched a movie for a little bit until Brandon returned with his parents. We wanted to venture out of the room, and Kate desperately wanted to go to the playroom there on the second floor. We checked with her nurse who agreed to the field trip, but she recommended that Kate wear a mask. Her white blood cell count was dropping to where she was at high risk for infection.

White blood cells are in charge of fighting off infections, so if the white blood cell count is low, immunity is low. This makes it easier to get sick. One type of white blood cell that is in charge of fighting off infections is the neutrophils. Doctors measure the ability to fight off infections by the absolute neutrophil count, or ANC. A normal ANC can range anywhere from 1,500 to 5,000. An ANC of below 500, however, is considered neutropenia and there is a high risk for infections. Precautions must be taken, such as a low bacteria diet in which the patient cannot have food or drink that has sat out for more than an hour, and can't eat fruits and vegetables that can't be peeled such as berries and broccoli. The patient also has to avoid other potential bacteria-bearing food and drink such as tea, fresh deli meat, and soft cheeses. Another neutropenic precaution is that the patient must avoid exposure to germs by staying out of crowds and by wearing a mask around others.

The mask is not the typical mask a doctor might wear. Instead, it is a thick, sturdy green mask that presses tightly to your face, sealing every possible crevice through which a germ might enter. There is a piece of metal that can be adjusted over the bridge of the nose to make it even more uncomfortable.

It is scratchy. It is itchy. It is tight. It is hot.

And this was the mask Kate was supposed to wear.

We were interested to see how this new intrusion was going to go.

We unhooked Kate's pole from the wall and attempted to put her mask on. Kate was fairly amiable at first about wearing the mask, but her hair was so silky, the elastic band kept on slipping down to her neck, leaving her nose and mouth exposed. She quickly became disenchanted with it. By the time our awkward party had made it to the playroom, Kate was extremely upset. We tried to fix her mask and calm her down, but it was to no avail. Disheartened, our party headed back to her room, the adventure having only lasted a grand total of five minutes.

Papa Don and Grammy visited for just a little bit longer and then Kate was tuckered out again. Brandon walked his parents out and then headed to the Grizzlies House for a much deserved good night's sleep. It had been a big day for all of us, but especially for Kate who had been through so much that week already. I tucked her in to bed, sang her a few songs, made sure she had her toy car to hold, and turned off the lights.

I sat in the reclining chair in the corner of the darkened room for a long time and just cried. The vision of a happy reunion with my girls had been overwhelmingly disappointing to me. Frankly, I was jealous and bitter that everyone else got to go home while we were stuck at St. Jude. And I was exhausted. Once again, everything I'd bottled up all week spilled forth. It was a long time before I fell asleep.

The next morning was Sunday, but not just any Sunday. It was Easter! When I awoke that morning, I thought sadly about the pretty light blue Easter dresses I had picked out for the girls. I thought about how I would miss seeing Jenna all dressed up to go to worship and would miss the look on her face when she saw the goodies in her Easter basket. I looked over at Kate, still sleeping in her bed, and hated that she was going to spend Easter in the hospital.

Brandon was heading to worship with a friend from college who now lived in Memphis, and I was going to stay with Kate. After Kate awoke, I ordered breakfast and brainstormed some ideas of things to do that morning. We watched a movie after breakfast and settled on the end of her bed to play Go Fish. As we sat there playing cards, we heard a knock on her door. We looked up and saw the Easter Bunny peeking in at us through the window. His escort motioned to see if they could come in. I looked at Kate, wondering if she would be afraid of this monstrous bunny with the frozen smile, but she had the biggest grin on her face.

"Look!" she squealed. "It's the 'Measter' Bunny!"

I smiled and the Easter Bunny and his escort came in Kate's room. I grabbed my camera and began snapping away as Kate hugged the "Measter" Bunny and gave him a big high five. The Easter Bunny handed

Kate a pink plastic basket filled with goodies and she excitedly began to examine the basket.

"Mmmm, chocolate!" she squealed again and immediately began to peel the foil off of one piece. The Easter Bunny and his friend wished her a happy Easter and began to head out the door.

"I'll see you later, 'Measter' Bunny!" Kate called after him.

How refreshing that moment was to my heart!

That was the first time I had seen her smile in almost a week. For just a few minutes, happiness filled the hospital room like rays of sunshine. After the Easter Bunny left, I asked Kate if she wanted to try and go play for a little bit in the playroom down the hall and her eyes lit up.

"But if we leave the room, you're going to have to wear your mask," I warned her. She began to whimper a little. Her nurse entered the room at this point and cast a questioning look in my direction when she heard Kate's whimpers.

"She wants to go play, but doesn't want to wear her mask," I explained.

Her nurse paused for a moment in thought before she spoke. "I think it would do her good to get out and play. Her ANC is 600, so technically she is not neutropenic yet." She kneeled beside the bed. "Kate, would you wear your mask around your neck just as practice?" Kate nodded her head in agreement. Her nurse turned toward me. "Let's start with it around her neck and go from there." I nodded my head in agreement, making mental notes on the baby steps I would need to take to get my three-year-old to cooperate with these many new intrusions in her life.

The nurse began her chemo for the day (pegaspargase), and then we unplugged her pole from the wall and lowered the railings on her bed. Kate slid off the side of the bed and I slipped her green mask around her neck.

"There," I declared. "Now you look like a superhero!"

Kate smiled and padded in her stocking feet to the door of her hospital room. I followed close behind with her pole and we headed out of her room. We walked down to the common area first. Kate's eyes lit up at the jukebox in the corner and we picked out songs and danced around and around until we were dizzy.

A few girls around Kate's age walked into the common area with their moms and sat at a table nearby. Kate's eyes lit up again and she immediately began marching in their direction, with me following close behind pushing her IV pole.

"Hi!" she said. "My name's Kate. What's your name?" she asked.

The girls introduced themselves and they all were instant buddies. They played together for a little while, and once again it did my heart so much good to see Kate smile again and to hear her sweet laugh.

Eventually, Kate began to tire out. We headed back to her room, both refreshed from our adventure. I ordered lunch for Kate and she settled down for a nap after her meal.

Soon after Kate fell asleep, Brandon returned from morning worship services and brought up an Easter lunch for both of us from the cafeteria downstairs. The delicious smells of turkey and dressing and sweet potato casserole filled the room. We snuck out of Kate's room and into the family room next door, opening the blinds so we could see into her room. We settled onto the couch to eat, grateful for some time alone.

I told him all about our morning and he smiled at Kate's excitement over the "Measter" Bunny and at her making new friends. We chatted as we ate and enjoyed whatever sense of normal we could grasp as we sat in a hospital room eating an Easter lunch with our daughter who had just been diagnosed with cancer sleeping in her hospital bed in the next room.

Kate began to stir a couple of hours after she'd drifted off and we cleaned up from lunch, and headed back into her room. Brandon agreed to stay with her while I headed back to the Grizzlies House for a quick shower and to go through some of the items our friends had brought the day before.

As I walked out the front doors of the hospital, I glanced at the gloomy sky and reflected on how dreary the sky had been since we'd arrived. The weather had been fitting for all that had transpired. As I walked to the Grizzlies, the clouds suddenly parted and the brilliant rays of the sun shone down. I smiled at God's timing. He knew how much we'd needed a day like today. As I whispered thank you, the warmth of the rays of sunshine whispered a reply: "You're welcome."

My spirits rose even more as soon as I set foot in our room. The couch was overflowing with care packages and cards that our friends had brought us the day before. I was amazed at how quickly our brothers and sisters in Christ had put everything together. Tears lingered in my eyes as I sorted the gifts, making piles of art supplies, books, toys, and more. There was also an envelope containing a large sum of money and I sat in shock, completely humbled by the generosity displayed to our family.

As I climbed in bed that night and reflected on the day, I thought, "Today was a pretty good day!" Immediately, I marveled at that thought. My perspective on what a good day was had certainly changed!

Monday was a big day for Kate! She began her morning with anesthesia for another lumbar puncture and intrathecal chemotherapy and was ravenous by the time she woke up. We ordered her lunch once she was brought back to her room and she anxiously waited for it to arrive. While we were waiting, her nurse, April, slipped in.

"I have exciting news for you," she announced pushing her short auburn hair back with one hand. "Kate will be discharged this afternoon! After she finishes eating, I'll go over your discharge papers with you, so just let me know when you're ready."

Brandon and I smiled nervously at each other. While we were excited about being discharged from the hospital to the Grizzlies, we were also apprehensive about Kate's care being put completely in our hands. The hospital felt so safe with a nurse just outside our door. The world outside the walls of the hospital seemed formidable.

Kate fell asleep after lunch and we headed into the adjoining family room with April, who was shuffling through a stack of discharge papers. Brandon and I sat down on the couch as she went over Kate's information with us.

"Once you are out of the hospital, you will be in charge of giving Kate her medicine. You will give her Prednisone, her steroid, three times a day with food. Dr. Pui has also prescribed Ranitidine twice a day to help combat acid reflux caused by the steroids. She will also need two doses of leucovorin tomorrow at eighteen hours and twenty-four hours after her lumbar puncture that she had today. The leucovorin will stop the chemo that she had with her lumbar puncture before it damages her kidneys. If you miss the time, even by a few minutes, you need to call the hospital so we can give you further instructions. I would recommend that you set alarms on your phones to remind you to give her this medication. Also, it needs to be refrigerated. She will take trimethoprim and sulfamethoxazole, antibiotics to prevent pneumonia, three times a day, but only on Mondays, Tuesdays, and Wednesdays. We will send ondansetron and diphenhydramine with you. These are nausea meds and you can administer them as needed. Her last medicine is her oral chemo, mercaptopurine, or 6mp. It needs to be refrigerated as well and she will take it every night at bedtime. She needs to fast for two hours before she takes it.

"It is also imperative that you wear medical gloves when you give her the oral chemo to protect yourselves from it. You will also need to wear medical gloves when you deal with any of Kate's bodily fluid such as her urine or vomit. It will have traces of chemo in it and we can't have you two on chemotherapy as well!"

Brandon and I glanced at each other out of the corners of our eyes. The smiles on our faces were already starting to slip. How in the world were we going to do this? Were we really responsible enough for them to put Kate's health and medical care into our hands?

April continued, "You will need to monitor Kate for fevers as well. Her ANC is now below 500, so her immunity level is very low and she is at high risk for infection. She will need to wear her mask at all times unless she is in her room. If she runs a fever of 100.4 or greater, give us a call immediately and bring her to the medicine room here. If she has a fever, she needs to be treated within an hour. I can't emphasize this enough. Last month, we had two little boys die because they started running a fever and were not brought in immediately. Their immune systems were too weak to fight off the infection." She shook her head. "So sad, so sad."

By this time, my eyes were wide and my mouth was hanging partially open.

She continued, not missing a beat. "You will also need to make sure she adheres to the low bacteria diet. Everything she eats must be fresh and cannot have been left out for over an hour. If it's been out for over an hour, throw it away. She may not have fresh fruit or vegetables unless they can be peeled. Do not use the salt in the shaker on any table—use salt from a packet. Make sure she doesn't eat or drink after anyone else. And if you have any questions, you've got a pamphlet here that covers everything." She waved a pamphlet in the air before setting it on top of our growing stack of paperwork.

Brandon and I glanced at each other again. Did we really want Kate to be discharged from the hospital? Ever?

"Well, are you ready?" April asked.

Brandon took a deep breath. "Umm…"

"Great. Then sign here that I've gone over everything with you and I'll get you on your way!"

Brandon signed Kate's discharge papers and April left to collect the medications that we would need at the Grizzlies. We woke Kate up, got her dressed, and loaded our belongings into a wagon from the hospital lobby. Brandon and I coaxed Kate into her mask by slipping on masks of our very own that a child life specialist had found for us. Now we could all be superheroes together! Brandon pulled the wagon holding our belongings, I pulled Kate in her own wagon, and we triumphantly—and nervously—waved farewell to all the nurses as we headed to our home away from home at the Grizzlies.

Kate was excited to be out of the hospital and amazed at all the toys and books waiting for her when she arrived in our suite. Her chocolate radar went off and she honed in on a care package filled with sweets from a friend. She and I munched on a few pieces of chocolate, and as I was reaching for another piece Kate slid the box out of my reach and chastised me. "Mommy, I'm going to have to move this away from you so you don't eat all my chocolate."

Brandon and I laughed, but then our tone grew serious.

"Kate," Brandon began. "We wanted to talk to you about what all has happened this past week. Have you ever heard us say when you were sick that you had a 'bug'?"

Kate nodded her head indifferently as she continued to plow her way through the bag of chocolate.

"Well, you have a bug in your blood. And this bug was being mean to some of the cells in your blood," Brandon explained.

"Kate, can you say leukemia?" I asked.

Kate slowly repeated the word and then asked, "Can I go play with my toys now?"

Brandon and I smiled and then decided that we would not press the issue. She would let us know when she was ready to talk or if she had any questions. And we would be ready and willing to talk with her whenever that time came.

Later, we ate dinner in a quiet cafeteria before heading back to the Grizzlies for an early bedtime for a tired Kate. We measured out Kate's medications and then tucked her into bed. As Brandon and I climbed into bed together a couple of hours after Kate had dozed off, we smiled at each other as we gazed over at the tousled blonde hair sticking out from under the covers in her bed. We were relieved to have survived the first week of a very long journey and were thankful to God to have our little girl sleeping next to us. And she was alive. It was with these last thoughts that we drifted off to sleep.

Tuesday marked our first day as "outpatient" at St. Jude. We were scheduled in assessment triage for labs at 6:45 that morning. Kate has never been a morning person, so Kate, plus an early wake-up call, plus having to wear her mask, plus not being able to suck her thumb, plus being on steroids made for one really grouchy girl. She made sure everyone within earshot knew just how unhappy she was too. I held her in my lap and tried to soothe her by rocking her from side to side while she desperately tried to shove her thumb in her mouth through her mask. It wasn't long before her mask had a permanent indention in the middle from where she'd tried to poke her thumb through.

We met with Dr. Pui after Kate's bloodwork had come back. He was pleased with her numbers and shared with us that her spinal fluid from her lumbar puncture the day before had been clear of leukemia cells!

"You may have a day off tomorrow to rest," he informed us.

The next day, we packed up all our belongings and moved to the Ronald McDonald House. We realized we had an ever-accumulating amount of toys and coloring books that were being hurled our way. We arrived around lunchtime at the two-story sprawling brick house with red trim. A statue of Ronald McDonald himself sat on a bench outside, waiting to welcome us to his house. Once inside, we met with one of the employees in her office. We filled out some paperwork and she took the three of us on a tour around the house. Kate was excited to see the various play areas, but was disappointed that we weren't stopping to play at any of them.

"You will have *plenty* of time to play," we reassured her.

We first peeked in a room on "B-side," which was the newer addition to the Ronald McDonald House, and the lady told us the rooms in B-side were a fair bit larger than the ones in "A-side."

"We are totally full in B-side, so you will be staying in A-side," she informed us as we made the trek back to the front part of the house where the rooms for A-side were located. We passed through brightly colored living and dining areas and smiled at the friendly giant animal statues. It was quiet since most of the families were at the hospital for the day.

The lady took us down the hall on A-side, opened a door on the right, and there we stood face to face with the room in which we would be staying. The room was a very bright, colorful green with cute paintings of animals over the beds. There were two queen beds, side by side, covered with patchwork quilts. It was very clean. And it was very small. It might be generous to say it was two hundred square feet.

It was all I could do not to cringe. We had planned on bringing Jenna to Memphis to live with us once we were settled in the Ronald McDonald House. How in the world would we manage with a three-year-old and a one-year-old in this room with us? As soon as this thought popped in my mind, I felt ashamed. I kept reminding myself that we were being given a place to stay—for free—and I needed to be thankful for that.

The lady handed us the key to our room and asked if we needed anything else. We thanked her and told her no. After she'd left, we ventured to Dining Room A and inspected the free food pantry for lunch. The pantry was filled with boxes of cereal, canned goods, snacks, and treats—all donated to the House. Every family was also given a grocery gift card each week with which to purchase groceries. For now, we just selected a few items off the shelves for lunch. Once we had finished eating, Brandon headed to the car to unload our suitcases and I went back to the room to get Kate settled down for an afternoon nap.

As Kate snuggled down into her bed, I headed to the bathroom. As soon as I shut the door, the tears began to flow. I was overwhelmed at the thought of cramming the four of us into this tiny room. I was exhausted. I missed Jenna terribly. And all I wanted to do was to go home and resume our lives as normal again. After a few minutes, I wiped away my tears and tried to calm myself down before I left the bathroom. But as I slipped out the door of the bathroom, Kate, who has always been very intuitive and observant, noticed my watery eyes.

"What's wrong, Mommy?" she asked, crawling out of bed and coming to my side.

I tried my best to smile through my tears as they welled up in my eyes again. "Mommy's just sad," I explained.

"Are you sad because you miss Jenna?" she asked somberly.

"Yes," I answered as the tears spilled down my cheeks once again. "I miss Jenna. And I miss our home."

Kate patted my arm and sweetly whispered, "It will be okay, Mommy. We'll be home soon."

Oh, that precious girl.

I hugged her for a long time, then helped her back into bed and lay down next to her. We stared at each other for almost an hour, neither sleeping, before we decided to go play in one of the playrooms she had seen earlier.

Kate was scheduled in assessment triage for more blood work that afternoon. After her appointment and a quick supper, I attended the Bartlett Church of Christ for Bible study while Brandon stayed with Kate.

Everyone was friendly, asking if I was "Kate's mom." They, too, had been praying for our little girl. I met a couple, the Molloys, who knew Brandon from his college days. I mentioned to the wife, Beverly, how small our room was at the Ronald McDonald House and that I was trying to come up with a way to put some dividers up in the room to give us some privacy. We brainstormed together for a few minutes and she said she would think on it some more and let me know if she came up with something.

Friday was the usual LPIT (lumbar puncture and intrathecal chemotherapy), but this day was a disaster from the beginning. Because of the steroids, Kate was ravenous at nearly any given hour of the day and woke up even more eager to eat. However, because she had to be given anesthesia (or "sleepy milk" as we began calling it due to its white color) for her LPIT, she was NPO for eight hours prior to the procedures.

Kate's first appointment of the day was not scheduled until nine o'clock in the morning. We reported to assessment triage to have her blood drawn and then sat in the A Clinic waiting area until her appointment with Dr. Pui at ten. When we sat down in the exam room with Dr. Pui, he explained that Kate's platelets were too low to have her lumbar puncture to be done right away and she was going to need a platelet transfusion before she could be put to sleep. Brandon and I groaned inwardly. Kate was already starving and crying off and on with hunger. A platelet transfusion would add at least another two hours before her LPIT could begin.

Later, as we sat in the medicine room with Kate as her bag of platelets infused, her eyes began to glaze over. She'd stopped crying by this point, as if she'd realized it was futile. It was nearing one o'clock and Brandon and I were both starving. Brandon and I took turns slipping out to the cafeteria to grab a quick bite of lunch while the other sat with Kate.

Finally, at two o'clock, her platelets were done and she was called back to procedures. Everything went smoothly from that point on and the poor kid was finally able to eat for the first time that day at four o'clock in the afternoon. However, she wasn't done with her day yet. She still had two more chemo treatments to go, both vincristine and daunorubicin. She ended up not getting back to the Ronald McDonald House until late that evening.

I, however, missed the last half of the day with Kate.

While she was getting her platelet transfusion, I slipped out of the hospital into our black sedan waiting in the parking lot and headed for Huntsville, Alabama. Home! I had a surprise for Kate that came in the form of a squishably soft, energetic eighteen-month-old named Jenna!

Brandon and I had debated the logistics of all four of us staying in our room at the Ronald McDonald House and, while it would be difficult, we wanted to make it work. My parents had offered to keep Jenna for as long as we needed, and we were thankful for that, but we wanted her with us. We wanted to be together as a family.

When I pulled into our driveway later that evening, Jenna was playing in the driveway with her Nonna and P-Daddy. She squealed with joy when she saw me behind the wheel of the car. I threw it into park, hopped out, and ran to scoop up my sweet Jenna, covering her with kisses and squeezing her as tightly as I could. Oh, how I'd missed her!

"Hi, Mommy!" she kept saying, putting her chubby little hands on either side of my face and gazing with delight into my eyes. I soaked up the moment of holding my baby in my arms once again and relished the feel of her soft skin against mine as we hugged.

We played in the driveway for a little while longer and then headed inside for supper. After supper, while Nonna gave Jenna a bath, I packed a suitcase for her and added a few other items for Kate, Brandon, and myself. I snuggled in bed with Jenna, read a Bible story and a book to her, and then kissed her good night. I visited for a little while longer with Mom and Dad before I headed off to bed. I checked in with Brandon who said Kate was tired, but doing well. He also said that some members from Bartlett Church of Christ had come by with three floor-to-ceiling cardboard partitions to help divide our room and give everyone some privacy. I was amazed at their generosity and thrilled with this news. I couldn't wait to see the room!

The next morning, we ate breakfast and I tossed a little blonde-haired, blue-eyed girl into her car seat and headed west. Mom and Dad hung around for a little while to clean and straighten up before packing up their belongings and heading back to their home in Birmingham. I was beyond thankful for all their help the past week and a half!

Jenna and I pulled in at the Ronald McDonald House parking lot just before lunch and I texted Brandon to tell him to get the camera ready!

As we stood outside our door, Jenna looked up at me questioningly, wondering where we were. I told her, "I have a surprise for you!" and opened the door. We walked into the room and saw Kate lying pitifully on her bed in the far corner of the room. As soon as they saw each other, they both lit up as bright as the sun. Jenna ran squealing with excitement to Kate's bed and Kate crawled to the edge of her bed with a huge smile on her face. Kate hopped down off her bed and grabbed Jenna in a bear hug. And there they stood, just grinning and hugging while the camera clicked away. Brandon and I smiled the biggest smiles of our lives. After a good long hug, they started playing Ring Around the Rosie, dancing, giving each other kisses, and hugging each other more.

Then Jenna turned to Brandon to give him lots of loving as well. She'd missed her daddy, too. The pictures we took during those few minutes were, needless to say, priceless. My heart was full.

And so we began our adventures of living together as a family of four in a two hundred square foot room! All that mattered, though, was that we were together again.

One year.

One year is approximately the amount of time that Noah and his family lived in the ark…with a ton of animals…smelly animals.

And the wives of Shem, Ham, and Japheth had to live in the same ark as Mrs. Noah—their mother-in-law—for a year. Bless them.

Can you imagine the wide range of emotions running through these eight people when they stepped off the ark for the first time?

I can only imagine their sense of relief in finally being off the ark. I can only imagine their sense of awe coupled with fear at being the last remaining souls on earth. How very small they must have felt!

I can only imagine how they must have looked to the heavens, desperately seeking a sign—a sign to know they weren't alone. A sign to know that God was still there. A sign to know that He was still watching over them. A sign to know that everything was going to be okay.

And suddenly, they saw it—the rainbow.

The rain has certainly poured over us this past week, Kate. Our first few days in Memphis were the hardest days of our lives. Our bodies were tired and our souls were weary. But God knew just when our spirits needed a rainbow the most. He sent us a rainbow on Easter by giving us a good day filled with smiles, play time, and the "Measter" Bunny. Oh how my heart needed some encouragement then! That special day with you was enough to get me through the next few hurdles.

The tears came again as we moved into the Ronald McDonald House, but God sent me a rainbow in the form of you, Kate. Your tenderhearted words and your loving touch washed my tears away. You, who had just been diagnosed with cancer at the age of three, reassured me that everything was going to be all right.

And as my heart ached and yearned for our family to be together again, God sent a rainbow by giving us a reunion that blew every fairy tale out of the water. Today, Kate, rather than dwelling on the rain, I am going to praise God for all of His rainbows!

Love,

Mommy

"In my distress I called upon the Lord; to my God I called. From His temple He heard my voice, and my cry came to His ears" (2 Samuel 22:7).

"But You, O Lord, are a shield about me, my glory, and the lifter of my head. I cried aloud to the Lord, and He answered me from His holy hill" (Psalms 3:3-4).

"I am weary with my moaning; every night I flood my bed with tears; I drench my couch with my weeping. My eye wastes away because of grief; it grows weak because of all my foes. Depart from me, all you workers of evil, for the Lord has heard the sound of my weeping. The Lord has heard my plea; the Lord accepts my prayer" (Psalms 6:6-9).

Chapter 4: The Family of Christ

April 26, 2013

Dear Kate,

Your story is spreading far and wide. At the age of three, you are impacting the lives of many and becoming an inspiration to others. While you were impacting the lives of others, our lives were being impacted by others as well.

Our hearts have been humbled over the past few weeks at the outpouring of love shown to our family by so many people. St. Jude has taken care of us by not only providing us with medical care but also giving us a place to live as well as money for groceries. We have been amazed by St. Jude.

We were absolutely amazed at the love, compassion, and concern shown by our friends, family, and brothers and sisters in Christ. Care packages, cards, money, and prayers poured in from home and beyond—some from people we'd never even met! And thus we began learning a tremendous lesson in generosity and the power of prayer.

The Ronald McDonald House was an amazing place. We were given a room and absolutely everything we needed during our stay there. We had a kitchen that we shared with a few other families. It was fully equipped for me to cook meals for my family, but I didn't have to cook very often! Each month, we were given a calendar that listed special events. Volunteer groups signed up to provide dinner for all the families living in the Ronald McDonald House for most of the nights each week. What a blessing it was to not have to worry about dinner while we had so much else going on! Many times these groups also provided entertainment, such as musical performances, crafts, and games.

While the Ronald McDonald House was amazing, it obviously also had some drawbacks. Imagine putting sixty different families from all walks of life in the same house, expecting them to live together for a couple of months. Then throw in the added stress that their children have cancer.

While there was a family or two who caused problems in the house, we found a few families with whom we enjoyed visiting. Across the hall from us was another little three-year-old girl who had been diagnosed with ALL, B-cell the week before Kate. She was there with her mom and grandmother. There was also another little three-year-old boy with ALL and he was there with his mom and newborn brother.

Most of all, however, our family became friends with a family from Texas—the Cassidy family. Michael and Cathy had four kids—Dakota, Danny, Darcy, and DayLyn. Darcy had been diagnosed with a brain tumor a few years before and achieved remission, but now at age nine the tumor had come back and was wrapped around her spinal cord. When the doctors took a look at the scans of her brain and spine, they couldn't believe that Darcy was sitting in front of them. Judging from the scans, they fully expected her to be paralyzed or in a coma; yet there she sat!

Jenna took a special liking to seven-year-old DayLyn and would holler for her wherever we were in the Ronald McDonald House. "Layla! Layla!" Jenna yelled in her toddler's interpretation of "DayLyn." When DayLyn appeared, Jenna would wrap her arms around DayLyn's neck as tightly as she could and refuse to let go. We were happy to find some friends so far away from home.

Jenna also found a few other older friends at the House and amused us as she ran around with them as if she were the same age. Jenna absolutely loved living at the Ronald McDonald House.

When one of the other kids commented to me that she wished Jenna was her sister, I thought about how blessed Kate was to have such a fantastic little sister. The first day that Jenna was with us at the Ronald McDonald House, we were heading to the dining room for dinner. Brandon and I slid Kate's mask on and then ours as well, as we had become in the habit of doing to support her. When Jenna saw all of us wearing masks, she began pointing at our masks saying, "I want! I want!" We laughed, shrugged our shoulders, and grabbed an extra mask from Kate's box. As soon as we slipped Jenna's mask on, she was ready to go and we marveled at this eighteen-month-old who so readily and willingly wore this hot and scratchy mask.

Kate, on the other hand, was not as interested in making buddies. She felt awful from the chemotherapy and the steroids she was taking. Because of the steroids, all Kate was interested in was eating! Breakfast usually started with a pack of peanut butter crackers around five in the morning. For a more official breakfast, Kate would eat a grilled cheese sandwich, a bowl of grits, yogurt, two pieces of fruit, and an entire bowl of popcorn. She usually requested more food after the popcorn, but we had to hold her off as lunch was approaching by this point.

Grits became an insatiable craving for Kate. She requested a bowl of grits with every meal. We would meet her after she woke up from her lumbar punctures with a steaming bowl of grits from the cafeteria. She would devour it in less than two minutes.

Whenever Kate had a lumbar puncture scheduled, she was not allowed to eat. This was sheer torture to this ravenous little thing and torture for us as her parents as well. She made sure everyone knew how unhappy she was! On these days, we distracted her by building up excitement for who she was going to get to see that day at the hospital.

A few people quickly won Kate's heart. Martha May, or "Marfa May" as Kate called her, was Dr. Pui's nurse practitioner and always peeked in on us during our visits with Dr. Pui. With her short curly auburn hair, long face, easy smile, and relaxed nature, she was a favorite among Dr. Pui's patients. Kate also loved Mr. Tony, her nurse in procedures where she would be put to sleep for her lumbar puncture and intrathecal chemotherapy. In stark contrast to Martha, Tony was tall with a shaved head and colorful tattoos covering his arms.

Kate was also greatly intrigued and amused by Dr. Pui himself. When we first came in the exam room, he rarely acknowledged that we were there. I usually tried to make small talk and he would grunt his replies. But once he finished going over Kate's lab reports on the computer, he would swivel around in his chair with a great big smile and an enthusiastic "Hi!" for Kate. Her fascination with him increased once she discovered his pockets were always filled with neat toys.

While Kate loved seeing Martha May, Tony, and Dr. Pui, none won the heart of Kate as much as Dr. Pui's nurse, Justine. Tall with dark skin and hair and a winning laugh, Justine's cheery disposition and loving nature immediately melted any "roid rage" Kate might be experiencing. Kate looked forward to seeing Justine each day and loved listening to her banter back and forth with Roberta, another nurse in A Clinic. It wasn't long before Kate declared that Justine was her best friend.

We settled quickly into our lives in Memphis. We had no other choice. Kate's treatments took off running and we had to sprint to keep up. For the first couple of weeks, we reported two to three days a week for labwork, therapy visits with Dr. Pui, and her regularly scheduled chemotherapy. Kate was also scheduled two days a week to be put to sleep for her LPIT.

Brandon and I both prefer routines and schedules, but we quickly learned to be flexible with our time and plans. We would show up at the hospital for an appointment only to find out Kate's hemoglobin or platelet levels—or both—had reached critical levels and she would have to have a transfusion immediately. This added anywhere from three to five hours to our day. We spent many, many hours in the medicine room where Kate received her transfusions as well as whatever chemo was scheduled for that day. Some chemotherapy treatments were merely a five minute "push" where the nurse would push the chemo in a syringe into Kate's port over a period of five minutes. Others could take as long as two hours. For these, we were given a room in the medicine room and we passed the time watching movies, reading books, and coloring. Kate usually had two or three chemos back to back in the same day—a "chemo cocktail."

While these long days at the hospital were exhausting and certainly took their toll on all of us, the days off took their toll even more. We were away from home and going through the most difficult time of our lives. We didn't want any down time. We didn't want to just sit and wait. We wanted to cram all her treatments into a short period so we could hurry up and go home. We just wanted to be done with this induction phase. But we had to learn patience. This was not a sprint but a marathon we had to endure.

In a little over two weeks, we had reached day fifteen of induction. Day fifteen was the day that the doctors would do another bone marrow aspiration to determine if there were still leukemia cells present in her blood. As soon as we had been given the road map for that week and day fifteen was explained to us, I felt anxious. We prayed and prayed for Kate's cancer to be gone and to hear that wonderful word—remission.

I had asked at her appointment if we would be able to get the results the next day, Saturday. Clinic would be closed, but the nurse said they would call with the results or I could call the medicine room's weekend clinic to get the results.

On day fifteen, Kate had her usual LPIT in the morning with the addition of a bone marrow aspiration, followed by two rounds of chemo—pegaspargase and vincristine.

The next day, we waited and waited for the much anticipated phone call. Finally, around four o'clock that afternoon, I called the weekend clinic.

"Hi, my daughter had her bone marrow aspiration done yesterday and I was wondering if I could get her results," I politely asked.

"The results? You'll have to wait until your therapy visit on Monday to get those results, ma'am," the nurse explained.

"Oh, I was told that I could call today and get her results," I explained.

The nurse must have heard the disappointment in my voice and she speculated that she might be able to get someone to look at the results and call me back. "What's your daughter's medical record number?" she asked.

I gave her the five-digit number and waited as she looked up Kate's records.

"Ma'am, I see here that Dr. Pui is Kate's doctor," she began.

"Yes," I affirmed.

"I can tell you right now that Dr. Pui would *not* want anyone discussing these results with you other than himself. I've worked at this hospital for over twenty-five years and am on a first name basis with every doctor in this hospital...except for Dr. Pui."

I smiled in spite of my disappointment. I understood completely. And so we would wait.

We met with Dr. Pui first thing Monday morning. We waited anxiously as he settled into his chair in front of the computer in the exam room. He pulled up Kate's records on the computer and began scanning her road map for the week. He went over a few of the items listed on her schedule, and while we waited patiently, on the inside we were screaming, "Just tell us if she's in remission or not!"

Finally, the long awaited moment came. He looked up the results of her bone marrow aspiration and his face fell as he explained to us that Kate was not in remission yet. Her bone marrow aspiration showed that 0.123 percent of her blood still contained leukemia cells. We would continue with her chemotherapy as planned and Kate would have another bone marrow aspiration on day forty-two.

We mistook his disappointment for something worse than it was and fear and worry crept into our hearts. Once Brandon and I were alone while Kate was asleep in procedures for yet another LPIT, we cried for our daughter, wondering what her fate would be and what plan God had for her and for us.

We were disappointed with this news. We had been asking "big"—to hear the word "remission." We knew that our God was big and powerful enough to heal our sick little girl. But just because it hadn't happened yet didn't mean He wasn't powerful enough to do it. It just wasn't in His plans and in His time to heal Kate completely yet.

We knew there was a purpose for us being at St. Jude and that there was a purpose for this journey, so we prayed as we waited for day forty-two. We prayed that through us, through Kate, and through our friends and family, God would be glorified.

It wasn't until later that we understood Dr. Pui's reaction. His nurse Justine explained to us that Dr. Pui strives for perfection. He wants every patient of his to achieve remission immediately. We understood Dr. Pui's reaction even more when we watched a video that St. Jude had published on Kate's doctor. A colleague commented that he knew Dr. Pui would not give up his research and would push for new developments in the treatment for leukemia until the survival rate for leukemia patients was 100 percent. Dr. Pui had never married or had kids, simply stating that he was married to his job and his patients were his kids.

And this man was our daughter's doctor. We were certain that God had a hand in placing Kate in the care of world-renowned Dr. Ching-Hon Pui.

And for that, we were thankful.

We had surprised ourselves and caught on very quickly to Kate's medication schedule, but soon after day fifteen, we had another set to add to her plethora of medications. In addition to her steroids each day, ranitidine, 6mp, leucovorin, trimethoprim and sulfamethoxazole, and her nausea and pain meds that we gave as needed, we now had to add prophylactic antibiotics. The chemotherapy treatments had almost completely wiped out Kate's white blood cell count as well as her ANC and she was at extreme risk for infection. The prophylactic antibiotics were precautionary in an attempt to keep Kate from getting sick and came in an Eclipse.

The Eclipse was a plastic ball that contained her medicine, and we were trained on how to hook it up to her port to administer her antibiotics.

We would take the cap off Kate's access line, clean the end of her line for thirty seconds with an alcohol wipe, unclamp her line, flush her port with a syringe of saline, and hook up Kate's medicine. Once the medicine finished infusing, we unhooked the Eclipse, cleaned the end of her line again, flushed her port with saline, flushed her line with Heparin, clamped her line tight, and put a new cap on the tail of her access line.

The Eclipse had to be refrigerated, but would not infuse properly until it was at room temperature. We had to pull the ball out of the refrigerator an hour before the antibiotic was scheduled in order to get it to room temperature. One was also light sensitive so we had to keep it in a special bag, similar to a fanny pack, while it infused. The antibiotics took anywhere from thirty minutes to an hour to infuse, and usually had to be given every twelve hours. This schedule wasn't too bad, but a week later, a third antibiotic was added that had to be given every eight hours. This meant we were getting up in the middle of the night to hook her up to her antibiotic, letting it infuse for thirty minutes, and then unhooking it. We soon became skilled enough at hooking and unhooking the Eclipse that Kate never even stirred during the night infusion.

On top of all of her medications, we had to keep track of when her port was last accessed because the needle could only stay in for seven days. As long as Kate's port was accessed, she couldn't get it wet nor could she get it wet for twenty-four hours after she had been de-accessed. If she ever had more than a couple of days in between appointments, we would usually opt to have her de-accessed so that she could get a bath.

Kate, however, stayed accessed nearly round the clock because she was due for chemo or bloodwork almost every day. On days that she had to have her port accessed, she screamed hysterically from the moment I put numbing cream over her port to the moment the needle was pushed into her chest. She would scream "All done, all done!" over and over again. As soon as the needle was in, she was fine, albeit a little sweaty and snotty from all the screaming.

One nice distraction from our rigorous medication schedule was our visit to patient services to pick up Kate's mail. We received hundreds of sweet cards, dozens upon dozens of gift cards, and many care packages from far and wide! We spent many afternoons opening up cards and packages and it was sometimes difficult to keep up with everything coming in. We were constantly amazed and humbled at this outpouring of love.

One morning, I ran down to patient services to pick up our mail. When the lady asked for the patient's name and I replied, "Kate Miller," she froze. "Kate Miller?" she repeated incredulously. "Oh boy, do I have some mail for you!" She disappeared from behind the glass window and reappeared a minute later carrying seven care packages of different shapes and sizes. I exclaimed, "Wow!" and she said, "Honey, this is only half of it!" I had to get a wagon to haul all of the packages and letters back out to our car. That was not the only time I had to do that!

Visitors were also a wonderful distraction from the medications and hospital visits. Once we'd settled in to the Ronald McDonald House, we had multiple visitors come every week. Some stopped by as they passed through Memphis on business trips, others brought their kids up for a day or two to visit, and some even flew in to visit! Our visitors helped out with both girls and even ran errands for us.

And of course, not a weekend went by that our family didn't come see us. They were always eager to give Brandon and me a break, medication schedule permitting. The Tuesday after we met with Dr. Pui regarding the results of Kate's bone marrow aspiration, Brandon's parents, Papa Don and Grammy, came to spend the day with us.

"We want y'all to go out and enjoy an afternoon together," they informed us. "We'll keep the girls."

Brandon and I looked hesitantly at each other. A whole afternoon? After thinking things through, we realized we could give Kate her medications just after lunch, go out for a late lunch and possibly a movie, and be back before her next medications were due that evening. We joked that we were getting more dates now than we ever had before Kate had been diagnosed. We gave Kate her meds, hugged the girls goodbye, and bolted!

Brandon and I headed first for a leisurely lunch. For the first time in over two weeks, we finally sat down and talked about what had happened on the day Kate had been diagnosed, filling in the gaps for each other in the events of the day.

After we finished our meal, we looked for a movie theater to see what movies were out and at what times they were showing. We decided on a movie to see and shopped for an hour or so until the movie began. The movie was good, but the best part about it was letting myself get completely absorbed in another world. Gone for the moment were the fears that haunted me. Gone were the lists of medications whirling through my mind over and over again. Gone was the world of cancer. All that mattered at the moment was that the lead character saved the day by the end of the movie. As soon as the movie ended, reality crashed down on me and the fantastic illusion that everything was okay was shattered.

"I have this terrible feeling in the pit of my stomach," I told Brandon as we were in the car returning to the Ronald McDonald House. "It was so wonderful to get swept away into the movie, but now that it's over we have to go back to the world where our daughter has cancer. I don't know if I ever want an escape from reality again. Coming back to what our life has become is too hard." I fought back the tears that threatened to spill down my cheeks. Brandon took my hand in his and gave it a soft squeeze and we held hands until we arrived back at the Ronald McDonald House.

It was growing dark by this time and a volunteer group had come to serve dinner to the residents. We urged Papa Don and Grammy to stay and eat with us, but they needed to get back on the road and make the three hour drive back to Florence, so our family of four collected our masks and headed down the hall to Dining Room B to eat.

After dinner, we were getting the girls ready for bed and as I was changing Kate's clothes, I noticed that her needle in her port looked like it was dislodged. I called Brandon over to examine it and he agreed that it looked funny, so I called the medicine room at the hospital to ask what we should do.

"Can you draw blood from her line?" questioned the nurse. She quickly explained what I needed to do. I took one of Kate's saline syringes from our stash of medical supplies in the bathroom, removed the blue cap, and attached it to her line. I flushed her line first by pushing the saline into the line and then, following the nurse's instructions, gently began to pull back on it. Dark red blood slowly began to fill the syringe.

"I am able to draw blood," I confirmed with the nurse. She said it was up to us. We could bring Kate in and let them look at it or just wait until her next appointment. We had to administer her antibiotics via her port that night, so we decided to play it safe and take her to the medicine room for the nurses to check it out. We certainly didn't want her antibiotics leaking everywhere during the night if her needle was dislodged.

I loaded a tired Kate into the car while Brandon continued getting Jenna ready for bed. Kate and I easily found a parking space in front of the hospital and headed for the medicine room. They ushered us into a room and a nurse lifted up the front of Kate's shirt to examine her.

"It does look like it may have pulled out," she observed. "Part of it is probably still in, which is why you were able to draw blood, but we'll go ahead and de-access, then access her again."

Kate, who was sitting in my lap, began to scream as we lifted her shirt over her head. "Don't take my shirt off! I don't want a needle! All done!" she screamed over and over again.

A couple of other nurses came into the room to see if her nurse needed any help. One helped hold Kate down while the other watched quietly over the shoulder of Kate's nurse.

Kate's nurse ever so gently and ever so slowly began to pull the dressing off of Kate's chest. Kate screamed in pain as the dressing pulled at her skin and left red welts behind. After a few minutes of meticulously peeling off the dressing and stopping occasionally to attempt to calm Kate down, the nurse had only successfully pulled off one side out of four.

Finally, the nurse who was watching spoke up. "I don't think you are going to be able to calm her down," she said. "The key is just to get it over with." She stepped forward, and with a firm but gentle hand pulled

Kate's dressing off in three seconds flat. Kate screamed for every bit of those three seconds, but once the dressing was off, she stopped crying immediately. We all breathed a sigh of relief and I mouthed a quick "thank you" to the nurse who had stepped forward.

The nurse cleaned Kate's chest with alcohol and, after it dried, pushed the needle back into her port. Kate screamed again, of course, but that didn't slow the nurse down this time. A minute later, Kate's new needle was covered once again with its dressing and it was over.

From then on, I immediately informed any nurse who was de-accessing or accessing Kate that she was going to scream. There was no sense in trying to calm her down. The key was just to get it over with quickly. From that moment on, we saved ourselves and Kate a lot of drama and angst in the months and years to come.

Kate had labs drawn the following morning and was not scheduled for chemo until the following afternoon, which meant she could have a break from her needle for a day! This also meant we had an hour window during which the poor kid could finally get a bath! It had been weeks since she'd had a bath, and, although we had sponge bathed her, there is nothing like getting in a tub full of warm water and scrubbing the germs away.

Twenty-four hours after Kate had had her needle removed, we filled the tub in our bathroom full of water and gave her a bath. Then we closed the curtain and let her splash to her heart's content. I will never forget the way her hair swirled around her in the tub and treasured that moment, knowing that in just a short while, there would be no more hair to swirl, no more hair to dry, and no more hair to stream behind her as she ran.

After her bath, Brandon took Kate to the hospital for her assessment triage appointment to get yet another needle and to have blood drawn for her appointment the following day. Jenna and I headed to Dining Room B, where a group was providing dinner, and I enjoyed my time with my little girl as we ate.

As soon as Brandon and Kate came back, I knew something was wrong. Kate was crying uncontrollably in Brandon's arms as he carried her across the dining room toward Jenna and me.

I threw him a questioning look and he shook his head.

"She's been like this ever since she got her needle," he explained. "She keeps on saying that her chest hurts."

"Did you say something to the nurse before you left?" I asked.

"Yes," he nodded. "I told her that she always screams while she is getting her needle, but she always calms down as soon as it's in. Kate told her the dressing hurt and was too tight, but the nurse just told her it would stretch out as she moved around."

I pulled a pitifully wailing Kate into my lap. "What's wrong?" I questioned her.

"I just want to go to bed," she sobbed.

"Does your chest hurt?" I asked.

"I just want to go to bed," she cried again, curling up in a ball in my lap.

Brandon spoke up. "Why don't you eat something first?"

We pushed a plate of food toward her and coaxed her to eat. She refused to eat anything and just sat sobbing in my lap. After a few minutes of trying to get her to eat, we gave up and decided just to take her to bed. When we got back into our room, Brandon changed Kate into her pajamas and she climbed into bed where she curled up, still sobbing.

"I think we need to take her back," Brandon said.

"They're going to love seeing us again in the medicine room," I smiled ruefully at Brandon. "But I think you're right. Do you want me to take her so you can go eat dinner, and then you can get Jenna to bed?"

"That's fine," he agreed and I called the medicine room to tell them we were on our way with more needle issues.

Kate continued to cry as I loaded her into the car and drove the short mile to the hospital parking lot. Her crying escalated as we entered the medicine room. A couple of nurses stood ready to greet us and escorted us into the same room we were in just a few days before.

The nurse who had taken charge the other night quickly got Kate's dressing off of her chest. We saw right away what the problem was. The nurse who had accessed Kate had used an infant-sized dressing over Kate's needle. It was so tight that it had pulled her needle completely sideways and the plastic edging on the end of the needle was pressing into her chest. There was a deep red imprint where the wings of the needle had been digging into her chest.

As soon as the dressing was removed, Kate stopped crying. The nurse covered her needle again with an appropriate sized dressing and we were sent on our way. When we arrived back at the Ronald McDonald House, Kate declared she was hungry and I fixed her a peanut butter and jelly sandwich along with some fruit and popcorn. She ate every bite. We gave Kate her medications for the evening and then sent her off to bed.

We had one morning off this week and ventured out to the zoo for a brief visit. St. Jude patients and their families can go to the Memphis Zoo for free, so we waved Kate's medical bracelet for the ticket attendant to see and walked right on in. We guessed that Kate wouldn't last very long at the zoo, but we filled the pink-flowered diaper bag with snacks to appease her insatiable appetite and rented a stroller so she wouldn't have to walk. Kate had to wear her mask, even outside, so we made the deal that she could take the mask off in the stroller whenever she was ready to eat. Other than that, she had to keep it on at all times.

Jenna loved looking at all the animals. She ran from exhibit to exhibit, squealing over each new and exciting animal she met. Kate, however, was only interested in eating. We coaxed her out of the stroller once or twice to look at the giraffes and elephants. She gave each animal a quick once-over and then climbed right back into the stroller, resuming her popcorn munching. We eventually just left her alone to eat while we toured the zoo.

The mask hung loosely around her neck the whole time because she ate the whole time. Even though Kate was stowed away in the stroller and we were outside, my stomach was in knots every time we passed a group of people. I feared one of them would sneeze as soon as we walked by and

Kate would get sick. Every now and then, I pulled out the hand sanitizer and gave us all a little bath just to appease my anxious heart.

We had made it through about half of the zoo when Kate suddenly declared that she was done and burst into tears. She had lasted a little over an hour and we really couldn't have asked for any longer! We hurried to the car and loaded everyone in before sighing in relief that we had survived an outing with our little chemo patient.

The next visit at the hospital would be a fourteen-hour day. Fourteen hours is a long day for an adult and so much more for a three-year-old! Kate had her usual LPIT that morning, and then she headed to the medicine room for a nine-hour chemo treatment. The chemo itself, Cyclophosphamide, actually only ran an hour, but then she had to have eight hours of fluid afterward. This particular chemo could cause ulcers in her bladder if it sat for too long, so the fluids' purpose was to flush out the chemo to keep it from sitting in her bladder.

I took her for the first half of the day while Brandon chased Jenna around the Ronald McDonald House and then we swapped out. Before Brandon and Jenna came up to the hospital, they were able to meet a celebrity who had come to visit the cancer patients and their families at the Ronald McDonald House—Phil Robertson from *Duck Dynasty!*

I asked Brandon how his visit with Phil went when he and Jenna arrived in the medicine room where Kate was getting her chemo.

"Good," he reflected, setting Jenna down, who immediately crawled into the bed with Kate to watch a movie. "But Jenna was scared to death of him. I think it was the beard."

I laughed. "What did she do?"

"She just wrapped her arms around me and buried her face into my neck," he replied. "Phil tried to get her to touch his beard and she petted it twice and then buried her face again."

While it was pretty cool to get to meet a celebrity, we were more appreciative that a celebrity had taken time out of a busy schedule to come and visit the residents of the Ronald McDonald House. Even more than that, we were thankful for the many celebrities who donated millions of dollars to St. Jude every year. This money saved the lives of children from all around the world.

Jenna and I left the medicine room to head back to the Ronald McDonald House for a nap. Brandon and Kate did not get back from the hospital until nine o'clock that night, and Kate was very ready for bed. Brandon and I were too.

During this week, Kate's hair gradually began to come out. It made us fully appreciate the awesomeness of God in that He knows the very number of the hairs on our heads. Kate's hair seemed unending. We would brush and brush and pull handfuls out every time. This went on for weeks as it slowly thinned out more and more.

We tried to talk Kate into a head-shaving party and she readily agreed at first. But when the time came, she refused and got upset. We tried to run the electric razor on our arms and then her arm to show her that it didn't hurt, but she wouldn't budge on her decision. We didn't push the issue and just continued to sweep up piles of hair off the floor each day.

Jenna actually helped speed up the process a little bit. Kate and Jenna were both fighting with each other one afternoon and Jenna, in a fit of anger, reached up to pull Kate's hair…and pulled out an entire handful! Brandon and I, who were swooping in to break up the two of them, froze in mid-stride. Jenna and Kate's mouths both fell open as their eyes fell on the handful of Kate's hair clutched in Jenna's pudgy fingers. I wasn't sure if I wanted to laugh or cry, but as Jenna attempted to hand Kate her hunk of hair back with an "uh-oh," we all burst out laughing. I figured that was one less dustpan of hair I had to sweep up.

While Kate was losing hair rapidly, she was gaining weight rapidly as well. After being on steroids for over a month and having a ravenous appetite, her belly was filled out and her cheeks were so fat that she could have been mistaken for a chipmunk. In fact, at one of her appointments with Dr. Pui, he checked her weight as recorded in assessment triage that morning and commented to Kate on how fat she was getting. *Very tactful, Dr. Pui. Very tactful*, I thought, smiling to myself.

While the steroids drastically changed Kate's outward appearance, they also drastically changed her behavior. In an instant, she could turn into a stark-raving-mad lunatic and throw a fit that would put any toddler to shame. She took most of her "roid rage" out on her poor sister. Jenna would walk by Kate and Kate would kick her down onto the floor. Jenna would sit next to Kate and Kate would outright slap her in the face.

We let none of this behavior slide. How could we? We most certainly didn't want Jenna to think this kind of behavior was acceptable and we also did not want to have a monster on our hands when we were through with this cancer journey.

Our discipline and reprisals to Kate were met with demon-like resistance. Kate would rear back and scream in our faces with every ounce of her being. It was hard not to get angry when she acted like that. There were times when we reacted with anger, but quickly learned that it only escalated the situation. Because of the steroids, Kate had no self-control.

Instead, we tried to get her to calm down by talking to her in calm voices and by getting her to take deep breaths. One time she was screaming at me in my face, and I just wrapped my arms around her in a big bear hug. She immediately stopped screaming and started sobbing in my arms. They were the tears of a little girl who could not make any sense of the way she was feeling—of a little girl who could not understand the magnitude of the rage she felt inside. My heart broke for her.

As her hair continued to fall and her weight continued to rise, we plugged along day by day, week by week, through Kate's road map of chemotherapy and doctor's appointments. About four weeks into treatment, Kate began a new chemo, cytarabine; it was a forty-five minute infusion for four days in a row and then she would have three days off chemo before repeating the rounds again.

During this first set of cytarabine, we went for dinner one evening at the Target House with our friends from Texas. While the Ronald McDonald House housed patients and their families who were expected to stay three months or less, the Target House was for patients who were expected to be in Memphis for three months or more, some for even a year.

The Target House was amazing. When we turned into the driveway, we couldn't believe our eyes. Sponsored by the Target Corporation, the red brick building was huge and beautiful and looked like it should be on a college campus rather than in the middle of downtown Memphis. We headed to the dining room where we ate dinner with our friends Cathy, Darcy, and DayLyn. Her husband Michael had taken the older two kids back home to Texas for school and a few other events on their schedule. Cathy stayed to care for Darcy, and DayLyn stayed as a buddy for her sister.

After dinner, we all ventured out to the playground. The kids played for a few minutes on the playground, but soon became more interested in the steep hill located next to it. All four girls climbed up to the top of the grassy hill, joined hands, and began running down the hill at full speed. They would crash halfway down and roll into a heap of giggling girls at the bottom. Kate and Darcy looked so full of life, and we had not seen Kate have so much energy in a long time. Brandon and I smiled at each other, our hearts tugging in our chests, knowing that we would treasure this moment forever.

Cathy stood quietly next to me and I asked her how Darcy was doing.

She smiled bravely. "The radiation and chemotherapy are not working. Her tumor is not responding to treatment so they are talking about sending us home next week."

My heart stopped as I absorbed this news.

Cathy continued, "The girls and I were taking a break in between appointments today and I noticed that Darcy had suddenly gotten very quiet. I asked her what she was thinking about and she immediately began to cry. I asked her why she was crying and she said she didn't want to go home. She knew that the doctors were sending her home to die."

I protested. "God can still save her."

Cathy nodded in agreement. "I know that God will save her."

I nodded along with her. "Yes, you never know. A new treatment could open up…"

Cathy stopped me. "No. Either way, God is going to save her. Darcy will be saved, no matter what happens."

Tears filled my eyes at Cathy's words of wisdom. She was exactly right. Her words exemplified strong determination and faith and I marveled at the attitude of my new friend. We stood quietly, watching our girls having the time of their lives. It was a bittersweet moment that was filled with so much life, love, and laughter. However, the knowledge of what our girls had been through and still had to endure hung heavy on our hearts.

A couple of days after our Target House dinner, my sister Haley flew in from Colorado for a week-long visit. Her trip to see us was a combined effort of caring and compassionate friends who knew how much Haley longed to be with us during this difficult trial. One of Haley's friends had been planning on flying out to visit Haley and her husband Bryan during the upcoming summer, but when she heard of Kate's diagnosis, she gave her flight points to Haley instead and flew her from Colorado to Memphis. Another set of friends jumped in with hotel points and gave Haley enough points to stay for a week at a hotel just down the road from the hospital and the Ronald McDonald House. Our hearts were so grateful for these wonderfully selfless people who jumped at the chance to help our family be together.

Leaving Brandon in charge of the girls, I hopped in the car and drove the short drive down the interstate to the airport. There was Haley waiting on the curb, tall and thin, her long brown hair pulled back in a ponytail. It had only been a couple of months since I'd seen her. I'd taken a long weekend trip out to visit her and Bryan back in February. Even though it had only been a couple of months, I felt as if I'd lived a lifetime since then. After putting the car in park, I jumped from the driver's seat and ran around the car for a giant hug from my little sister.

"You look good," I commented, stepping back to survey her. "How was your flight?"

"Thanks, it was fine," Haley replied as she loaded her luggage into the trunk. "How are you holding up?"

I gave her the most decent smile I could muster. "I'm good."

We climbed into the car and headed back to the Ronald McDonald House. As we drove, I tried to prepare Haley for what she was going to see—a chubby little demon-possessed girl with a thinning head of hair.

"I remember Kate's dramatics well," Haley said with a hint of a smile.

"Kate's dramatics have taken a turn for the dark side," I clarified as we pulled into the parking lot of the Ronald McDonald House.

Haley and I headed straight for our room where we found everyone just waking up from an afternoon nap, Brandon included.

Kate looked cautiously at Haley as she climbed off her bed. Kate and Jenna were used to only seeing Aunt Haley on the computer, and Kate looked at her as if to say, "Now how did you get out of my computer?"

Jenna, on the other hand, took one look at Haley, screeched at the top of her lungs, and bolted into her arms. Haley gave her a big hug and then reached her arm out for Kate to join them. Kate looked doubtful and reached to cling on my leg.

After dinner that night, Haley attempted to break the barrier again. Kate lay down on the bed sucking her thumb, and Haley climbed on the bed next to her for a cuddle.

"Please don't lay by me," Kate slurped through the thumb in her mouth.

Haley smiled and nuzzled Kate's side.

"Please don't lay by me," Kate repeated again and Haley, sighing, slid off the bed.

Jenna, who had been getting a bath, suddenly came running into the room completely naked. Kate laughed at Jenna and the two began to dance around the room. Jenna grabbed some Mardi Gras beads that had been handed out at dinner a few nights before and threw a tangled mess around her neck. There she danced around the room, completely naked save for a dozen necklaces jangling around her neck. Brandon and I decided then and there that we were going to have to keep our eyes on that child!

Kate had sailed through the first four days and doses of cytarabine and had earned herself a three-day break from chemotherapy before the next round was scheduled to begin. Kate had no appointments the next day and we hung around the Ronald McDonald House with Haley.

This day was huge because it was Kate's last day of prednisone. Prednisone was the steroid she had taken for forty days, three times a day. After dinner that night, we gave Kate dose number one hundred twenty of that terrible yet essential drug and smiled in relief at each other as she swallowed the last drop in the syringe.

We had no appointments the next day either, and while Brandon and I were cleaning up from lunch that day we noticed Kate was actually in somewhat of a pleasant mood. Later, after she and Jenna woke up from their naps, our hearts filled with joy. Kate was happy. She was laughing. She was ready to play! Our Kate was back!

That evening, two clowns from a traveling circus came to put on a special performance for the kids at the House. Kate and Jenna were mesmerized by the clowns as they pulled out their special props from their bags to set up for their performance. The girls plopped on the large sectional couch to get ready for the show, joining a few others who were already waiting there.

To begin the show, the clowns passed out red clown noses for everyone to wear and Haley, Brandon, and I obliged by pushing them onto our noses. The clowns were funny and their antics brought a lot of laughter from their audience, but not one other kid found the show as riveting and hilarious as Kate did. We smiled as huge belly laughs erupted from her and relished the sound of her happiness. The show was fantastic, but nothing was more fantastic than seeing the joy on the faces of all the children who were enduring so much, yet still took such childlike joy in something as simple as a couple of clowns.

As the show was ending, another surprise was waiting for the girls behind the couch. Kate and Jenna turned around to see P-Daddy and Nonna sitting behind them, both sporting bright red clown noses too. The girls squealed and ran to throw themselves in the arms of their grandparents.

P-Daddy and Nonna had come to stay for a long weekend so that they could visit with Haley as well.

After dinner that evening, Kate and Jenna grabbed some toy grocery carts from the play area beside the dining room and took off. We were enjoying watching the two girls play so much that we just let Kate's mask hang around her neck. She was so happy and feeling so great that we hated to taint that moment by covering up her smiling face. Kate and Jenna chased each other around and around the play area giggling like only two sisters, two buddies, could. Kate kept on calling out, "Let's go, Jenna! Follow me, Jenna! Jenna, can you go this way?" Kate's laughter pealed through the play area and we beamed to see our little girl feeling so well, so happy, and so alive.

But then that moment was over.

One of the many blessings of being a Christian is the bond of brotherhood with fellow Christians. When one member suffers, we all suffer. Kate, as you were facing this tremendous trial, many members of the church rose with you to face this monster by the name of cancer.

Without a single question, our brethren opened their wallets and gave to us financially to ease any burden we might face. They cleared their busy schedules and drove the four-hour lonely road between Huntsville and Memphis to be of whatever help they could. Some only got to see you for twenty minutes because of unexpected appointments, but it was enough for them.

The care packages filled with toys, books, and activities spoke volumes of the love. One afternoon, your daddy stood in shock, surveying the overflowing wagon of packages from the mailroom. "How do we ever pay everyone back for all they've done for us?" he whispered to me. We decided then and there that we would never hesitate to help someone else in their time of need.

But more important than the money, care packages, and visits were the earnest prayers being lifted up to the throne of God on your behalf. Christians from all over the world were praying to God for your healing. One of our members from our home congregation was currently in South Africa and, after receiving word of your diagnosis, e-mailed us to let us know that Christians in South Africa were praying for you too. "They love her because I love her," he wrote.

So Kate, cling to these wonderful examples of generosity and always have the heart to help those in need. Even more so, cling to the avenue of prayer. Trust always in the power of God to heal and to answer your prayers as He sees fit.

Love always,

Mommy

> *"Iron sharpens iron and one man sharpens another"* (Proverbs 27:17).
>
> *"Two are better than one, because they have a good reward for their toil. For if they fall, one will lift up his fellow. But woe to him who is alone when he falls and has not another to lift him up! Again, if two lie together, they keep warm, but how can one keep warm alone? And though a man might prevail against one who is alone, two will withstand him—a threefold cord is not quickly broken"* (Ecclesiastes 4:9-12).

Chapter 5: God's Perfect Plan

May 10, 2013

Dear Kate,

As you grow up, you may wonder from time to time, "Why me? Why did I get cancer?" I would be lying if I said those questions never ran through my mind. Why you? Why our daughter?

A few months before you were diagnosed with cancer, I began following the story of a family whose three-year-old daughter was tragically killed when a swing set flipped over and landed on her. It was Christmas Eve, and her mom was eight months pregnant with their second daughter. I was humbled by the grace and faith her mother showed during a time of immense grief. While she could have chosen to be angry at God, she chose instead to praise Him and sought His comfort to guide her through her pain.

Just a few weeks before you were diagnosed, I watched a reality show on television in which a couple lost their baby girl about halfway through the pregnancy. Again, I was humbled by the mother's reaction at the loss of her daughter. The first words out of her mouth were, "The Lord giveth and the Lord taketh away. Blessed be the name of the Lord." And then she asked her husband to pray.

I was impressed by these women who chose to praise God in their darkest hours. I prayed to have the same grace, the same faith, and the same trust in the Lord if ever faced with a seemingly insurmountable trial. And then, not more than a month later, our trial came in the form of Acute Lymphoblastic Leukemia.

I n the middle of the night, Kate awoke soaked from head to toe with urine. This had become almost a nightly occurrence. We had tried everything to keep her pull-up from leaking during the night. We tried an overnight pull-up on her and an overnight diaper on top for good measure. We also put a bed liner on the bed that we could pull off and toss whenever it got wet instead of having to change the sheets in the middle of the night. We even started to set an alarm in the middle of the night to get up and change her pull-up so that it wouldn't overflow.

However, this night, Kate was soaked and shivering too.

I led her quietly into the bathroom and after slipping on a pair of blue medical gloves to protect myself from the chemotherapy in her urine, I stripped her of her pajamas and gave her a quick sponge bath. She shivered the entire time. I didn't think twice about it, assuming she was cold from being wet. I dressed her in a clean pair of pajamas, replaced her soaked pad on her bed with a new one, and tucked her back into bed.

For the next hour, I could hear Kate on the other side of the cardboard partition, tossing and turning in her bed until, finally, she cried out for me.

"Mommy, I need to go to the bathroom!" she cried.

I helped her out of bed quickly before she woke Jenna up and hustled her into the bathroom. She sat on the toilet for a minute, straining, and then began to cry. I noticed that she was shivering again and it suddenly occurred to me that she might have a fever. I rummaged through our bag of medical supplies we kept on the metal shelves in the bathroom until I found the thermometer the hospital gave us. I placed the thermometer under her arm and watched anxiously as the numbers slowly began to climb until they reached 99.6. Because it was an auxiliary temperature, I added a degree, which made her temperature 100.6.

We needed to call the hospital.

I took a deep breath, adrenaline pumping through my veins, and woke Brandon up as Kate crawled back into her bed to lay down.

"Brandon," I whispered, shaking him from his sleep. "Brandon," I repeated more urgently when he didn't budge.

"Huh?" he mumbled, rolling over in bed to face me.

"Kate has a fever," I began, already starting to change my clothes. "It's 100.6 and we need to call the hospital. Do you want to call?"

Brandon sat up and fumbled for his phone, which was lying on the windowsill beside the bed. He blearily rubbed his eyes, trying to focus on the screen as he scrolled through his list of contacts in search of the number for the medicine room. I finished getting myself dressed and began to dress Kate, who began crying when she realized we were going up to the hospital.

"I'm fine, Mommy! I'm fine!" she protested, her teeth chattering away. How I wished I could just give her medicine and put her back to bed! But that was against the rules when dealing with someone who had a port and a fever. The medicine could mask the fever and this was a grave concern if the fever was being caused by an infection in the port.

We heard a squeal from behind us and saw Jenna's head peeking around her cardboard partition. She was grinning and ready to play before the sun even rose.

Brandon talked with one of the nurses in the medicine room who instructed us to bring Kate straight over. They would draw blood to determine what the problem might be.

"She's on her way," he affirmed before hanging up the phone.

I grabbed a few snacks as well as Kate's backpack filled with books, crayons, and coloring books. Brandon curled up in bed with Jenna, attempting to get her to go back to sleep again as Kate and I headed out the door.

"Keep me posted," he called out as we opened the door.

"I will," I replied before the door shut behind us.

After parking, we entered the hospital through the revolving doors of the Chili's Care Center. I was a mom on a mission, so much in fact that I walked headfirst into the revolving glass doors of the hospital. *At least I got a smile out of Kate*, I ruefully thought as I rubbed the sore spot on my forehead.

Once we arrived, the nurses immediately got us into a room and began assessing Kate. They drew blood and took her temperature, which was surprisingly normal. I was confused. She was still shivering and even if our thermometer had been off by a degree, she still would have had a fever. Kate continued to cry and complained that her stomach hurt. I urged her to try to go to the bathroom and as she sat on the toilet, she screamed and screamed, but nothing would come out.

A half hour later, Kate's blood counts were back and her ANC was zero.

"With her ANC being zero and your report of a fever earlier, Dr. Pui will want you admitted to the hospital," the nurse explained. "They are getting a room ready for you now."

Disappointment filled my heart. While we waited, I texted Brandon, my parents, and Haley to let them know the news. Brandon said he would come up before lunch to swap out with me and let me get a nap while Jenna was napping. I readily agreed.

We waited about another hour before we were escorted up to the second floor. Kate continued to scream in pain intermittently, complaining about her stomach, and nothing seemed to ease her discomfort.

I got Kate settled and texted Brandon her room number. A couple hours later, my dad and Brandon showed up at the door. Just a minute or two before they arrived, Kate's stomach pains intensified and she was hysterical. As soon as Brandon and Dad opened the door, Kate threw up everywhere. We stood stunned for a moment, and as a second wave seemed imminent we searched frantically for something in which to catch the next round. Dad produced a pink plastic basin filled with various items from a cabinet and, after dumping everything in the basin on the bed, I caught the second wave of vomit as it came flying. It didn't really matter though because she and her bed were already covered.

Brandon alerted Kate's nurse that we would need her sheets changed on her bed and a new gown. The nurses quickly got the situation under control before I headed back to the Ronald McDonald House to assist Mom and Haley in corralling Jenna.

Brandon checked in with me throughout the day and relayed the news that Dr. Pui had come by and wanted to do an ultrasound on Kate's pancreas. He believed that one of her chemos may have caused pancreatitis, hence the fever and vomiting. Brandon also relayed that Kate had thrown up once more, but ondansetron had eased her nausea. Later that afternoon, Kate began running a fever. We were glad that she was safe in the hospital and under the care of the wonderful St. Jude doctors and nurses.

Dr. Pui held Kate's scheduled chemo during her hospital stay. Kate's fever spiked off and on over the next couple of days, but antibiotics kept it from getting out of control. Brandon reported that she used the bathroom the second night of her hospital stay and was a different kid after that. After all, who doesn't feel better after a really good poop? The ultrasound showed that everything was just fine with her stomach and her pancreas.

Haley and I spent the third day of Kate's hospital stay with her. By this time, a rat's nest the size of a softball had formed on the back of her head with the remaining hair she had, so Haley and I set about the task of trying to brush all the knots out. It probably would have just been easier to have shaved it all off right then and there. It took an entire hour to comb out the mess and we pulled out handful after handful of long blonde hair. Kate screamed and cried the entire time, but finally the tangles were out!

By Tuesday, the fourth day of her hospital stay, she'd been fever free for forty-eight hours and was released back to "Old McDonald's" as Kate had begun calling it. She was ecstatic to be free again! This was also the day that Haley was flying back to Colorado though. It was disappointing that our visit together had been interrupted and tainted by a hospital stay, but this was the new normal for our lives. My sister and I tightly hugged each other goodbye, and it was hard to let go.

Shortly after Kate had been discharged from the hospital, Brandon also packed a bag to head back to Huntsville. He had been attempting to make it back to work for the past week and things kept coming up to prevent his return—visitors, exceptionally long chemo days, and then Kate's hospital stay. While his coworkers insisted there was no rush and for him to return only when he was ready, we finally decided that there was never going to be a good time for him to go back to work. He would just have to do it.

After missing almost six weeks of work, Brandon was heading home. I would be left to tend to Kate and Jenna by myself, which was very sobering. I kept reassuring Brandon—and myself—that we would survive.

Jenna made sure she sent her daddy off with a bang. Or, I should have said, a ring.

After Kate and I had settled back into the Ronald McDonald House that afternoon, Jenna and I headed to the kitchen to fix a quick supper before Brandon left for Huntsville. I kept an eye on her as I pulled pots and pans out of the cabinets and a few items out of our pantry. She desperately wanted to go out the side door to the playground and stretched to reach the black button on the wall that would release the door to be opened. I smiled, knowing that she would not be able to reach that black button try as she might. It was just far enough out of reach.

The fire alarm next to the black button, however, was not quite out of reach. Suddenly, I heard a piercing bell jangling and looked over to see a startled Jenna bolting for my arms.

"Jenna!" I groaned and, picking her up, I ran to find some help.

We quickly came across a custodian headed our way and I gave her a quick explanation of what had happened. She followed us into the kitchen and attempted to fit the plastic cover of the fire alarm that Jenna had knocked loose. Instead the custodian accidentally knocked it completely off, which set off the alarms for the entire house. Horns were blaring outside, shrieking whistles trilled up and down the corridors of the house, residents were beginning to stream out the doors, and Jenna and I just stood in the kitchen watching the drama unfold before our very wide eyes.

L. Erin Miller

We headed out into the dining area where it was a little less noisy just as Brandon came running into the dining room, carrying Kate. Kate had her face buried in Brandon's shoulders, crying at the horrendous racket all the alarms were making.

"Let's go! We need to get out!" Brandon insisted urgently, motioning for Jenna and me to go out the door. I grimaced and slowly shook my head no.

Brandon stopped in his tracks, a confused look spreading over his face. I pointed at Jenna and realization dawned. He rolled his eyes and came to wait with us.

Just then, the house manager and a few other custodians rushed to the kitchen area. The first custodian informed them that it was a false alarm and subtly pointed a finger at Jenna who had her head buried in my chest. The house manager pulled out her walkie-talkie, told the guard at the gate to turn the fire truck around when it pulled up, and then dispatched one of the custodians outside to round up the residents of the house who had evacuated and were congregated on the far side of the playground. Our little family stood huddled in the dining room as the chaos continued for another minute or two. And then, finally, all was quiet again.

The house manager came over to us and jiggled one of Jenna's dangling legs.

"I usually give a stern speech to any kid who sets off the fire alarm," she began. "But you're too little for a speech!"

"We're sorry," I feebly offered and the house manager waved it off with a smile as she walked away.

I turned to Brandon and moaned, "This is not a good way to start off keeping the two of them by myself!"

My time of caring for the girls, however, went well because I ended up having a lot of extra help. I survived three hours of appointments the next morning with both girls, but the last thirty minutes were pretty tough. I felt like a circus act as I tried to entertain Kate, wrestle Jenna, and listen to Dr. Pui.

Dr. Pui determined at this visit that Kate did not have to make up the chemo that she missed while she was in the hospital. She would receive her last regularly scheduled dose of Ara-C that day and then she would be done with induction, the first phase of treatment! We would monitor her counts over the next few days to determine if she was ready to press forward with the next phase of treatment called "consolidation." Even though it would have only added a few extra days to induction, I was thrilled that she did not have to make up the chemo she missed and we could stay on schedule. Home was that much closer!

We had more visitors over the next few days who helped tend to Jenna or tagged along with me to Kate's appointments. A few friends from my hometown—Rachel, Lacey, and Amy—came for the day. Rachel and Lacey stayed with Jenna while Amy came with me to the hospital for a short visit with Dr. Pui.

Dr. Pui pulled up Kate's records on the computer and made some observations on her counts.

"Counts look good and are starting to rise now that induction is over," Dr. Pui mused as he considered the numbers on the screen. "We'll give it the weekend and see what counts do before we move into next phase—consolidation. If they continue to trend upward, we plan for her to be admitted to hospital for first round of high-dose methotrexate on Wednesday of next week. After she clears methotrexate, you can go home."

My heart skipped a beat. "Home?" I repeated, not sure if I heard him right.

"Yes, home," he confirmed as he headed out the door.

I turned to Amy after he left. "I think I may cry."

Amy's blue eyes were wide as well. "That's so exciting!" she exclaimed. Then she lowered her voice and asked, "Did you understand what he was saying? I didn't understand a word!" I laughed.

Home. I savored the sound of that word. I'd had no idea we were this close to getting to go home. Our road maps, which mapped out the course of Kate's treatment plan, were given to us in small doses. They usually only showed one week at a time. The nurses explained that so much could change in the schedule depending on Kate's health that they didn't like to give the schedule out too far in advance. While this was true, I also think that it would have been too overwhelming to process it all if it was given to us more than one week at a time.

Justine entered the room and gave us a brief synopsis of what we could expect in the upcoming week. Once we began consolidation, Kate would have four treatments of high-dose methotrexate. She would first be hooked up to a bag of fluids the day before her chemo was scheduled in order to protect her kidneys from the harsh chemotherapy. Hydration would be essential during this phase of treatment. The morning after getting hooked up to fluids, she would have her usual LPIT. This time only, she would also have a bone marrow aspiration to check again to see if her cancer was in remission. After these procedures, she would be admitted to the hospital to begin the high-dose methotrexate, which would run for twenty-four hours. As soon as Kate's body had cleared the methotrexate below a certain level, she could be discharged from the hospital with the bag of fluids and as soon as she cleared it to an even lower level, we could go home. We would be at home for roughly ten days and then return to repeat the process again until she'd had four treatments in all.

It was a lot of information to take in, but we were used to that by this point. After making some notes, Amy, Kate, and I headed back to the Ronald McDonald House to check in on Jenna and her babysitters.

I took a few minutes to call Brandon and share the good news with him. Because Kate would be admitted to the hospital the following week, he decided to return to Memphis that weekend to stay. He'd only been able to squeeze in three days at work, but one of us needed to stay with Jenna while the other stayed with Kate. I was excited for him to be coming back to us a lot sooner than I had expected.

My friends helped me get the girls down for naps, and then we settled in the living room of A-side to visit while the girls slept. We chatted for a couple of hours while I kept an eye on the baby monitor I had plugged in, and then it was time for Amy, Rachel, and Lacey to head back home to

Birmingham. Kate, Jenna, and I ate dinner and then straightened up our room a little bit in preparation for the visitors who would be coming the following day—both sets of grandparents, some friends, aunts, uncles, cousins, and most importantly, Brandon! The girls reveled in their visitors that weekend.

Monday afternoon, Brandon took Kate to the hospital for a count check while Jenna and I stayed behind. When they returned, both were smiling from ear to ear.

"Tell her," Brandon urged Kate with a slight nudge on the shoulder.

"I can go to Chick-fil-A!" she squealed, wiggling with excitement.

"What?" I asked, confused.

"'Marfa' May said I can go to Chick-fil-A!" Kate repeated again and began to do a happy dance.

Brandon explained, "Kate's counts are outstanding and have rebounded much faster than they expected. They want us to come to the medicine room tonight to get hooked up to a bag of fluids and start the next phase of treatment today! We should be home by the end of the week!"

In an instant, my feet were on the floor and I was doing a happy dance right along with Kate. I was amazed at how fast everything was moving. Nothing had moved fast at the hospital for the past six weeks and now my sluggish mind was racing to catch up with this new pace!

We called our parents to share our news and then headed to Chick-fil-A. The girls had a blast playing in the play place and devoured the savory chicken nuggets with fruit and fries. Brandon and I soaked up the happiness of our daughters.

We couldn't stay at the restaurant for too long—Kate was due back at the hospital late that afternoon. At the hospital, they hooked up a very heavy bag of fluids to Kate's port and showed me how to change the pump's battery should it die before her hospital admission the next day. I slung the bag of fluids over my shoulder like a purse and held Kate's line in my hand as a leash. I quickly realized how cumbersome this bag would be as Kate would be literally attached to me for the next few days.

The next morning, Tuesday, Kate and I headed to the hospital for her lumbar puncture, intrathecal chemotherapy, and for her bone marrow aspiration. It was day forty-two! Once again, it was time to check to see if Kate's cancer was in remission. After she was asleep in procedures, I paused outside her room as I always did and offered a quick prayer for God to watch over her and protect her. But this time, I also prayed that we would hear that wonderful word, "remission."

After Kate woke up in recovery, she and I reported back to A Clinic to be admitted upstairs and finally, late that afternoon, we were taken to the second floor.

During our first stay in the hospital, we had learned the drill of recording Kate's food and liquid intake and her output as well. But this stay required a little more monitoring due to the chemo she would be receiving. The nurse would begin her high-dose methotrexate once she had taken a urine sample from Kate to establish a baseline of the chemistry in her urine.

Our potty-trained girl had regressed almost back to square one after all that she had been through during the past six weeks. I either had to get Kate to tinkle in a cup or I could slip an absorbent pad in her pull-ups and wait on her to go. Once Kate went to the bathroom, her nurse could hook her up to her chemo. Then I would have to deliver samples of Kate's urine or the absorbent pads from her pull-up to her nurse every time she went to test and make sure she was clearing the methotrexate efficiently.

Fortunately, Kate cooperated and used the bathroom in a cup and her first round of high-dose methotrexate began! The next morning, I was cleaning up from breakfast when the phone in Kate's room rang.

"Erin?" I heard Martha May's familiar voice ask.

"Good morning, Martha!" I replied.

"Has Dr. Pui been by to see you yet?" she asked.

"No," I answered.

"Well, I am sitting here looking at the results of Kate's bone marrow aspiration from yesterday and her Minimal Residual Disease is negative. Kate is in remission! May 7th will now be known as Kate's remission day!"

Tears filled my eyes and for a moment, I was too happy to speak. I smiled at the sweet little wispy-haired girl sitting in the bed beside me, looking curiously at the blubbery face of her mother.

"I am so happy," I choked out to Martha. "Thank you for calling to tell me."

"You are welcome," she replied, "but you'll have to act surprised when Dr. Pui tells you when he makes his rounds this morning. I don't want to steal his thunder."

I laughed. "It's a deal."

When I hung up the phone, I pulled Kate into my arms for a giant hug and a flood filled my heart.

Kate's little body was so sick when she was diagnosed that remission seemed a long way off. But through the power of prayer and the omnipotence of God, Kate had responded perfectly to her chemotherapy.

How amazing to consider the power of God! Our God who spoke this world into existence, our God who parted the waters of the Red Sea to save the Israelites from the Egyptians, our God who raised His Son from the dead so that we, through His sacrifice, could have remission of our sins—that same God had healed our Kate! What a mighty God we serve!

Just a half hour later, Brandon walked into Kate's room to swap out with me for Kate's hospital stay. His mom had come to tend to Jenna for the day so that I could start packing up our room at the Ronald McDonald House. As soon as he set his blue duffel bag down, I grabbed him by the hands and turned him to face me.

"I just got off the phone with Martha May," I began, a huge smile breaking across my face. "She received the results from Kate's bone marrow aspiration. Kate is in remission!"

Brandon smiled and enveloped me in a bear hug. Then we crawled on either side of Kate and prayed together, thanking God for healing our girl.

After visiting for a few minutes, I kissed everyone goodbye and went to see Jenna and Grammy. I was thrilled to begin packing for home!

In twenty-four hours, Kate's chemo was done and the drinking and waiting game began. The nurse urged Kate to drink as much as possible to flush the methotrexate out of her system, and she obediently, albeit begrudgingly, drank as she was told.

The following day, Thursday, Kate's methotrexate level was tested. It needed to be below 0.5 percent to be able to go home. Kate's level was 0.58 percent. We were so close!

Kate's methotrexate level was acceptable enough to be discharged from the hospital and we would stay another night at the Ronald McDonald House. Even though I'd already packed up our room, I'd had enough foresight to pack a small overnight bag for us just in case. This trial had definitely taught us to expect the unexpected and be prepared for anything.

We had an extra day, so we cut what was left of Kate's hair into a little bob so it didn't look so stringy. We scattered the thin locks under a tree outside the House.

"It's for the mommy birds," Brandon and I explained to Kate. "They can use it to build a nest for their baby birds." She was okay with that. It helped her loss feel purposeful.

Also with the extra day, Kate had a chance to paint a sign to go on the wall of the Ronald McDonald House. All patients got to choose a clear plastic cut-out to put their handprints on and decorate when they left the house. Kate chose a fish and the house manager helped her paint her hands blue and put her handprints on the fish. Once the paint was dry, I wrote Kate's name, diagnosis, remission day, and copied the passage from Deuteronomy 20:3-4 on the fish. Kate added the finishing touch on the fish when she wrote her name all by herself.

The next day, Brandon took Kate back up to the hospital to have her methotrexate level checked again. When they came back, he greeted me with words that sounded sweet to my ears.

"We're going home!"

It still took us a couple of hours to finalize our packing and to check out of the Ronald McDonald House. By late that afternoon, we were pulling out of the parking lot. We had accumulated so many toys, books, games, and crafts over the past two months that both my car and Brandon's truck were packed to the max.

We stopped in Corinth, Mississippi for a quick dinner at a McAlister's Deli. When we pulled in the parking lot, Kate asked in a pitiful voice, "We're not going home?"

Over the weeks, we had grown accustomed to Kate's very sparse head of hair and her slightly rotund figure from forty days of steroids. Now that we were out of Memphis, away from St. Jude where Kate blended in, we braced ourselves for stares and odd looks as we entered the deli. Our reception at the restaurant, however, was actually quite the opposite.

After ordering, we settled down at a table and it wasn't long before our sandwiches were brought out. As we neared the end of our meal, an employee slipped four jumbo-sized chocolate chip cookies onto our table, told us to enjoy them, and walked away. The manager also came by the table and handed a card for a free meal to Brandon. Our hearts smiled at the generosity of these strangers, and we vowed then and there that McAlister's Deli would be a regular stop of ours whenever Kate's health would permit it.

Once we had finished dinner, we continued our trek to Huntsville and arrived home late that evening. It was dark outside, but my parents had come the day before to make sure the house was ready for us and had left the front porch lights on. Some thoughtful friends had hung a "Welcome Home" banner over our front door, left some flowers on the doorstep, and tied balloons to the mailbox. When we stepped into our house, it smelled fresh and clean. Mom and Dad had cleaned the house from top to bottom and my grandfather had paid for someone to clean our carpets while we were gone. It didn't take long for the tears to start falling.

The girls were ecstatic to be home! They flew to see the colorful balloons tied to the mailbox, went squealing from one end of the house to the other, and ran to see their rooms while Brandon and I unloaded the truck and car. The boxes of toys that had been generously given to the girls during our stay completely filled the bonus room upstairs, and the kitchen and dining room downstairs were filled with our luggage. There was a lot to unpack, but I pushed that from my mind, and we began to get the girls ready for bed.

From day one of being diagnosed, Kate had attached herself to that little blue toy car that she clutched in her hands as she slept. Every time we put her to bed in the hospital and at the Ronald McDonald House, we had to make sure she had her car.

As we tucked her into her bed that night, I handed the car to Kate and kissed her good night. She sat up and stopped me before I walked away.

"Here, Mom." Kate held out the toy car and a puzzled look crossed my face. "I don't need this anymore." She lay her head back down, thumb in mouth, and closed her eyes to sleep.

Kate was home.

Over the past two months, your daddy and I have asked "Why?" from time to time. Why us? Why you? Why cancer?

Your daddy and I have posed these questions occasionally, but every time, the conclusion we came to was the same.

Because God's plan is perfect, whether we understand it or not.

We already saw the unfolding of God's plan long before you were diagnosed with cancer. God had an amazing plan when He created the avenue of prayer. He knew that we, as Christians, would need the opportunity to communicate with our Creator and lay our cares on Him. Do you have the best doctors in the nation treating you? Yes! Do we live in a time in which modern medicine can treat above and beyond our expectations? Yes! But no doctor or medicine can compare to the thousands of prayers being offered up all over the world on your behalf. God's plan is perfect in that we can come together as brothers and sisters in Christ, help to bear one another's burdens, and make our requests known to God.

God had a plan when your daddy started traveling for his job and was gone for a week, sometimes even two weeks, each month. While his absence was difficult on all of us, I see now that God started preparing us for this moment over three years ago. Because of all his travel, your daddy had accrued over twenty weeks of comp time, sick leave, and vacation days. What an amazing blessing it is that he has been able to be here, and that we were able to support and relieve each other during this time!

When you did not achieve remission on day fifteen, it would have been easy to doubt God. Instead, we had to acknowledge that God's plan for you was greater than our plan. While we waited to hear the word "remission," we submitted in total dependence on Him and solidified our trust in God's power to heal.

The moment we began this new chapter of our lives, we were desperately determined to see what God's plan might be for this journey. We just knew it had to be some big, grand, intricate scheme in which we would play a part. While there may still be a grand scheme, we are already reaping a great deal from this journey.

We have been given time to grow closer together as a family. Between business trips and all the daily activities that consumed our time at home, we have never had this much time together as we've had over the past couple of months.

More importantly, though, we have been given an opportunity to grow closer to God. We have learned to depend on Him completely, rely on Him to help us carry this heavy load, and have learned to trust His plan.

So even after this journey is complete, my Kate, if all we have gained from it is being closer together as a family and closer to God, I'd say God had a pretty grand plan for this journey after all.

Love,

Mommy

"Behold, these are but the outskirts of his ways, and how small a whisper do we hear of him! But the thunder of his power who can understand?" (Job 26:14).

"For my thoughts are not your thoughts, neither are your ways my ways, declares the Lord. For as the heavens are higher than the earth, so are my ways higher than your ways and my thoughts than your thoughts" (Isaiah 55:8-9).

Chapter 6: Be Still

July 1, 2013

Dear Kate,

I have never been very good at being still or waiting. If we ever had a free weekend, I filled it. If I ever had a spare five minutes, I crammed in a fifteen minute chore or activity. I have never been a huge fan of down time and have always tried to keep myself busy.

The past few months have been a steep learning curve for me in building patience. I have learned that just because an appointment is scheduled for a certain time doesn't mean the appointment is actually going to take place at that time. And we just had to wait. I have learned that all plans come to a screeching halt when your counts are not good. And we just had to wait.

I must learn to be content with waiting and being still because waiting and being still are part of God's plan too.

We ended up coming home on Mother's Day weekend. Kate's counts had been good when we left Memphis on Friday, so we went to worship as a family on Sunday morning. It thrilled my heart to worship together on Mother's Day. However, I worried at the reception Kate would get from everyone that morning. Kate looked so different than when we left. She was about ten pounds heavier from forty days of steroids and had a very thin head of hair.

As soon as we entered the building, we were greeted with lots of smiles and hugs and only a few gave pained looks at Kate's altered appearance. We returned the warm hugs and then hurried the girls off to Bible class just in time for class to start. Brandon and I slipped into the class on prayer and sat up front in the only seats that were left. The teacher had already passed out a song for the class to sing and began leading it after we sat down. I'd held it together through the greetings upon our arrival, but as we sang the words, "But He careth more for thee, But He careth more for thee?" the tears began to pour.

Oh, how we knew just how much God cared! A kind lady sitting behind us passed me a tissue. I gratefully wiped away the tears streaming down my face and struggled to force back down the sobs that were threatening to erupt from my chest. I was desperately wishing we had sat in the back row instead of the front! We were happy to be back amongst our spiritual family at our home congregation and enjoyed catching up with everyone after worship that morning. The girls happily played with their friends, but it wasn't long before Kate began to droop. She was physically exhausted from our big morning, so we headed home for lunch and her afternoon nap.

Soon after getting Kate and Jenna down for their naps, Brandon's parents and grandmother came to visit for the afternoon and go to worship with us that evening. I had already been leaning toward staying home with Kate that evening to let her rest, and when Kate woke up from her nap with her sucking thumb covered in blood, I knew she would definitely not be going to worship that evening.

The nurses in Memphis had warned us about the aftermath of the high-dose methotrexate Kate had. One side effect was mouth sores. Kate had developed these sores all inside her mouth and they had begun to bleed.

Memphis had given us the phone number for the St. Jude Affiliate Clinic in Huntsville, and Brandon spoke with Dr. Carolyn Russo, the doctor on call for the weekend. She instructed us to take Kate to the emergency room to get her checked out right away and that she would notify them that we were coming. Because Brandon's family was visiting, I offered to take Kate to the hospital so that he could stay with his family. Knowing her port would have to be accessed, I smeared the cold numbing cream on the skin over it and covered it with the dressing before loading her into the car. Kate knew immediately what the numbing cream meant—she was going to get a needle. She screamed hysterically the entire twenty-minute drive to the hospital.

As we pulled into the parking lot by the emergency room, all the memories of the day Kate was diagnosed came flooding back. I fought back tears as I picked up a screaming Kate, strapped her mask over her face, and grimly walked through those doors once again. As soon as we stepped through the sliding glass doors, a nurse was waiting to greet us and immediately guided us to a room. I was very grateful I did not have to sit in the waiting room with a bunch of sick kids and my immune-suppressed child!

When we went into the room, Kate now knew that a needle was in her very near future and her hysterical screaming escalated to a whole new level. She was writhing in fear and the mask strapped over her face did very little to muffle her piercing cries. The nurse seemed very scattered as she continued to come and go out of the room, gathering materials to access Kate. She put on a mask and then passed one for me to put on as well. She ran a thermometer over Kate's forehead and briskly informed me that Kate had a fever of 100.8. My throat tightened as fear took hold of me. I knew the gravity of a cancer patient getting a fever.

"What kind of port does she have?" the nurse asked.

"A subcutaneous port," I replied and her eyebrows furrowed before she left the room again. Kate still continued to scream. Anxiety began to fill my chest and I never thought I would long to be back at St. Jude as I did at this moment.

The nurse returned a few minutes later with another nurse and a pack containing all the materials necessary to access Kate. The first nurse laid the pack on the metal tray right in front of the sobbing Kate and hesitantly began opening it. Kate saw what was in the pack and began twisting in an attempt to get away. I had to put her in my lap and wrap my arms around her arms and my legs around her legs to restrain her.

After the pack was open, the nurses both stood looking at the contents. Because of their masks, all I could see of each nurse's face was her eyes. And both pairs of eyes were filled with uncertainty. The first nurse asked the other in a loud whisper, "What do we do now?"

Tears began filling my eyes and I prayed to God for everything to be okay. I turned to the first nurse.

"Do you know how to access her port?" I asked.

Exasperated, the nurse replied, "She is just screaming so loud and I can't concentrate when they act like that." With that, she abruptly left the room.

You can't concentrate when a kid is screaming? You work in the pediatric ER! I thought to myself.

I turned to the other nurse. "Do *you* know how to access her port?"

She calmly replied, "I do. I think the other nurse was just confused when you called it a subcutaneous port. She's not familiar with that terminology."

"I have never heard it called anything else," I explained over Kate's crying, bewildered.

The second nurse began cleaning Kate's chest with alcohol. After it dried, the nurse blessedly got that needle in her port and covered over it with its dressing. As soon as the needle was in, Kate immediately stopped crying. The nurse drew some blood for labwork and left the room. In all, Kate had sat for forty-five minutes waiting to be accessed. I felt sick to my stomach and wondered if this was what it was going to be like every week while we were at home.

Kate and I watched a few cartoons on the television while we waited for her counts to come back. The first nurse, upon orders from Dr. Russo, went ahead and began an infusion of an antibiotic through Kate's line to prevent any infection from developing in Kate's mouth. The antibiotic ran through one line and was sitting on the table next to the hospital bed in a large awkward box that pumped the medicine. Kate had another line attached to her IV pole, through which fluids were being pumped.

118

A little before seven, Kate informed me that she needed to go to the bathroom. I tried to decide how I was going to help her down the hall to the bathroom, keep her from tripping over her lines, push her pole, and carry the large box containing the antibiotic at the same time.

At that moment, the first nurse came back in the room.

"Oh good!" I greeted her. "I'm glad you're here. Kate needs to go to the bathroom. Would you carry the box of Kate's antibiotic while I push the pole and help her down the hall?"

The nurse immediately turned around and headed for the door, stating, "My shift is over at seven. The next nurse can help you." And she was gone.

I was dumbfounded. It wasn't too much longer before the new nurse came in the room to meet us and she was absolutely wonderful. She immediately helped us to the bathroom, got us some snacks because supper had come and gone, and chatted with us for a little while as we waited for Kate's counts to come back.

Another hour or so went by before her counts were back. Her ANC had dropped dramatically from 1800 when we left Memphis on Friday to 900 that day. The methotrexate was most assuredly doing its job. The new nurse checked Kate's temperature again and it was completely normal. She commented that it was probably high earlier because Kate had worked herself up into such a frenzy over getting her needle.

In all, we spent about five hours in the emergency room on Mother's Day and were scheduled to report to the St. Jude Affiliate Clinic first thing in the morning to follow up with Dr. Russo.

It wasn't long after that Kate declared she did not want me to use numbing cream anymore. Anticipation was her worst enemy. She chose the pain of the quick stick of the needle over the numbing cream and the thirty minutes of nervous agony that gripped her heart while she waited to get that needle.

The next morning, I followed the directions to the Affiliate Clinic and realized I knew exactly where it was! It was in a building attached to the

119

hospital on the floor just above my gynecologist. All those years of going for my baby appointments and I never knew there was a St. Jude clinic on the floor above it. There had never been a reason to have known that before now.

As soon as we walked in, I breathed a sigh of relief. We were home. It was clean, very kid-friendly, and most importantly the nurses knew exactly what they were doing. The front of the clinic was a waiting room with chairs, the secretary's office, and a small play area. Down the hall were several exam rooms where the patients were assessed and accessed. The back of the clinic was where chemo and transfusions were administered. It contained several pairs of blue reclining chairs that could be made private by pulling a curtain around each pair. A television hung from the ceiling in front of each pair and patients could pass the time watching shows or movies.

But the best part was the play area! It had a large round table for crafts, a couple of stations with video games, storage cabinets filled with games and toys, and shelves displaying a large assortment of kids' movies. Kate and Jenna immediately occupied themselves at a table with toy dinosaurs and greeted anyone who approached with a mighty roar!

For the first time, we met Dr. Russo in person. She would be Kate's primary doctor when we were home in Huntsville. Dr. Russo was petite with olive skin and short dark hair, peppered with gray. She seemed very serious, but smiled easily and was friendly with Kate.

Dr. Russo examined Kate thoroughly and within an hour or so, we were ready to start for home. Our instructions were to report back to the clinic on Thursday for a follow-up visit and to check Kate's counts again.

We reported back that Thursday. While Kate's white blood cell count, ANC, and platelets were holding steady, her hemoglobin had dropped to critical levels again, so we came back again the next day for a blood transfusion.

In our ten days at home, we spent almost half of those days at the clinic. The other half were filled with catching up on everything we had missed while we were in Memphis for the previous two months. I stayed up late almost every night trying to unpack, to sort through all the boxes and boxes of toys the girls had received, and to wrap wedding and graduation gifts.

We were scheduled to go back to Memphis on Wednesday for the second of four rounds of high-dose methotrexate. Kate, who apparently couldn't wait to start our road trip westward, hopped into bed with us bright and early at six in the morning. That should have been a sign of the day ahead.

I packed bags for myself and the girls and we went first to the clinic to make sure Kate's counts were okay before we began our trek to Memphis.

Kate's nurse for the day was Caroline. A New Zealand native, Caroline's accent immediately intrigued Kate. Add Caroline's dark hair, mischievous eyes, and equally mischievous spirit, and Caroline quickly became one of Kate's best buddies.

Caroline pricked Kate's finger for a quick count check and we headed to the play area. I visited with the child life specialist Ms. Beth while the girls played with the toy dinosaurs and roared at the nurses and patients. A couple of hours went by and knots began to form in my stomach. "What was taking so long?" I wondered.

Slowly, Kate's counts began to come back, one report at a time. Her white blood cell count was borderline acceptable to proceed with her next round of methotrexate. Another thirty minutes or so passed. Her platelet count came back and was just barely acceptable as well. Eventually, her hemoglobin and ANC came back as well, both as sketchy as the two previous counts.

Caroline wasn't sure that we would be able to go forward with Kate's next round and contacted Memphis to see what Dr. Pui wanted to do. I thought I was about to have an anxiety attack as I thought about all the careful packing I had done and how we were supposed to have been in Florence an hour earlier to drop Jenna off with her Grammy. We were also pushing it to make it in time for Kate's appointment to be accessed that evening in Memphis. Finally, the word came back from Dr. Pui that he wanted to press forward, and while I was relieved, Caroline expressed her concern to me over how low Kate's counts were.

I didn't quite understand her concerns then, but I would soon enough.

We stopped at a sandwich shop on our way out of town, although lunch time had come and gone. The girls had snacked heavily at the clinic so they barely touched what I ordered for them. I hungrily ate my sandwich, but was constantly having to discipline the girls during lunch. Irritated at their behavior and stressed at how our morning had gone, I was becoming increasingly snappy. When neither girl would eat their food, Kate would not sit still in her seat, and Jenna pinched me, I'd had enough.

I grabbed their food and tossed it in the garbage as I hauled them both back out to the car, seething the entire way. As I buckled them into their car seats, I ranted and raved, yelling at them over their behavior and losing all self-control. When I stood beside the car after finishing my rant, I noticed a truck driver who had witnessed every second of my ugly meltdown. I was mortified and ashamed. I plopped down into the driver's seat of my car and burst into tears, the anxiety of the morning and exhaustion from the past week and a half catching up to me.

An hour later, I pulled into the gas station where we were meeting Grammy. Kate was just starting to doze off. I pleaded with her to stay awake for just a few more minutes. Grammy was waiting on us and kept an eye on the girls while I ran inside to go to the bathroom after I pumped the gas. Once I arrived back at the car, I passed Jenna over to Grammy with a quick hug and kiss goodbye and hopped back into the car. We were cutting it close, but it looked like we could make it just in time for Kate's appointment that evening in Memphis. As I hopped in, I noticed Kate had fallen asleep while I'd been inside using the bathroom. Hoping for some peace and quiet for the rest of the ride, I quietly shut the car door and turned on the engine. Slowly I shifted the car into drive and eased out of the gas station and back onto the highway. As soon as I pulled onto the highway, Kate abruptly sat up, rubbed her eyes, and asked perkily, "Where's Jenna?"

Inwardly, I groaned. So much for a quiet drive! Kate was very good, though, and entertained herself with some coloring books for the rest of the way. As we drove onward, dark clouds loomed, and we drove through four separate torrential downpours over the course of the next three hours. By the time we got to Memphis, my hands were achy from gripping the steering wheel tightly in the gusting wind and the buckets of rain.

We pulled into the parking lot of the Memphis Grizzlies House with ten minutes to spare before Kate's appointment. I saw the hospital shuttle sitting in front of the hotel, ready to go to the hospital. I slung Kate's backpack on my back, scooped her up in my arms, and sprinted through the pouring rain just in time to catch the shuttle before it left.

Kate was successfully accessed and hooked up to her bag of fluids and we made it to the cafeteria a few minutes before it closed to grab a bite to eat for supper. We walked back over to the Grizzlies, both very ready to settle down for a good night's sleep.

"Hi!" I said to the receptionist standing at the front desk. "We're ready to check in." I gave him Kate's name and he shuffled through his stack of papers for me to sign.

"We are booked for the night and are sending people to a nearby hotel," he began as he shuffled through the papers, "but it looks like you are going to be staying at the Ronald McDonald House," he stated, pulling out Kate's information from the stack.

I sighed as he handed me our meal cards and paperwork to give at the front desk of the Ronald McDonald House. Just then, I noticed that the shuttle heading for the Ronald McDonald House was sitting outside of the Grizzlies. Not even thinking, I grabbed Kate, the paperwork, and our meal cards, and hopped onto the shuttle just as it was pulling out from the Grizzlies.

It took all of about a minute for me to realize my error.

I was so embarrassed. "I'm sorry," I told the driver. "We have our car here and we need to get off."

"You can leave your car parked here. That's fine," he reassured me.

I shook my head, even more embarrassed. "Well, our luggage is in the car," I sheepishly explained.

The driver pulled over and Kate and I hopped off and began walking back to our car. We drove down the road to the Ronald McDonald House, checked in, and I got Kate and her heavy bag of fluids settled on the bed in our room. I put in a movie for her to watch while I went to unload the car.

I pulled the luggage cart laden with our bags behind me to the door of our room. I reached into my pocket for my keys, only to discover that my pockets were empty! I had left the keys in the room with Kate! I reached my hand up to knock on the door and call for Kate to come let me in, but stopped when I remembered that she was attached to that heavy bag of fluids. If she tried to come open the door for me, she would probably pull her needle out from her chest. Instead, I went to find a janitor who graciously let me back into the room.

What a day it had been!

Neither Kate nor I slept well that night. I'd set my alarm for every two hours to change Kate's overnight pull-ups since she was hooked up to the bag of fluids. Morning came all too soon and we headed to the hospital for Kate's LPIT and to be admitted to begin her second high-dose methotrexate afterward. Everything went very smoothly that morning, and I was grateful for something to have been easy after such a difficult day the day before. Whoever would have thought I would consider a lumbar puncture and intrathecal chemotherapy easy?

As soon as Kate's twenty-four hours of methotrexate finished running the next afternoon, I began pushing fluids on her, determined to flush out this methotrexate in record time and go home. I watched the clock and every ten minutes, Kate had to take ten sips from her drink. I did this as long as she was awake and also during the night whenever the nurses awakened her to check her vitals.

As before, I also had to deliver a sample of Kate's urine to her nurse to test and be sure she was clearing the methotrexate efficiently. Because of the amount of fluids she was drinking in addition to her being hooked up to fluids, Kate had to go to the bathroom every forty-five minutes exactly.

This was an ordeal in and of itself as I unhooked plugs, wires, and lines and then hooked her back up again after she was done. In between making her drink and all her bathroom trips, I recorded her intake of food and beverage as well as her output on a chart hanging in the room.

She had cleared enough methotrexate by the following day to be discharged back to the Ronald McDonald House. We were scheduled to meet with Dr. Pui the following morning to see if she had cleared enough to be able to go home. In those thirty-six hours, Kate drank over 120 ounces of fluids and I was pretty sure I could hear her sloshing when she walked.

We sat in the back of the medicine room on that Saturday morning, eager to hear the word "home." The pharmacist came to meet with us first and shared the good news that Kate had indeed cleared her methotrexate. I was thrilled and ready to be discharged, and then the pharmacist added, "But…"

But? But what? It was very clearly explained to me that if Kate cleared the methotrexate, she could go home. We should be in Memphis for four days and at home for ten. There were no "buts" about it!

"But Dr. Pui wants to talk with you about Kate's counts," the pharmacist finished.

My heart sank, and just a minute later Dr. Pui entered the room along with a nurse.

"White blood cell count is too low," he began in his brisk manner. "It is not safe to go home." He must have seen my countenance fall because his manner softened. "If you absolutely need to go home, you can. You live by Affiliate Clinic, right?" I nodded my head in affirmation, my spirits lifting momentarily. He continued, thinking out loud, "It is Saturday. Monday is Memorial Day so clinic will be closed. I will be on plane on Tuesday and will not be able to be reached with counts…" his voice trailed off.

As he spoke, I realized how critical Kate's condition was even before the methotrexate began to take its toll. I took a deep breath before speaking, "Dr. Pui, if it is safer for her to be here, we will stay here."

He considered me for a moment and then nodded. "I want her right by hospital." He stood to leave and before he walked out the door, he turned and said, "I was wrong. I should not have gone forward with her chemo. I am sorry." Then he left, leaving the nurse and the pharmacist behind with us.

As soon as he left, my tears began to flow. The nurse ran to grab a box of tissues while the pharmacist offered words of sympathy. After composing myself, we scheduled another count check for Monday and then headed back to the Ronald McDonald House for the afternoon. When we went back into our room at the Ronald McDonald House, Kate asked in a tremulous voice, "Mommy, are we going home?" Tears started streaming down my face again and I tried to explain that her counts were too low for us to leave and go home. Kate started crying, too, and we sat down on the chair in the room and hugged and cried together. In about ten seconds, Kate had moved on and was ready to go play, but I still needed a few more moments to grieve. I missed my husband and my daughter. I missed our home.

And so we sat and waited. It was mind numbing not to have any appointments at the hospital to occupy our time, so Kate and I tried to break up our day as much as possible. We went to the playroom for a little while and then back to the room to watch a show and take a mask break. We had a meal card so our outings each day were to the hospital to eat at the cafeteria. We sometimes ate outdoors on a little bench outside the café to break up the monotony of it all. We could have gone to the zoo or to a baseball game that the residents of the Ronald McDonald House were offered, but Kate's counts were so low that I didn't want to risk exposing her to anything.

The following Monday was Memorial Day, and Kate's counts were still terrible. Her hemoglobin had reached a critical level and she was going to need a blood transfusion. She and I spent a few hours in the medicine room that afternoon for her transfusion. As soon as I'd told Brandon that we weren't going home again that day, he and Jenna came to be with us and were waiting on us when we got back to the Ronald McDonald House. They stayed the night and then my parents took off work and came up the next day for a visit.

Kate had another appointment that day to have her counts checked, but her counts still remained critical. She and I stayed behind while everyone headed home. Brandon dropped Jenna off with Grammy again because he had to go back to work, and Kate and I planned to pick her up once Kate's counts rose.

Seeing them had been a breath of fresh air. It occurred to me how much stronger I felt because of them. I knew how much I needed them and their support to make it through this difficult time. I felt like I could conquer the world with my family by my side!

As I lay in bed that night, I thought about how the next day was Brandon's and my ninth wedding anniversary. My heart ached at the thought of spending our anniversary apart, and it ached more so for the reason we were having to spend that anniversary apart.

How I longed to hear the word "home"! The word "home" came soon enough, but not in the way I had envisioned. We reported back again Thursday for a count check. When Martha May paged us to come to A Clinic, I pushed Kate's stroller with an eager and confident smile. My countenance fell though as soon as Martha approached, shaking her head in dismay.

"Kate's counts are even lower," she reported sadly. "And her monocytes, the cells responsible for cranking out white blood cells, are at 1 percent. Her counts are not going to budge for a while."

"Oh, no," I moaned.

She observed my crestfallen face for a moment before saying, "Just go."

"Go?" I repeated, confused.

"Yes, I am going to send you home. I know you will do a good job taking care of her and Dr. Pui trusts you as well. However," she warned, "if Kate begins running a fever on the way home, you absolutely must get her to a hospital within an hour." She pulled up a map on her phone and highlighted the cities that would have a hospital on our path home. "Always have a plan," she continued, "and know which hospital you are going to try to make it to if she starts running a fever."

I took a deep breath and considered offering again just to stay so that Kate would be safe, but my selfish desires and longing for home won over. "Okay," I agreed.

We gathered our belongings from the Ronald McDonald House and were on our way home in less than thirty minutes, only planning to stop momentarily to pick Jenna up from Grammy at a gas station along the way. I may or may not have driven well over the speed limit. Even including our few minutes that we stopped to pick up Jenna, we made it home in record time.

We were scheduled to report to the clinic in Huntsville first thing on Monday morning and, judging from the bruises covering Kate, I wasn't surprised when Dr. Russo said she was going to need a platelet transfusion immediately. Kate's counts were still terrible. Her platelets had reached the lowest ever at 9,000, white blood cell count was 900, ANC was 0, and hemoglobin was 7.2! She received her platelet transfusion and then we came back the following day for a blood transfusion.

By this point in her treatment, Kate was down to about eight strands of hair that hung limply from her head. She looked pitiful. One morning Jenna asked for a ponytail on top of her head and when I complimented her on how cute she looked, Kate asked for one too. Hesitating only for a second, I gathered up all eight of those strands and gave the pony tail holder about ten twists, and Kate had one too! I made sure I complimented Kate on how cute she looked as well.

Soon after this, Kate consented to the shaving of her head and we did it immediately before she changed her mind. It didn't take very long since she did not have much hair left and when I got done, she looked adorable. The best part, though, was that Brandon wanted to shave his head as well. This would be something special for him and Kate to share. His hair went flying and the girls squealed in laughter as I buzzed their daddy's hair off. The picture I got of Kate and Brandon with their matching "hairstyles" was priceless. Some people say a picture is worth a thousand words, but to me that picture was worth a million!

Other members of the family joined in on the fun and her uncle and some of her cousins shaved their heads for Kate too.

During our couple of weeks at home waiting for Kate's counts to rise, another family member received some very scary news. Papa Don called Brandon one evening to tell us he had been diagnosed with prostate cancer. We were shocked and worried, but he was quick to reassure us.

"The doctor said I could choose to do nothing about this and I would probably die from something else other than cancer. However, I'm not crazy about the idea of letting cancer stay in my body, so I'm exploring my options for treatment right now."

While we were relieved to hear that his prognosis was good, it was discouraging to hear that another family member had been diagnosed with cancer. We added Papa Don to our ever-growing list of people battling cancer whom we prayed for every day.

It was two more weeks before Kate's counts finally began to rise. It was a worrisome time filled with several blood and platelet transfusions, and we were very careful to keep Kate well. We made sure she wore her mask if she went outside to play, monitored her food to be sure it was safe and in accordance with the low bacteria diet, limited her exposure to others, and washed hands regularly.

One afternoon, I was sitting in the office when Kate walked in crunching on something in her mouth.

"What are you eating?" I questioned curiously.

"Candy," she casually replied.

"Where did you find that candy?" I asked her incredulously, unable to recall the last time I'd seen a box of that tiny, sour candy in the house.

"On the garage floor."

I threw my arms up in exasperation.

Once Kate's counts were acceptable enough to begin the third round of high-dose methotrexate, we headed back to Memphis, only stopping to drop Jenna off with Grammy in Florence.

After such a difficult second round of methotrexate and the news about Brandon's dad, God knew that we would need a boost to our spirits. We prayed and prayed and Kate drank and drank and she cleared her methotrexate in one day for the third round! We were elated to be headed home so early! However, we didn't get to leave without a warning. Kate's counts were slowly starting to plummet once again. We were instructed to hold Kate's daily oral chemo and to report to the Huntsville Affiliate Clinic first thing Monday morning.

The girls and I went to the clinic Monday morning. As we got off the parkway and stopped at the red light, Kate began to complain that her stomach was hurting. She had not gone to the bathroom in a few days, a side effect of her chemotherapy, and I just thought she was constipated. Then she began to burp and I realized what was about to happen.

Kate threw up everywhere and all I could do was watch helplessly as I had nothing to catch it in. I offered words of reassurance as we drove the last mile to the clinic. She screamed in between each wave of vomit and all I wanted to do was wrap her up in my arms. Well, I would clean her up first, and then wrap her up into a big hug.

I had no extra clothes for Kate so I grabbed the pack of wipes from the diaper bag and tried to clean her up as best as I could. Her blue jean shorts were a lost cause so I ditched them right away and then wiped up her shirt with all the baby wipes I had left. I put Kate in the stroller, slid her mask on over her head, and swung Jenna onto my hip, pushing the stroller with my free hand.

We loaded into the elevator and I just smiled at the man holding the door for us like nothing was unusual about my child, sitting in the stroller with no pants, a damp shirt, a glistening bald head, a mask strapped over her face, and smelling slightly of vomit.

Crystal, the receptionist at clinic, ushered us quickly back to the treatment room where Ms. Beth, the child life specialist, met us with a clean T-shirt for Kate. Dr. Cox, after examining Kate, wanted to give her fluids and monitor her for the day. I surveyed the little room where we would be and immediately called in reinforcements for Jenna. Brandon was there within thirty minutes and took Jenna, as well as the soiled car seat, off my hands. I felt bad that he was going to have to be the one to clean up that car seat. Okay, maybe I really didn't feel *that* bad.

Kate's counts had dropped by the time of our clinic visit later that week. By the following Monday, they had risen again and she had an almost normal ANC. Because her ANC was so good and she had only had a finger prick at the clinic that morning to check her counts rather than a needle in her port, Kate could get wet! We called all our friends that afternoon and they met us at a nearby splash pad.

This impromptu play date was a true testimony to what wonderful friends we have. Each one of them dropped everything they were doing and hauled their kids to the splash pad with just a couple hours' notice.

Kate was ecstatic. She was with her friends, playing in the cool water, eating ice cream, and just being a normal kid...except that she had a bald head. We hadn't really talked with Kate about how others might react to her lack of hair. At one point, we could tell that a couple of kids there were asking Kate about her bald head. We were too far away to hear what was being said, but when Kate leaned over and let them rub her head, we knew everything was just fine!

It was wonderful to be among our friends again, even if it was only for an hour. It was enough to carry us through our last visit to Memphis in our consolidation phase.

We left the next day for the fourth and final treatment of high-dose methotrexate. I was definitely eager to finish consolidation and move on to the next phase of Kate's treatment plan.

We had the routine down pat by now. We dropped Jenna off in Florence with Grammy, arrived at assessment triage Tuesday evening, and Kate was accessed and hooked up to her bag of fluids as usual. We reported the next morning for her appointment with Dr. Pui to review her counts and then headed to procedures for her LPIT.

While Kate was sleeping in her hospital room later that afternoon, already hooked up to her high-dose methotrexate, I hurried to our car to unload our overnight bag for our hospital stay. On my way back up, I ran into the nurse practitioner for the second floor of the hospital. She and I chatted about how this was Kate's last high-dose methotrexate in consolidation and that we were getting ready to begin the last phase, continuation.

"Hey," I began. "Can you show me the entire treatment plan for continuation?"

The nurse practitioner hesitated. "I'm not sure. We usually only show up to two weeks at a time because things can change so much."

"I understand. I just want to see the big picture so that I can know what to expect."

She reluctantly agreed to stop by with the protocol that afternoon and was true to her word. She stopped by an hour later, just as Kate was waking up from her nap.

"Here's the treatment plan," she said as she laid the plan on the table in Kate's room. The plan filled three pages of paper, single spaced, and listed 120 weeks of chemotherapy during continuation, the final phase of treatment for Acute Lymphoblastic Leukemia.

"Kate is standard/high risk, so this column here shows the chemo she will be getting every week," she explained.

"Every week?" I mumbled faintly.

As I stood, soaking in the next two years of our lives, I began to cry. It wasn't just a few tears trickling down my cheeks. It was a downright ugly cry.

"Mommy, what's wrong? Why are you crying?" Kate's voice caught on her last question, tears threatening to spill down her cheeks as well.

I tried to compose myself, angry at myself for crying like that in front of my daughter. The harder I tried to calm down, the harder I cried.

"Mommy is just sad," I explained in between sobs.

I turned to the nurse. "I'm so sorry. It's just really hard to see the next two years of chemotherapy—the next two years of our lives."

The nurse's face was stricken. "I'm so sorry. I shouldn't have shown it to you," she apologized.

My voice suddenly became firm in spite of my tears. "No. This is exactly what I asked you to do. This is exactly what I wanted—to know what to expect. And now I do. So thank you."

She gathered up the papers, asked if we needed anything, and left the room with a small wave goodbye. I was pretty sure that from that moment on, she would never agree to show another parent the 120 weeks of continuation again.

Later that evening, I had settled on the bed with Kate to read some books when a hospital volunteer popped her head in the door.

"Hey guys," she greeted us enthusiastically. "If you're interested, we are throwing a superhero party down the hall and it will start in about five minutes." She waved a quick goodbye and headed to the next room.

Kate's eyes lit up. "Mommy, can we go to the party?"

I smiled. "Sure, but I think we have time to finish our book." I continued to read, but about every thirty seconds, Kate would interrupt to ask if it was time to go to the party.

"Not yet," I would reply.

"Okay, mommy, but you need to hurry, hurry, hurry! I don't want to be late!" she urged and I smiled at her excitement.

We finished reading the book and after slipping some shoes on Kate's feet, unplugging her IV pole, and donning our masks, we headed down the hall for some superhero fun.

Some volunteers had a superhero movie playing on the TV in the common area outside the elevators. They had also set up a station where patients could color pictures of action heroes or make their own superhero mask. Kate colored and chatted with a little girl sitting across the table from her. After a few minutes, however, Kate grew bored with coloring and asked if we could go look out the windows. These windows overlooked the entrance to the hospital and we stood and watched people going in and out of the hospital.

As we stood there, I suddenly became aware that my foot felt wet and when I looked down, my heart lurched in horror. Kate's chemotherapy was pouring out of her line all over my foot and the floor. I stood in shock for a second, but tried to remain calm. I knew that how I reacted would determine how Kate reacted. I picked her up with one arm, grabbed her pole with the other, and started to run the long way back down the hall to the nurses' station. After a couple of steps, I stopped when I realized what a terrible hazardous mess I was going to leave along the way.

I sat Kate back down, my mind scrambling frantically to formulate a new plan. That's when I noticed that her blood was pushing its way out of the line in her chest until it too began pouring out all over the floor!

"What in the world is going on?" I wondered, my panic level rising as I searched for someone to get help.

Right at that moment, another mom we knew came walking up and asked, "How's Kate doing?" I wheeled around and barked at her, "Go get a nurse now!" She took in the scene before her and took off running for the nurses' station.

Another mom sitting nearby realized what was going on and swooped in, closing the clamp on Kate's line. She offered a smile, "This has happened to us before too." She gestured towards the closed clamp. "Closing the clamp won't fix the problem, but it will at least keep everything from spilling out over the floor."

Kate began to whimper at this point and I hugged her with a forced smile, my heart still pounding. In my best attempt at lightheartedness, I told her, "Wow, you're really making a huge mess!" She smiled uncertainly and then four nurses swarmed us. Two took charge of cleaning up the area while the other two escorted us back to our room.

Kate's nurses set to work getting her tubing changed out and I got Kate settled in bed with her dinner that had arrived from the cafeteria while we were at the superhero party. One nurse explained that a cap had come off the end of Kate's tubing and the change in pressure caused her blood to flow backward out of the tube. She said that it happens more often to the little kids because they like to get up and play while the older kids usually just lay around in bed all day.

I asked the other nurse, "What do I do about my foot?"

He shrugged. "Wash it."

What else could I do?

While they worked and Kate ate, I vigorously scrubbed my foot and my shoe in the bathroom sink. I wondered if I might have superhero powers in my right foot now that it had been bathed in chemotherapy!

As soon as her methotrexate finished the next afternoon, I began pushing fluids down Kate, making her take ten sips every ten minutes just as before. The next day, we were free to go back to the Grizzlies, but were instructed to report the following day to see if Kate had cleared her chemo.

I continued to push the fluids down Kate until she'd drunk 120 ounces in two days! One thing Kate understood was the word "home." She knew the more she drank, the sooner she could go home. In fact, occasionally she took a few sips and asked, "Can we go home now?" She broke my heart when I was reading Peter Pan to her. We got to the part where the Lost Boys wanted to go home with Wendy, but Peter didn't. Kate asked very suddenly, "Peter Pan didn't want to go home?" I told her no. She paused for a moment and then whispered, "I want to go home."

When we reported to have her methotrexate level checked, however, we missed going home by .06 percent! It usually took Kate two days to clear her chemo anyway, so I wasn't too devastated. Her white blood cell count and ANC were good, so we decided to spend the afternoon at the Memphis Zoo. We scurried back to the Grizzlies just for a moment to regroup and then headed to see some animals!

Kate loved seeing the animals again and it was nice to be able to enjoy some sunshine after being cooped up in the hospital for the past couple of days. I had the stroller for Kate in case she got tired, but she opted to walk most of the time, eager to stretch her legs. The only problem was that Kate was still hooked up to her bag of fluids because she had not cleared her methotrexate yet. I had to carry the bag because it was so heavy, so Kate was literally attached to me. I had to constantly remind her not to run ahead, for fear of pulling the line out of her chest.

When we went to see the sea lions, my apprehension grew. It was fairly crowded, and I was worried about someone tripping over Kate's line. I told her she had to stick to my side like glue and we weaved in and out of the crowd until we made it to the glass wall of their tank. We stood there for a few minutes, gleefully watching the sleek black sea lions swim.

The next moment happened so quickly, I was fairly certain I had indeed gained some kind of superpower from the chemotherapy that had spilled all over my foot. Kate stepped away from me for one second to put her drink down on the bench behind us just as a heavy-set middle-school-aged boy came barreling through the crowd. Kate's line hung in the air in between us and just as his foot touched the line, I wrapped both arms around him and tackled him, throwing him backward.

"Her line! Her line! Watch her line!" I commanded him and he brushed himself off, mumbled a brief apology, and continued on his way.

I hauled Kate into my arms and told her we were getting out of there! A sweet lady came up and offered to help. She pushed the stroller and helped get us safely outside the sea lion area. I thanked her profusely and we returned to the car because it was getting close to dinner time.

We reported the next day to have Kate's methotrexate level checked, but her level was still a little too high. I was so bummed. It was hard calling Brandon and Jenna and telling them that we wouldn't be coming home that day either. Jenna's voice sounded so sweet as she chirped, "I miss you, Mommy. I love you!" My heart ached for her.

We decided to make the most of yet another day in Memphis and went back to the zoo again to see a few more exhibits that we'd missed the day before. Kate finally cleared her chemo the next day and we were sent home. We were so glad to be done with consolidation and moving on with the next phase of treatment, continuation!

The characteristic of being still requires a lot of patience, and the lesson of patience in waiting rang clear during consolidation, didn't it, Kate?

During consolidation, frustration, bitterness, and discouragement definitely crept into my heart. These are all tools of Satan. While we have been waiting, Satan tried to tell me that God had forgotten us, and he worked to bring doubt into my heart.

But I know God has not forgotten us. God is teaching me the beautiful design of waiting on and trusting in Him.

I considered David, who was promised by God to be anointed king over all Israel and then had to wait twenty years for that promise to be fulfilled. During those years, David fled for his life from Saul, refused to kill the Lord's anointed even when given multiple opportunities to do so, and thus showed his trust that God would give him the throne in His own time.

David waited on the Lord.

The hectic life we lived, created by a too-full schedule, never left any time to wait on the Lord. To wait on the Lord, you must be still. I read the passage in 1 Kings 19 recently in which the Lord passed by Elijah. God wasn't in the great strong wind. He wasn't in the earthquake or the fire. However, He was found in the "gentle blowing" or the "still small voice." God cannot be found in the rush of a chaotic life, but only in those still and quiet moments when our hearts can truly seek Him without distraction.

As we enter this last phase of treatment—and the years upon years that will follow—we must remember that God, at times, will make us wait for what is best.

So we must wait on God, knowing that He is working in us for the good things that lie ahead and that His plan is most assuredly worth the wait.

Love,

Mommy

"Be still, and know that I am God. I will be exalted among the nations, I will be exalted in the earth!" (Psalms 46:10).

"Therefore the Lord waits to be gracious to you, and therefore He exalts himself to show mercy to you. For the Lord is a God of justice; blessed are all those who wait for him" (Isaiah 30:18).

Chapter 7: A Deeper Understanding

September 25, 2013

Dear Kate,

In the 1950s, the survival rate for leukemia was zero. It was a death sentence as ninety percent of children died within a week after diagnosis. And, without being too graphic, it was also a bloodbath, a nightmarish end for any parent to watch and for any child to suffer through.

An American doctor of Hungarian descent was intrigued by these children and threw himself into finding a cure for leukemia. He told the parents of his patients, "I'm not here to give you a shoulder to cry on. I'm here to give you hope." He pushed the envelope, made a lot of people angry, and many people thought he was insane. But he plowed ahead anyway.

This doctor and his partner were the first to realize that they needed to figure out a way to stop the bleeding first so they could address the underlying problem of leukemia. After much research and many experiments, platelet transfusions bought them enough time to try to figure out how to destroy the leukemia cells. This doctor was also the first to push for a "chemo cocktail," or combination of chemos given at once rather than one at a time. With these efforts, the leukemia cells were destroyed and his patients achieved remission. However, they always relapsed. He was the first to realize that leukemia needed to be treated with prolonged, regimented, and *regular chemotherapy. Suddenly, the survival rate for childhood leukemia soared!*

Kate, I thought the day you were diagnosed with cancer was the closest to death you would ever be.

I thought that, from that moment on, we would always be taking steps forward to your healing. I thought that as each day passed, we would see our little girl's health being restored.

I was wrong.

At diagnosis, I didn't understand that the purpose of chemotherapy was to bring you to death's door—not just once, but over and over again as your bone marrow was repeatedly wiped out by the drugs. I didn't understand that I would have to watch you suffer for a long time. Not for just days, weeks, or months…but for years!

No parent wants to watch their child suffer. Every parent wishes they could take away their child's pain and bear that burden for them. But this monster was something you were going to have to fight physically on your own. We, as your family, were standing by your side and holding you up with love and hugs and kisses and encouraging words and prayers to carry you through this long journey.

We knew you were going to have to get much sicker in order to get better one day. You must get sicker in order to live!

*H*ello, continuation!

We survived induction and consolidation and moved into the third and final phase of continuation therapy that lasts 120 weeks. The term "final phase" sounds so great. And then they have to throw in the "120 weeks" part.

The purpose of continuation therapy was to continue chemotherapy for a prolonged amount of time to thoroughly eradicate any lingering leukemia cells present in Kate's blood. Just because the machine didn't detect any leukemia cells when Kate was deemed to be in remission didn't mean there weren't any there. In fact, there could have been even a million leukemia cells still floating around in Kate's blood that the machine couldn't detect. If Kate were to stop treatment right now, her leukemia would almost certainly come back. However, this prolonged treatment plan has been shown to have a high survival rate of 94 percent. While 120 weeks seemed formidable, the years we were gaining with Kate were more than worth it.

In continuation, Kate was scheduled to have bloodwork done every week and receive chemotherapy each week as well, with only a few random weeks off at the beginning. She would receive the majority of these treatments at the St. Jude Affiliate Clinic in Huntsville. The weeks off were scheduled after some of Kate's harsher chemos to give her body a chance to recover. She would receive an assortment of doxorubicin, pegaspargase, and vincristine for the first twenty-three weeks with no rhyme or reason as to what chemo she got and when she got it. After the first twenty-three weeks, Kate's chemotherapy schedule would settle into a four-week rotation of different chemos.

During continuation, Kate was also scheduled to be on the dreaded steroids once again, this time in the form of dexamethasone, or DEX for short. She would be on DEX for five days every four weeks and take three doses each day. Her nurses had warned us of how DEX was much worse than its cousin prednisone, and we wondered how anything could be much worse than the forty days of prednisone that Kate had been on during induction. We would soon find out.

Continuation also included two re-inductions in which Kate would be hit again with some harsher or higher doses of chemos in order to wipe her bone marrow of any lingering leukemia cells. Re-induction one was scheduled from weeks seven to nine and re-induction two from weeks seventeen to nineteen. We would return to stay in Memphis for three weeks for both of these re-inductions.

We were also slated to go back to Memphis every four weeks for Kate's LPIT. She would receive pegaspargase during our visit to Memphis.

However, because of allergic reaction concerns, she would have to wait four hours after anesthesia before she could begin the two-hour infusion of this chemo. So our stay in Memphis would be three days until she swapped pegaspargase for another chemo later down the road.

We started week one of continuation with a bang. That day, Kate was scheduled for all three chemotherapies—doxorubicin, pegaspargase, and vincristine—so Grammy came over to keep Jenna. Kate was also scheduled to start DEX that day as well. Before she and I left for clinic, Grammy and I jokingly belted two fluffy white pillows to Jenna's front and back, put a football helmet on her, and snapped a quick picture. Jenna was ready for Kate's steroid week!

At our clinic visit that day, a middle-school-aged boy was celebrating the end of his treatment. The nurses and doctors all gathered for his "No Mo' Chemo" party and sang a farewell song to him. I attempted to join in, but could not for the tears streaming down my face. Here we were at week one, the beginning of such a long, long road, and while I tried to be happy for this boy who was at the end of his, I couldn't hold back the tears. Crystal, the receptionist at clinic, came over to talk to Kate after the song and very subtly patted my leg and handed me a tissue. I offered a weak smile and appreciated her kind gesture.

After Kate's counts had come back that morning, I was told to go ahead and give Kate her first dose of DEX. I filled her syringe with the strong smelling medicine and she obligingly swallowed it, cringing as it went down. That afternoon before we left, I squeezed in another dose and she gagged a little as it went down her throat. I asked Dr. Russo if I could mix it with something and she suggested something very sweet like maple syrup to balance the foul tasting medicine. I stored that tip away for her dose that evening.

Kate's counts had been good and she was begging to go to Wednesday night Bible class, so we agreed that she could go. I was a little concerned because she had not had a nap that day, but we couldn't say no to that little pleading face when she asked to go to Bible class. So off we all went, Grammy included because we'd gotten back so late from a long day at the clinic. Kate reveled in being in Bible class with her buddies and played hard afterward, running up and down the aisles as fast as her tired little body would go.

We still had one more dose of DEX to give her that day, so after we got home I filled her syringe once again with the steroid and held it out to her. She vehemently refused.

I had learned a while back that there was no rationalizing with Kate when she got to this point. I had learned to be firm but to also be her cheerleader. I held the syringe to her mouth and told her she needed to take her medicine. She screamed and cried and screamed and cried some more. Grammy hoisted her up on the counter so that she was sitting eye level with us and we both began to tell her that she could do it. There was no choice. She had to do it.

"Kate, take your medicine. Open your mouth. I'll push the medicine in and then you will swallow your medicine. Take your medicine. You can do it. I know you can. Let's do this and be done." I repeated myself over and over again for twenty minutes. Kate continued to scream and cry the entire time.

Finally, she opened her mouth for the syringe and I squirted the medicine in her mouth. She swallowed, gagged once again on the terrible tasting medicine, and then threw up all over herself. My shoulders drooped. All that effort and we were right back where we started.

The next time, we tried to mix it with maple syrup as Dr. Russo had suggested, but she threw that right back up as well. The maple syrup concoction was just too sweet.

We paused for a few minutes while Brandon gave Kate a bath to clean her up and give her a chance to calm down. The poor baby was exhausted and her face was splotchy from screaming and crying for so long.

To say I was frustrated was an understatement. I wasn't frustrated with Kate but with the medicine and with cancer and with chemo and with doctors. I didn't want to go to the clinic anymore. I didn't want to give her any more medicine. I most certainly didn't want to watch any more poison course through her veins. I just wanted to be left alone and I wanted my baby to be left alone.

Brandon calmly tried to talk to Kate and convince her to take her medicine. He sat in our bedroom with her for thirty minutes, but to no avail. We resumed our forceful coaxing, but this time we mixed her steroid with some apple juice. We poured just a little juice into a cup and then added her DEX. We didn't want to do too much juice because if she didn't drink it all, she might not get all of the steroid down. We wanted just enough for a few sips, but also enough to drown out the taste. We dubbed the drink "tangy juice."

Kate eventually agreed to drink the tiny cup of tangy juice we offered her and after polishing off the juice, she was very ready for bed. So were we!

In all, it had taken over an hour to get Kate's steroid down.

The DEX definitely turned Kate into a nasty little demon after a couple of days. She felt awful and if she was awake, she was crying. It also caused severe mood swings. If she got upset, it would turn into an hour-and-a-half-long screaming fit. I was amazed that such a tiny thing could scream with that much force for that long. Sometimes, she would kick her legs on the floor while she screamed, her face angry and beet red.

The steroid also made her insatiably hungry at all times, day and night. She woke us up four to five times a night ready to eat, to go to the bathroom, restless from the steroid, or in pain…sometimes all four! By the end of the week, Brandon and I were exhausted.

Brandon and I had speculated before how the doctors who developed these treatment plans came up with the dosages for each chemo and the order that they would need to be taken. Well, we knew exactly why the doctors decided on five days of DEX. That was all any sane parent could take!

But a couple of days after finishing DEX, the sun would shine once again and I would think, "There you are, Kate."

Also as we entered continuation, Kate began not tolerating her chemo as well as before and began to throw up a lot. At first, Kate didn't understand what was going on and therefore didn't know to try to get to a toilet before she threw up. She also let out piercing screams of terror after she threw up, afraid of what had happened.

I learned pretty quickly the most telling sign of impending doom was that Kate would cough. I would hear her cough, take off sprinting for her, grab her up, and dash to the bathroom, usually making it just in time. There was one occasion when we were at my parents' house eating dinner and I heard Kate cough next to me. I was up, in the kitchen to grab a plastic bag, and back at the table to catch the wave of vomit before anyone else even realized anything was going on. Another time, I was cooking dinner, heard the cough, and managed to get Kate to the toilet just in time. As soon as she finished throwing up, almost in the same breath, she said, "I'm ready to eat dinner now." I told her, "Good, because now I'm not!"

Kate often got sick on the car ride to the clinic, but made me laugh on one trip. We had just pulled up to her usual "puking point" en route to the hospital when I heard what sounded like a gag from the back seat. I whipped open the console and had halfway pulled an emesis bag out when Kate said in a bored voice, "Mom, I'm not about to throw up." It was just a yawn.

We entered the blazing hot month of August in Alabama and slipped outside whenever we could. Kate would strap on that hot, scratchy green mask, throw a big floppy pink hat on her bare head, and she was ready to go! She never lasted too long because of the mask, but we enjoyed whatever freedom the great outdoors could afford us whenever we could!

We spent week three of continuation in Memphis for Kate's lumbar puncture and intrathecal chemotherapy and then arrived at the clinic in Huntsville for week four. Kate's counts were good so we decided to cautiously creep out of our bubble for the weekend and have some fun. We celebrated her being potty trained again with an ice cream sundae, and she savored every bite! On that Friday, however, Kate looked a little pale. I wondered if I should call to have her counts checked to see if she needed a blood transfusion, but brushed the thought from my mind and plowed on into the weekend. I later regretted not following my instinct.

On Saturday, we went swimming and then played at a friend's house that evening. We took Kate to worship Sunday, but we kept her out of Bible class and just sat in the training auditorium by ourselves during worship.

This room was perfect for our situation! The training auditorium was a room in the back of the church building that had a television so you could sit and watch the service in the main auditorium. If Kate was neutropenic, she didn't leave the house at all other than to go to clinic. If her ANC was low, but not quite under 500, we let her go to Bible class with a mask. Then one of us sat with her in the training auditorium while the other sat out in the main auditorium with Jenna. On the rare occasion that Kate's counts were completely normal, we let her go to class and sit in the auditorium on the back row. We set these guidelines for ourselves and did our best to stick to them, although we did occasionally make a bad call.

Sunday morning after Bible class, Kate needed to go to the bathroom. We waited until everyone was in the auditorium for services before heading to the bathroom. I followed her in and waited while she was in the stall. A minute went by and I heard her exclaim that she couldn't reach the toilet paper. She had locked the stall door, but I just used my fingernail to twist the lock open from the outside.

When I opened the door, she asked in shock, "Mom! How. Did. You. Do. That?" She then gasped dramatically and asked in a whisper, "Was that a miracle?"

That afternoon, we put the girls down for naps, and then Brandon left early for a men's meeting before the evening services.

"Mommy!" I heard Kate crying out after she woke from her nap a little later.

I quietly opened her door and knelt beside her bed.

"Hi, baby girl," I said, kissing her forehead.

I froze. I leaned forward and brushed my lips across her forehead again.

Her forehead felt warm. Really warm.

I retrieved the thermometer from her bag of medical supplies and she cried as I slipped it under her tongue.

"Mouth closed," I instructed her and she obeyed.

A minute later, the thermometer flashed 101 and my heart sank.

Kate lay back down in bed, thumb in mouth, while I went to call Brandon. He answered his cell phone after a couple of rings.

"Hey, Kate just woke up from her nap and she's running a fever of 101."

"Oh, no," he replied, letting out a sigh.

"Can you come home and get Jenna and take her to worship with you? And I'll call Dr. Russo and get to the hospital."

"I'm on my way," he confirmed.

After hanging up with Brandon, I called Dr. Russo who instructed us to go to the emergency room. I reluctantly began packing a bag for Kate and myself. I woke Jenna up from her nap, gave her a quick snack, and dressed her for church. Brandon arrived and loaded Jenna into his truck while I loaded Kate into the car, each of us heading in opposite directions.

Kate was not happy about going to the emergency room. She vividly remembered our last visit there and was terrified about going back. I tried to reassure her, but I was scared, too, as I reflected on the difficult nurse we'd had at our last visit.

Fortunately, our nurses this time were fantastic and they quickly got Kate accessed. Her bloodwork came back showing that she needed a blood transfusion and that she was neutropenic with an ANC of 60! If I had requested to have her counts checked on Friday like my gut was telling me, we would have found out her counts had dropped drastically and we most certainly would not have taken her swimming or let her play with friends. We definitely made a bad call that time.

Dr. Russo came by and ordered an antibiotic as well as medicine to break her fever. Because Kate was a leukemia patient with low counts and a fever, she had to be admitted into the Pediatric Intensive Care Unit (PICU). She would stay in PICU until she was fever free for forty-eight hours and until her counts were trending upward. Brandon called his mom to come keep Jenna while we were in the hospital.

We ended up being in the hospital for five days. Sitting in a hospital room for that long can wear on you, but we stayed entertained by watching a lot of movies, coloring a lot of pictures, and reading a lot of books. Brandon also came by every evening after work to let me go home to eat, shower, and visit with Jenna and Grammy for a couple of hours. Escaping that hospital room was a breath of fresh air for me, but Kate didn't get to escape.

Kate did about as well as any three-year-old would do being cooped up in a hospital room. But by the end of the week, we were both very tired. The nurses came in every two hours throughout the night to check her vitals, and it was hard to get any rest.

When we came home, we had four days before we had to leave for Memphis for re-induction one, a three-week stay. During those four days, I unpacked from the hospital, cleaned the house, did laundry, and repacked for us to be gone for the next three weeks. I was a grouch!

The next week, we loaded up the car and all four of us headed west for Memphis to begin re-induction one at week seven. We received some surprising news at Kate's appointment the following morning, though.

Brandon took Kate to her appointments and called me while she was asleep in procedures for her LPIT.

"Hey," I answered my phone. I was sitting in the lobby down the hall from our room while Jenna napped. "Is she asleep?"

"She is. Everything has gone well except for her glucose being too low. She had to have an infusion of fluids before procedures this morning. Justine recommended getting Kate to drink clear soda each morning before her LPIT to make sure her glucose is high enough. But just make sure she finishes it two hours before anesthesia."

I made a mental note to add that to our routine.

"But guess what?" Brandon continued. "We get to go home!"

"What?" I asked, confused.

"Dr. Pui said that he trusts us to take care of Kate and that we can do the rest of re-induction one at home!" Brandon repeated.

I was glad and tried to push the thought of how much packing I'd done out of my mind. After dinner, I swapped out with Brandon and took Kate up to the hospital at seven for her three rounds of chemotherapy. It was a long night and we finished up just before eleven o'clock and then rested up before starting for home the next morning.

Kate had started steroids just after her LPIT as usual, but the steroid schedule for re-induction was a little different. Rather than the usual five days of steroids, Kate would be on dexamethasone for eight days straight, six days off, and then another seven days. If five days was rough, eight days of steroids was a nightmare. Kate was miserable and very snappy with Jenna and me. She ate almost every hour and I was pretty sure I spent half the day preparing food.

Kate, as usual, did not sleep very much while she was on steroids, which means we did not sleep very much either. After a week straight of being awakened four to five times a night for Kate's "munchies" and her many bathroom trips, I insisted that she take herself to the bathroom from then on. She was big enough to do it by herself. The next time she did, and I was awakened at four in the morning to a little voice in the hall, saying, "Mommy, I did it! I went to the bathroom all by myself! And I didn't even wake you up!"

We got a blessed break from steroids for week eight, and because steroids raise her counts we had about two days to play before her counts would plummet. We met some friends at Chick-fil-A during an off hour and played in the play area one day. I had called ahead to make sure there wasn't bingo or a birthday party that morning, explaining our situation, and came armed with a tub of disinfecting wipes. I was going to scrub that play area clean from top to bottom, but we arrived to find that the employees had just finished cleaning it…just for Kate.

During week nine, steroids made their return again and we were counting down the seven days with gritted teeth. Kate's hemoglobin dropped to its lowest ever at 6.5 (normal starts at 11.5), and she had to have a blood transfusion as well as a platelet transfusion. After our visit Friday at the clinic for her platelet transfusion, Dr. Russo instructed us to be back first thing Monday morning because Kate's counts were still very sketchy.

That Sunday night, Brandon and I had already gone to bed when we heard gut-wrenching screams coming from Kate's room. He and I both sat straight up, then bolted to Kate's room where we found her screaming and clutching her stomach.

"It hurts," she sobbed in between screams. "My stomach hurts!"

"Can you point to where it hurts?" Brandon asked.

"It just hurts!" she wailed again. "You need to take me to the hospital!"

We both tried to calm her down and stroked her in attempt to soothe her. I gave her some of her pain medicine in attempt to give her some relief, but it helped only a little.

Brandon and I debated on whether or not to take her to the emergency room. We were fairly sure that her stomach pain was caused by her steroids because a common side effect is acid reflux. Kate was already a dramatic child, and the steroids had raised her drama to an entirely new level. She had not slept through the night in almost three straight weeks, and she was exhausted. We followed our instinct and chose to wait until we saw her doctor in the morning rather than take her to the emergency room.

Brandon stayed in bed with her for a couple of hours and then I went in to her to give him some rest before he had to go to work for the day. Kate continued to cry and sometimes scream off and on throughout the night, and we were all exhausted by the time the first rays of light shone through her window.

Monday morning's clinic visit was just a count check and all of Kate's labs came back normal, so we were glad we had followed our instincts and stayed home the night before. We went home and enjoyed one day off before officially finishing re-induction one and beginning week ten.

The next night, we had put the girls to bed and I was sitting in our bed reading a book when I noticed Kate appear in the doorway.

"Kate, why are you out of bed?" I asked.

She began sobbing and hobbled slowly into our room. "My legs hurt. They hurt so very badly."

Kate clutched her legs with a shriek and fell to the floor, trembling and crying in pain.

I threw my legs over the side of the bed and was with her in a split second. I pulled her into my lap and held her like a baby, rocking her back and forth. She cried uncontrollably and occasionally her legs would shake violently in pain. My heart hurt so much for her.

Brandon, who had been in his office, heard Kate crying and came to investigate. He went to get another dose of pain medication and, after giving it to her, wrapped us both up in his arms and the three of us sat in the floor of our room until Kate had settled down.

The following morning, we headed to clinic for week ten. We felt accomplished that we had survived re-induction one, although it sure wasn't pretty. Week ten was a recovery week, so no chemo was administered and we were glad Kate's body would have a chance to rest after all it had been through during the previous three weeks. It needed the chance to rest because for week eleven Kate would receive all three chemos again! Her counts at clinic were decent with an ANC of 1,000, and we were thankful because we had a birthday to celebrate!

Jenna's second birthday was the next day, and we took a trip to the beautiful Huntsville Botanical Gardens. Kate and Jenna loved seeing the model train riding on its tracks, were thrilled to run up and down the paths through the woods, and enjoyed exploring the children's garden for almost an hour. Brandon met us for a picnic lunch at the children's garden, and then the girls ran through some sprinklers on our way out. That afternoon, we all went swimming at our neighborhood pool, and it thrilled my soul to have enjoyed such a beautiful, fun, *normal* day with my family.

The next night, we had our family over for a birthday party for Jenna. The girls were very excited to see their cousins, aunts, uncles, and grandparents. Every time the doorbell rang, Kate ran to see who it was. After one doorbell ring, she took off running from one direction while one of her cousins came running from the other direction and they both collided in the hallway. A wail immediately came from Kate and Brandon hurried over to assess the damage. She had a pretty nasty scrape up her right arm and he tended to it right away, applying ointment and a Band-Aid. Within a few minutes, she was as good as new.

Jenna was the prettiest little two-year-old I'd ever seen and enjoyed the attention from her family. I was happy that the world got to revolve around her for a change. It is quite a challenge to be a sibling of a cancer patient, but Jenna most certainly rose to the challenge.

In fact, Jenna had become a little mommy to Kate. When we were at the park one day, Kate wore out pretty quickly and lay down on the bench to rest. Her sister was not far behind her and promptly lay down on the bench, too. Another day, I was cleaning up from lunch, and Kate had already gone to lie down to get ready for naptime. I could hear Jenna bustling about in Kate's room, chirping away at her big sister. "Kate, you otay? I cover you up. Kate, you sweepy? Nigh', nigh.' I love you." Jenna melted my heart.

While Jenna had been known to leave a claw mark or three on Kate's bald head, she loved her sister fiercely and was always ready to stand up for her. At clinic one week, Kate was playing with the toy dinosaurs and roaring away, but the older brother of another patient kept taking the dinosaurs away from her. Kate asked nicely for the dinosaurs back the first few times, but then got upset and began to cry. We suddenly heard a loud, angry screech from one side of the clinic and the next thing we knew, a blonde blur went hurtling by and tackled the brother flat to the ground! Jenna wasn't going to let anyone mess with her sister! (Fortunately, the mom of the boy found it funny, and I was glad because I was having a hard time hiding my giggles.)

The following week at clinic was a doozy with all three chemos again. Grammy came to keep Jenna for the day and I hauled Kate off for a very long day. She didn't mind though. She had grown to love the clinic where she got to play video games, eat cheesy puffs, and watch movies—things she usually didn't do at home. Most of all, though, she had grown to love her nurses—Caroline, Lois, Jessica, Laura, and Heidi. They had become her best friends.

At clinic, Dr. Russo was examining Kate and noticed the scrape on Kate's arm and asked what had happened. I explained and she examined it more closely.

"It looks all right, but let's keep an eye on it," she instructed.

I nodded in agreement.

Late that same night, Kate began to run a fever and I took her to the emergency room while Brandon called his mom once again to come keep Jenna for us the next morning. At the emergency room, the doctor on call was examining Kate and when he lifted her arm, I noticed the mark on her arm had developed an angry red welt. I pointed it out to the doctor and he was dismissive of it. I made a mental note to point it out to Dr. Russo the next morning when she made her rounds.

The nurse had a difficult time getting a vein in Kate's hand and while Kate held very still for her, she screamed the entire time. It took almost ten minutes for the nurse to get the needle in Kate's vein, and at one point Kate yelled, "This feels *horrible!*" I had to smile briefly at her ability to communicate *exactly* how she was feeling and breathed a sigh of relief when the nurse triumphantly declared, "Got it!" (It took eight months for the bruise in her hand from that night to fade.)

Kate's counts were much lower, so we trudged upstairs to PICU once again. I smiled wanly at all the nurses who were becoming all too familiar. One nurse came up and said, "We were so excited to hear that Kate was being admitted. We are happy to see you!" I joked, "Sorry, but we don't feel the same about seeing all of you!"

We got settled in the room in which we would spend the next four days. Just as suspected, the wound on Kate's arm was infected, and once Dr. Russo ordered an antibiotic specific for skin infections Kate's fever went away. She also needed a blood transfusion the following morning, and there were some issues with her triglyceride levels that needed addressing, so the infected scratch on her arm ended up being a huge blessing. I couldn't imagine what her hemoglobin level would have been if we'd waited almost a whole week before our next scheduled clinic visit!

During this PICU stay, Kate was not a happy camper. She was incredibly grumpy, constantly had a sour expression on her face, and could throw the ultimate of fits at the drop of a hat. One poor nurse got stuck in the middle of a battle of wills between Kate and me in the bathroom in the middle of the night. Part of Kate's gown had gotten urine on it when she went to the bathroom and the nurse and I were attempting to change her into a clean gown. She wasn't having any part of it.

Unfortunately for Kate, I am just as stubborn as her and refused to let her get back in her hospital bed wearing a hospital gown wet with urine. She screamed and screamed about it, and at one point the mild-mannered nurse surprised me when he said very firmly, "Kate! You need to calm down. You are going to put this gown on!" It had no effect on Kate. She continued to scream and I, having learned this from a lot of experience now, knew the only way to get her to do what we wanted her to do was to wear her down. Eventually she'd give in. I continued to say, "Kate, you are going to put this clean gown on. I am not letting you wear the old one. It has your pee on it." It took about twenty minutes before she let go of the soiled gown and allowed me to pull it off and slip the other one on in its place.

The nurse left, and Kate climbed back in bed and went to sleep. I, however, lay there the rest of the night wide awake, too worked up to sleep.

At the end of our stay, our nurse was walking us to our car to help us load up and I told her, "Well, I told you last time we were discharged that I hoped I'd never see you again, and we lasted four weeks. Maybe this time, we'll go a little longer before we see you again."

She just smiled and reassured us, saying, "Hey, it happens."

We loaded our belongings in the car and did not look back as we pulled out of the hospital parking lot.

When we lived in Memphis for the greater part of the past few months, it was always hard. We were surrounded by cancer. Every single kid had either recently been diagnosed or, even worse, they had relapsed and were fighting this horrendous battle once again. While we shared the common bond of cancer with all of these families, it was also pretty depressing and discouraging at times.

Being at home was difficult too. We spent most of our weekdays at the clinic, traveled to Memphis for a few days every four weeks, and lived mostly in isolation. You also were suffering a great deal from nausea, leg pain, and stomach pain—all of which was sometimes unbearable to watch.

I often felt alone. No one at home fully knew what we were going through. How could they? No one can ever fully understand unless they too had watched their child suffer from cancer.

But I wasn't alone.

There was Someone who knew exactly what it felt like to watch His child suffer. God knew. God watched His only Son be tempted by the Devil, be reviled by His own people, be scourged and spat upon and beaten and mocked.

And God watched His Son be hung on the cross. He watched as His child cried out for Him. He watched as His child took His final breath.

God knew exactly what we were going through.

However, there was a difference.

While I would have never chosen this path for you, Kate, Jesus' suffering and death were all part of God's plan. God chose for Jesus to suffer for me. And He chose for Jesus to suffer for you, Kate.

I have always praised God for the gift of His only Son. But after watching you suffer for the past six months, Kate, I have found a much deeper—not complete by any means, but deeper—understanding of what God went through when He watched His child die on the cross...to save someone as unworthy as me.

God loves us so much Kate. He truly does.

Love,

Mommy

"How long, O Lord? Will You forget me forever? How long will You hide your face from me? How long must I take counsel in my soul and have sorrow in my heart all the day? How long shall my enemy be exalted over me? Consider and answer me, O Lord my God; light up my eyes, lest I sleep the sleep of death, lest my enemy say, "I have prevailed over him," lest my foes rejoice because I am shaken. But I have trusted in your steadfast love; my heart shall rejoice in your salvation. I will sing to the Lord, because He has dealt bountifully with me" (Psalms 13:1-6).

"For the Lord is good; His steadfast love endures forever, and his faithfulness to all generations" (Psalms 100:5).

Chapter 8: Thankful

November 27, 2013

Dear Kate,

There have been many moments in this journey when I thought we just couldn't handle anymore. But then we do. There have been times when I just wanted to run away with you, far from this world of cancer and pain and sadness. But we don't. There have been times when I thought God had forgotten us. But He hasn't.

God has given us many reasons to be thankful. Whenever I feel I am in the depths of despair, something happens to remind me to give thanks to God and to look for the little joys that can be found in each and every day.

Especially in little bundles of joy...

The first of October brought about some exciting news for our family.

A couple of weeks before Kate had been diagnosed, Brandon and I had hoped to start trying for a baby. As I sat in the ICU at St. Jude with Kate that very first night, I watched those plans fade away. Over the summer, Brandon brought the idea up again, asking if I wanted to go through with our plans, and I looked at him like he was crazy! However, as this journey became our new normal, I realized I didn't want to put our lives on hold just because of this detour we were taking. We knew it would be hard but both agreed that, in the end, we would be glad that we decided to go ahead with our plans. Cancer was not going to dictate our life.

Brandon and I diligently began to pray about this decision. We prayed for God to bless us with another baby if He thought we could handle it. We prayed for strength and wisdom. And we prayed that if He wanted to make this third baby a boy, we wouldn't complain!

A friend had shared some tips on how to try to determine the gender of your child that involved me taking ovulation tests. Now how many moms take ovulation tests while their daughter is in PICU? Each morning while Kate was in PICU during September, I took an ovulation test, and then after I checked the results I buried it under toilet paper in the trash can. I couldn't imagine the reaction of anyone who found an ovulation test in a PICU bathroom garbage can.

Shortly after we began trying for baby number three, I had a hunch that I was pregnant, but I didn't say anything to Brandon. I held my breath and waited.

The first week in October, a friend from Birmingham was going to come up to keep the girls for the day so that I could have a day to myself. She was a nurse, so I didn't even blink an eye about leaving Kate with her, but I did leave detailed instructions on the kitchen counter. Brandon and I were going to meet for lunch that day and then I was going to get a head start on Christmas shopping. But first, I was going to take a pregnancy test!

That morning right after Brandon left for work, I hopped out of bed and scurried into the bathroom, pregnancy test in hand. I put the stick in the sink after I finished and went to make the bed, my stomach fluttering away. After I waited a few minutes, I apprehensively crept into the bathroom and peeked into the sink.

Hmmm? There was one line—pink, bold, and clear. And…was that another line? I could detect a very faint pink line, but I had to strain to see it. It wasn't really screaming "I'm pregnant" like I wanted it to be.

I thought quickly as I climbed into the shower to start getting ready. I decided that after my friend got there, I would stop by a pharmacy on my way to meet Brandon for lunch and buy a digital pregnancy test. The digital test would clearly state "Pregnant" for my engineer husband. I decided to take a plastic bag with me to put the pregnancy test inside and then wrap it up inside his napkin at the restaurant to surprise him. I giggled with excitement as I finished getting ready.

My friend arrived a little later than scheduled due to traffic, so I had a serious time crunch. I went through with my plans though—I stopped by the pharmacy, bought a digital pregnancy test, and drove up to the outdoor shopping center where we were meeting for lunch. I ran into the public restrooms there and unwrapped the test.

Feeling confident, I sat on the toilet, did my business, and then glanced at my watch to begin the five minute wait for the results.

About a minute later, I heard a knock at the bathroom door.

"Cleaning services," a male voice called. "Anyone in here?"

Great. Just great.

"Umm, yes!" I called out in reply. "I'm going to be..." I glanced at my watch, "...about four more minutes."

There was a long pause followed by a slow "Okay" and the door shut.

I rolled my eyes at this crazy predicament and danced impatiently around in the stall muttering "Come on, come on."

Suddenly, the digital test flashed a clear definitive answer for my husband on the screen—Not Pregnant.

"What?!" I exclaimed. No way. I knew I was pregnant. Wasn't I?

I shoved the test into the plastic bag I'd brought and hurried to wash my hands. I waved at the janitor as I exited the bathroom, my mind whirring as I walked briskly to the restaurant.

I had brought the first pregnancy test with me just in case and debated if I would still surprise him or just wait until I knew for sure. The hostess at the restaurant seated me right away and I breathed a sigh of relief that I'd beaten Brandon to the restaurant. Nervously I wondered what I should do. Realizing I would not get another opportunity like this again, I finally slipped the bag with the "faint line" pregnancy test out of my purse, unrolled Brandon's napkin, slid it inside, and rolled it back up again.

Brandon appeared at our table a few minutes later and leaned in for a kiss before he seated himself across from me.

"Hi! How's your morning been?" he asked.

I smiled and answered, "Fine. What about yours?"

We chatted about our mornings and I anxiously waited on him to unroll his napkin. The waitress brought bread to our table and I smiled, hoping that he'd put his napkin in his lap, but my hopes were dashed as he began munching on the bread, napkin still rolled up. Inwardly, I groaned, but kept up my end of the conversation, knowing he'd eventually have to get his silverware out. It was about twenty minutes later when our waitress delivered our meal that he finally reached for his napkin. He unrolled it and a look of confusion came across his face momentarily, followed by a big smile.

"Are you serious?" he asked.

A smile broke across my face and he came over to my side of the table for a hug and kiss. As we hugged, I decided I wouldn't mention the "Not pregnant" test at all because to an engineer, if a digital pregnancy test says "Not pregnant," then you are absolutely not pregnant.

And then Brandon asked for another set of silverware.

October flew by with only a small bump in our regular weekly chemo routine—a literal bump. At clinic one day, Kate was sitting sideways in a chair at the round table and laughed at something one of her friends said. She slid backward as she laughed and slid right off the chair, hitting her head on the chair next to her as she fell. She let out a piercing wail and I immediately picked her up in my arms and stood, swaying with her as I murmured soothing words of consolation. One of the volunteers at clinic was there in an instant and threw her hands over her mouth and gasped.

"Is it bad?" I mouthed at her over Kate's shoulder and she nodded.

In less than thirty seconds, Kate's nurses had surveyed and assessed the situation, fixed her up with gauze and an ice pack, and summoned for

Dr. Cox. Dr. Cox hurried to the back with a look of concern. She checked the back of Kate's little bald head and determined that she would need staples.

My heart sank, but I figured if Kate was going to fall, she picked a good place and time to do it. I called Brandon to come up to clinic to tend to Jenna. Ms. Beth offered to watch Jenna until he got there. Kate's nurse Caroline led us over the bridge between clinic and the hospital to the emergency room where they were waiting for us. Kate was incredibly unhappy when they cleaned her wound and sprayed a numbing spray on it. She was even more incredibly unhappy when the doctor stapled her wound closed. In the end, she only had to have two staples, which were really not a big deal after all she'd already been through. She looked like Frankenstein with her stapled head and the gauze wrapped around it. I joked with her that she just wanted to get ready for Halloween early. Her ANC was really low that day, so we made sure we kept ointment on it to keep it from getting infected. We didn't want a repeat of the month before!

Re-induction two was scheduled for weeks seventeen through nineteen of continuation and would begin at the end of October. The plan was for Kate and me to make a trip to Memphis for week seventeen for her LPIT. Week eighteen of treatment would be done at our Affiliate Clinic back home. Then our whole family would head to Memphis for week nineteen, which included some heavy chemotherapy. We would remain in Memphis until Kate's counts recovered, an estimated three weeks, which was most of the month of November. Kate would also be on dexamethasone again for eight days, have six days off, and on again for seven more days. We were in absolute dread of fifteen days of steroids again!

Just a couple of days before Halloween, Kate and I dropped Jenna off with her Grammy and headed for Memphis as planned. We arrived at the Grizzlies in time for dinner and were excited to see a carnival set up. Kate ran from one booth to the next, playing games and earning small prizes. I hated to round her up, but she had a long day coming up and we headed upstairs for bed.

Kate's morning went well, and after she woke up from anesthesia we had four hours to kill before she was due for her chemo. We heard there was a Halloween party going on all afternoon in the pavilion just out the front door of St. Jude, so we ventured in that direction. When we walked in, my jaw hit the floor.

We might as well have been walking the streets of Gotham City. The entire pavilion was decorated in a superhero theme and the walls were decorated to look like a cityscape at night. There was a section for four different superheroes where patients could make different parts of their very own superhero costumes; they could also get their pictures taken with the superhero. There was a DJ playing music on stage, fancy cupcakes, popcorn, cotton candy, face painting, and more. St. Jude was amazing!

Kate and I walked around for a little while and snacked while we visited each superhero. She had her picture taken with each hero, made her superhero costume, and picked up some goodies to go. Then we went back to the medicine room for her two hour infusion of heavy chemo. Later that evening, we were glad to leave, eat, and crash for the night. As soon as Kate woke up the next morning around seven, we were on the road. It was Halloween and I was eager to pick up my sweet Jenna and get home for some trick-or-treating!

Kate had begun her fifteen days of steroids, had anesthesia the day before, and had two hours of chemotherapy as well, so she was not the happiest of princesses as I dressed the girls in their princess gowns for trick-or-treating. She was already bawling before we even made it out the door. It was cold, rainy, and very windy outside and after just a few houses, Kate declared that she was done!

"I do not want any more candy. I do not want to go to any more houses! I just want to go home and go to bed!" she wailed.

We persevered to a few more houses for Jenna's sake and then called it a night. We didn't make it to one of our neighbors' houses, and later that night we heard a knock at our door. It was our neighbor with two special Halloween cups filled with candy especially for the girls. We have such sweet neighbors.

The next eight days of steroids went as usual, but then we had the blessed break for six days and were thankful for a few nights of better sleep and a few days of a happier Kate. We sailed through week eighteen and its chemo treatment of another vincristine push at our Affiliate Clinic. We were so glad to be afforded the opportunity to be at home for that week before heading to Memphis for our long stay.

But before we left, we had a baby to check on! I had my first ultrasound the morning that we left for Memphis for week nineteen. It was scheduled for 7:30 in the morning, so once Brandon and I got ourselves and the kids ready and packed and loaded three weeks' worth of luggage into the car, we were worn out before we even made it out of Huntsville. We still had not told the girls that they were going to be big sisters, only telling them that Mommy had a doctor's appointment before we left for Memphis. We had decided we would keep our news a secret for a while.

The ultrasound tech called us back to a tiny dark room, and after undressing from the waist down in the bathroom I lay down on the reclined chair and she began the ultrasound. It wasn't long at all before we saw the tiniest of babies on the monitor and Brandon and I smiled at each other from across the room. It was time to tell the girls the good news.

Brandon pointed at the monitor and asked the girls, "Do you know what that is?"

They both looked confused and shook their heads no.

"That's a baby in Mommy's belly! You two are going to be big sisters!"

Smiles spread across their faces and immediately Kate asked, "Is it a boy or a girl?"

Brandon laughed. "We don't know yet. It will be a couple more months before we find out."

The ultrasound tech, who had been busy clicking away and measuring, spoke up. "Do you want a brother or a sister?"

Both girls agreed they wanted a little brother and Kate added, "And his name will be Bob."

I broke into laughter and had to explain. "Whenever we took walks and saw someone, Kate always wanted to know their name. 'I don't know' was not an acceptable answer, so if it was a woman I said her name was Suzy, and if it was a man I said his name was Bob."

And so our little baby became affectionately referred to as Bob.

After the tech informed us that everything looked fine and that our due date was June 17, 2014, she printed out some pictures for us and we were Memphis bound. Well, we were Memphis bound after we stopped to get a biscuit for the pregnant woman who was hungry again.

On the way, Brandon and I discussed what was in store for Kate for week nineteen. It was a doozy. Kate was scheduled for four doses of high-dose cytarabine, a three-hour infusion twice a day. Then she was also scheduled for another round of pegaspargase and another push of vincristine.

Martha May had given us the option to be admitted to the hospital for Kate's chemo. At first we had declined and opted to have Kate's chemo administered in the medicine room, knowing how much Kate hated being cooped up in the hospital. Now we were having second thoughts on that decision. I called Martha as we drove to Memphis and asked if we could have Kate admitted. She readily agreed as long as there was a bed available.

This change ended up being a huge blessing. Kate's counts came back showing that she was in need of a blood transfusion before her chemo could even begin. Her chemo ended up not even starting until midnight that night and ran until three in the morning. I couldn't imagine having to be in the medicine room for those crazy hours! Because she was admitted, however, Kate was able to sleep through all of it…and we were, too!

Brandon and I took turns again caring for Kate and Jenna. One of us would sleep at the Ronald McDonald House with Jenna and the other would sleep in the hospital room with Kate. It wasn't long before the two days in the hospital and the six rounds of chemotherapy were over. We all hunkered down at the Ronald McDonald House for the aftermath of these heavy rounds of chemotherapy and for another seven days of steroids. Kate cried almost constantly while we were there and we could not wait for this steroid time to end. It was one thing dealing with it in the privacy of our own home. It was another while living with complete strangers.

The first three nights at the Ronald McDonald House were miserable for me. Staying at the hospital and in housing always messed up my sinuses. After a night of broken sleep in the hospital, I had a terrible cold. Dr. Pui said I was fine to stay as long as I didn't get in Kate's face, made sure I wore a mask around the Ronald McDonald House, and let Brandon take Kate for her appointments.

Sleep was hard to find, too, because I was in my first trimester, nauseated, and had to go to the bathroom frequently. We had just potty-trained Jenna and Kate was on steroids, so the three of us just took turns waking up to go to the bathroom every hour or so during the first few nights.

Overall though, this stay at the Ronald McDonald House was somewhat enjoyable. We were acquainted with two other families in the house and that made the house feel more like a home. There were also more families there this time around. When we had been there for induction, it was usually just the mom and the patient. Brandon, for one, was thankful to have some more men around!

P-Daddy and Nonna came up to visit us the first weekend and Brandon and I had decided it was time to tell our parents our good news. We had just finished eating lunch on Saturday and walked back to our room when Kate, at Brandon's prompting, declared, "Mommy has a baby in her belly!"

Nonna was talking to P-Daddy and didn't seem to hear Kate the first time. So Kate spoke up again, a little louder this time. "Mommy has a baby in her belly!"

I held my breath, waiting for the reaction. I was sure at least one of them would exclaim, "What were you thinking?"

Nonna and P-Daddy laughed and cried and hugged us all. I breathed a sigh of relief. We rejoiced with them, but warned them that we wanted to wait a while before we told anyone other than family.

The fifteen days of steroids had raised Kate's white blood cell count and ANC, but two days after she finished the steroids, her counts crashed to nearly nothing. The high dose cytarabine certainly did its job, and Kate's white blood cell count and ANC weren't going to budge for a while. Dr. Pui put her on prophylactic antibiotics again and Kate had to have a couple of platelet transfusions as well as a blood transfusion until her body could start producing those cells again.

And so once again, we waited.

Activities abounded at the Ronald McDonald House during November, and celebrities made frequent appearances as Thanksgiving neared. One Sunday evening, Brandon took Jenna to worship services while I took Kate to have her port accessed and blood drawn. While we sat in the exam room, suddenly in walked a famous Houston professional basketball team! I quickly identified one of the star players by the big smile on his face and pointed him out to Kate. He and Kate chatted for a minute and the team was happy to pause for a picture with us.

Later, a local top models' group served us dinner at the Ronald McDonald House but were gone by the time Brandon and Jenna returned. Brandon lamented his poor luck that evening!

The Thanksgiving holidays rolled around, and we were still in Memphis. Nonna and P-Daddy came up the Wednesday before Thanksgiving to spend the next couple of days with us. We ate dinner that night and got ready to go to Bible class at Bartlett Church of Christ, but Mom wasn't feeling great. She complained that her hip was hurting badly and thought maybe the car ride had aggravated it for some reason. She opted to stay at their hotel and Brandon stayed with Kate while P-Daddy, Jenna, and I went to church.

On Thanksgiving Day, a special group set up camp in the dining rooms at the Ronald McDonald House. This group would be serving us lunch that day and had also prepared amazing crafts for the kids to do until lunchtime. Kate and Jenna made gingerbread houses, decorated ornaments, and painted T-shirts with the help of some teenagers from the group. The girls loved the attention! Papa Don and Grammy arrived during the craft time and Kate and Jenna were very excited to see them.

It wasn't long before a volunteer paged the families of the house over the speaker system, calling for everyone to make their way to Dining Room B where our meal would be served. Our Thanksgiving lunch was family style. The tables had been rearranged so that families could sit together and had been covered with tablecloths and decorated with centerpieces. One of the members of the group led everyone in prayer and then other members began bringing out an abundance of food to each table—macaroni and cheese, green beans, ham, turkey, corn, dressing, fruit, and more. A heavy-laden dessert table located at the corner of the dining room tempted us with delicious treats. Gratitude filled our hearts and we thanked God for these precious people who had given up their Thanksgiving to serve us.

After everyone had eaten dessert, Brandon nudged me and cut his eyes toward his parents. I nodded and leaned over to Kate.

"Kate," I called loudly. "Mommy has turkey in her belly, green beans in her belly, and corn in her belly. What else does Mommy have in her belly?"

Kate continued to eat as if she hadn't heard a word I'd said.

I prompted her again. "Kate, Mommy has turkey in her belly, green beans in her belly, and corn in her belly. What else does Mommy have in her belly?"

By this time, I had everyone's attention except for Kate's. Nonna and P-Daddy were about to burst from excitement and Papa Don and Grammy had their eyebrows raised in curiosity.

Kate continued to eat.

Of all the times to be difficult, I thought. "Well," I said rolling my eyes and turning to Brandon's parents. "She's supposed to say, 'Mommy has a baby in her belly too.'"

A shout of exclamation came from Papa Don and Grammy as they laughed and offered their congratulations. Grammy wiped a few tears from her eyes, just as my mom had. We asked them to keep the news under wraps for a little while, but that we would be sure to let them know when they could spread the word.

Naps for the grandfathers and Jenna followed lunch as well as a little football watching. Mom's hip was still hurting her a fair amount, so we wished them a safe drive home when they left later that evening and hoped that a good night's rest in her own bed would make it feel better. Brandon's parents left soon afterward as well.

Even though we were not at home for our usual Thanksgiving feast, it had been a wonderful day. We had been able to be together as a family and we were blessed by the generosity of those who had served us that day.

And I didn't have to cook.

Over the past eight months, God has given us many things for which to be thankful.

While we were in Memphis for the first six weeks of treatment, our neighborhood rallied around us and helped take care of our dog, Lily. When we came home, she had a new fluffy dog bed, multiple toys, and at least six different bags of treats on the back deck. One neighbor commented that they came over several times to walk Lily, but Lily was never there because someone else was always walking her!

P-Daddy and Nonna are teachers in the Birmingham area, and from day one of your diagnosis their schools and several surrounding schools joined the fight for you, Kate. One day, P-Daddy was sent on an errand from the high school where he teaches to the local elementary school. When he walked into the gym to deliver a package, the entire school was in the gym and started cheering. A little girl at this elementary school, who is also one of P-Daddy and Nonna's neighbors, helped organize the program. It was a kick-off for a fundraiser she wanted to do for St. Jude in honor of you. This little girl sold bracelets, pins, and pencils and raised $2,500 for St. Jude in your name!

We also have several friends whose children, in lieu of gifts at their birthday party, asked for donations to St. Jude and raised over $1,000 combined.

L. Erin Miller

Not a week goes by that a stranger doesn't express their sympathy in one way or another. A retired firefighter, whose own daughter had serious health issues when she was little, approached me one day with his checkbook in hand when we had stopped to see the dog at the fire station. A lady in line at the post office saw my "Fighting for Kate" shirt, asked who Kate was and how she could help, and pulled out her wallet. And just last week, we were leaving a restaurant and a lady walked up, pressed a $100 bill in my hand, and walked away without saying a word.

The list goes on and on from girls of all ages donating their hair to Locks of Love in honor of you, friends donating their bone marrow in your honor, teens from our home congregation selling bracelets and hair ties as a fundraiser for you, and a friend making "Courage for Kate" bracelets, not to mention all the prayers that have been offered on our behalf.

And I'm sure we don't even know the half of it. We praise God for these innumerable blessings. And thank You, God, for sending us an extra special blessing—the gift of the precious baby growing inside Mommy!

Kate, whenever you are in the midst of a storm with rain pouring, thunder crashing, and lightning flashing, watch and wait for the moments to be grateful. They will come. When they do, smile and whisper a prayer of thanksgiving to God for seeing you safely through the storm and for sending these blessings as a reminder of His love.

Love,

Mommy

> *"But now thus says the Lord, He who created you, O Jacob, He who formed you, O Israel: 'Fear not, for I have redeemed you; I have called you by name, you are mine. When you pass through the waters, I will be with you; and through the rivers, they shall not overwhelm you; when you walk through fire you shall not be burned, and the flame shall not consume you. For I am the Lord your God, the Holy One of Israel, your Savior... Because you are precious in my eyes,   and honored, and I love you'"* (Isaiah 43:1-3a,4a).
>
> *"I will turn their mourning into joy; I will comfort them, and give them gladness for sorrow"* (Jeremiah 31:13b).

Chapter 9: Tried by Fire

December 31, 2013

Dear Kate,

We are so glad to close the doors on the year 2013. While we have mostly adjusted to our new "normal," it is still hard to watch you suffer and endure things that no one, especially a child, should ever have to endure.

I remember reading through Job in high school in search of some encouraging verses to give my mom when she was having some health issues. I gave up after a while thinking how horribly depressing the book of Job was. I read through Job again last month, and my impression of the story has certainly changed. It helped me now. Job had to endure great pain and tragedy, and I could now relate to the way he felt as he coped with all of it.

Initially, I chastised myself for wallowing in our trial when Job's trials were far worse than ours. But then, we received news at the end of this month that made Job not seem quite so far away.

After Thanksgiving Day was over, I was ready to go home. The Thanksgiving holidays had been a nice distraction, but as the Ronald McDonald House began decorating for Christmas, all I wanted to do was to go home. Kate's counts still had not budged, but Dr. Pui did approve for her to go ahead and get the chemo scheduled for week twenty-one—pegaspargase—because it was not considered a "count dropper" chemo. That way we were able to stay on schedule. A few days after Thanksgiving, Kate's monocytes began to rise a little, which is always an indicator that her counts were about to start rising too. Sure enough, a couple of days after that, her ANC and white blood cell count began to rebound and we were granted permission to go home on December 1!

December was a blur. We did as many Christmas activities as Kate's immune system would allow. We went to the Galaxy of Lights at the Huntsville Botanical Gardens, drove around and looked at neighborhood Christmas lights, and baked until our little hearts were content.

We also squeezed in a trip to the mall to take our traditional picture with Santa. We opted to go on a Sunday after morning services and hoped it wouldn't be crowded. Kate wore her mask while we waited in line and both girls peered around us at Santa in his big red suit. Last year, neither girl would sit in Santa's lap and would only approach him if we went with them. I wondered what their reaction would be this year.

Jenna asked a lot of questions about Santa. She reassured us she was going to be brave and sit in Santa's lap. We tried to distract the girls by talking about things they could ask Santa to bring them. Kate's request was a train table and Jenna opted for a doll house.

When our turn came, Kate pulled off her mask and walked confidently up to Santa with a big "Hey Santa!" Jenna followed right behind her, smile plastered on her face, and declared loudly, "I would like a doll house!" Santa handed them each a coloring book and a candy cane and heaved both girls onto his lap. Brandon and I stood to the side as the photographer got the girls' attention and began snapping pictures.

"Jenna's about to lose it," Brandon whispered in my ear. While Jenna cooperated perfectly for the pictures, with a huge frozen smile, tears were welling up in her eyes. As soon as the pictures were over, Santa asked her another question and she burst into tears, slid out of his lap, and ran for her mommy.

Kate chatted with Santa for another minute and then waved goodbye as she climbed out of his lap and ran to us. We hugged her and told her that she did an awesome job! And then the mask went right back on!

During the first part of the month of December, Papa Don had his treatment for his prostate cancer. After much research, he had opted for a procedure called "High-Intensity Focused Ultrasound," or HIFU. This procedure used ultrasound energy to destroy diseased tissue through ablation. HIFU was still in the clinical trial phase here in the United States, so Papa Don and Grammy flew to Cancun, Mexico, where a doctor from the United States would perform the procedure.

While they were gone, the girls and I snuck over to Florence for the day. The girls played while I cleaned Papa Don and Grammy's house. We also left a couple of meals for them in the freezer and a banner that read *Bienvenidos a casa* or "Welcome home" hanging over their fireplace.

Kate's weekly chemotherapy continued, and on week twenty-four the chemo cyclophosphamide made its ugly appearance again. This time, Kate would receive half of the dose from induction. The cyclo would run for thirty minutes and then Kate would have four hours of fluids afterward to prevent ulcers from forming in her bladder. With the cyclo, Kate would receive a low dose of cytarabine, another chemo we'd seen before as well. Both of these chemos were considered "count dropping" chemos and generally took ten to fourteen days to take full effect. Cyclo/cytarabine days were long days at the clinic.

But most of all, December of 2013 brought a new trial to our family.

When Mom and Dad had come to visit us at the Ronald McDonald House for Thanksgiving, Mom's hip had been bothering her terribly. The Monday after Thanksgiving, her alarm went off for her to get ready to go teach school and she couldn't move. The searing pain in her hip almost caused her to black out and waves of nausea overcame her. My dad, a football coach, got in touch with one of the team's physical therapists at school. The physical therapist pulled some strings and got Mom an appointment that morning with an orthopedic doctor who ordered an MRI with contrast.

Mom and Dad called me that evening with the report from the MRI. Brandon was out of town on business and the girls and I were playing upstairs in the playroom.

Mom explained, "Erin, the MRI showed that I have lesions on my hip. The radiologist who interpreted the MRI is very concerned about what might have caused these lesions, and she wants me to see my gynecologist right away."

I was confused. "She wants you to see your gynecologist about lesions on your hip?"

"Yes," she replied. "She thinks there might be something somewhere else in my body that is causing these lesions on my hip. I don't really know much more other than that and don't want to assume anything, but we just wanted to prepare you."

I was still confused. "Prepare me?"

Mom paused. "There is the potential that this could be cancer."

My heart stopped.

Mom hurried on. "But we don't want you to worry because there is also the potential that this could be arthritis or…or it could be…" her voice trailed off.

Cancer. There it was. That ugly word again that changes people's lives forever. I tried to keep my voice calm.

"So when is your appointment with your doctor?" I asked.

"I'll have to call in the morning, but I will let you know."

We talked for a minute or two more before saying goodbye. After I hung up the phone, I sat in the recliner upstairs in a stunned silence.

Kate, who had picked up on the serious tone of the conversation, approached me.

"Mommy, who were you talking to?" she asked warily.

I forced a smile. "Nonna."

"Is Nonna sick?" she asked.

I wasn't going to hide it from her and my smile faltered. "Yes Kate, Nonna is sick."

She was quiet for a minute and then asked, "Is Nonna sick like I'm sick?"

A tear slid down my cheek. "Yes Kate, Nonna is sick like you are sick."

Kate considered that for a moment and then resumed playing with Jenna while I sat lost in thought. I determined I wasn't going to worry about anything until something was made official. Doctors had been wrong before and there was a chance that they could be wrong again.

The next week, Mom met with her gynecologist and he was very concerned about the lesions on her hip. He gravely explained that lesions like that usually meant that she had cancer somewhere else in her body and it had spread. He said he would thoroughly examine her from head to toe. Mom had her annual appointment for a mammogram already scheduled in a couple of weeks, but her doctor ordered one right away. Mom had the mammogram done and it showed that she had a tumor in her right breast, over one inch in diameter.

The next step was to do a biopsy of the tumor. Because the Christmas holidays were quickly approaching, Mom's doctor orchestrated perhaps the fastest diagnosis to surgery ever! Mom had a biopsy of the tumor done on the afternoon of December 17, the results came back the very next morning showing that the tumor was malignant, and Mom was scheduled to have a radical double mastectomy as well as a port placed on December 20.

That week was a whirlwind for my parents as they scurried to prepare for Mom's upcoming surgery and for the months of chemotherapy afterward. She had missed a few days of school in December due to numerous doctors' appointments, and many of her fellow teachers and students were wondering what was going on. Mom decided to read a letter to her class, sharing with them her diagnosis and what she was about to face. Many of her students cried.

Mom also decided to go ahead and retire, wanting all of her energy to go toward healing after her surgery and rounds of chemotherapy. She had dedicated twenty-four years of her life toward teaching junior high and high school English and toward preparing boys and girls for life beyond the classroom. But now it was time for her focus to shift to herself for a change.

In between all of Kate's treatments and all the activities that came with the holiday season, I had little time to grieve. The evening before Mom's surgery, I packed and tried to wrap up a number of things before I headed to Birmingham for the next couple of days. I felt as if my insides were tied up in a thousand knots and felt a constant tightness in my chest. It was hard to breathe. I had never had an anxiety attack before but was pretty sure that was what I was feeling that evening.

Early that Friday morning, I slipped out of bed and quietly dressed, tossing the last few items in my bag. I nudged Brandon awake and I kissed him goodbye.

He sleepily slurred, "Tell your mom we love her and are praying for her."

I smiled. "I will."

"I wish I could be there for you."

My heart pulled in my chest. "I know. But you are doing exactly what I need you to be doing right now and that's taking care of our girls." I gave him another kiss. "I love you. I'll keep you posted on today."

"Love you. Be careful," he called out as I left the bedroom.

It was a typical dreary winter day in Alabama as I made my way toward Birmingham. The weather fit the mood of the day perfectly. After I exited the interstate and neared Mom and Dad's house, tears welled up in my eyes and a sob erupted from my chest.

"Stop it," I told myself, but the tears continued to fall. *All right*, I thought. *Get it out now and then pull yourself together. You can't cry in front of her. You have to be strong for your mother.*

I let the tears fall freely for one minute. Just one minute. Then I took deep breaths and dried them up. I cracked the window as I drove the last couple of miles, letting the cold December air soothe my red eyes and splotchy face. I pulled in front of my parents' house, took one final deep breath to calm myself, and climbed out of the car.

Mom and Dad were busy getting ready to go to the hospital, but not too busy to stop and rub my baby belly for a minute and give me a hug. Mom had a list of things that needed to be done and I took the list, reassuring her I would tackle whatever I could over the next couple of days while I was in town.

Mom was scheduled to be at the hospital at eleven that morning. Around ten, Mom, Dad, and I gathered in the living room, ready to begin yet again a new chapter in our lives.

Mom and Dad loaded their luggage in the car and I grabbed my purse and headed to my car. After running a quick errand for Mom, I found a parking spot at the hospital and texted Dad to see where he and Mom were. They were already in the waiting room to go back for surgery and I quickly made my way there.

Mom was dressed in a light blue hospital gown and Dad was sitting in a chair beside the bed. He had a smile on his face, but I could tell his stomach was in knots just like mine. Nurses were in and out of the room, checking Mom's vitals and keeping us posted on the status of the operating room. Mom was shivering from head to toe, appearing to be cold, but I knew it was the trembling of a nervous anticipation of what was to come.

A few family members and friends peeked into Mom's room to speak to us for a moment while we waited. We still had not told anyone our baby news, so they were surprised by my baby bump. After hugs were given and well wishes and prayers offered, our family and friends gathered in the waiting room where Dad and I would soon join them.

At long last, the surgeon came into the room to go over the surgery. He reviewed the procedure for the double mastectomy as well as the procedure for her port placement and then paused and asked Mom if she had any questions.

Mom nodded her head in assent. "I do have one question," she began. "When you are operating and behold the human body and its amazing design, are you in awe of the great and mighty power of God?"

The doctor smiled at Mom's question and answered, "Well, I've never really thought of that before, but yes, yes I am."

"That was the right answer," Mom simply replied. "Now you may operate on me."

Mom's doctor informed Dad and me that they were just about ready and then he left. Dad and I crowded around Mom's hospital bed and we each bent over to give her a hug and a kiss. Dad asked if he could say a prayer and we all joined hands together as he prayed.

At the close of Dad's prayer, a nurse came to roll Mom's hospital bed down the hall toward the operating room. As she rolled the bed, I held on to Mom's hand as long as I could and only let go when they turned into the restricted area. Dad and I watched her go until the doors shut behind her and then looked at each other, both feeling a little lost.

"Well, I guess we'll go to the waiting room now," Dad decided and we asked a nurse to point us in the right direction. When we arrived in the waiting room, tears sprang to my eyes when I saw a section of the room filled with family and friends. It was so good to see all of these dear people, many of whom I had not seen in years, and it was also good to have a distraction while we waited. And we waited for hours.

Mom's surgery had been estimated to be complete by one that afternoon. One o'clock came and went. Two o'clock came and went. My uncle and I ventured downstairs for lunch because this pregnant mama was getting really hungry. Dad, however, refused to leave. He was too afraid there would be an update on Mom and that he would miss it. We offered to bring him something back, but he refused that offer as well. His focus was entirely on my mom, his wife.

Finally, at five o'clock that evening, we received word from the surgeon that everything had gone well and that Mom was in recovery. We sighed in relief, offered a prayer of thanksgiving to God, and bid farewell to the few remaining friends and family members who were still waiting with us. It took a few minutes to find our way to the wing where Mom would be staying, but we made it to the hospital room just before Mom arrived.

I paced back and forth by the window while Dad sat on the small brown couch. He pulled out his cell phone momentarily to make a phone call.

"I told Papa that I would keep him abreast of the situation," he explained as he began dialing the phone number of my grandfather.

I froze in midstride and choked back a laugh at Dad's choice of words. When he heard me snort, he realized what he'd said. "Well, I guess that was a poor choice of words." We both cracked up. The laugh that we shared together was exactly what we needed.

Ten minutes later, we heard a bed rolling down the hall and I stepped out of the room to greet Mom as she approached. I was surprised to find her still nearly unconscious.

Once Mom's hospital bed was situated in the room, her nurse introduced himself, went over a few post-operation guidelines, and asked us to let him know if we needed anything. He left, reassuring us that he would be back to check on Mom momentarily.

Dad and I both leaned over Mom's bed. "Mom?" Dad asked, stroking Mom's dark brown hair.

Mom groggily opened her eyes and tried to talk, but her mouth was as dry as cotton. I hurried down the hall to fill her cup with ice chips, cleaning my hands with sanitizer on the way out and on the way back in.

I spooned some ice chips into Mom's mouth, and after crunching and swallowing a few spoonfuls she whispered a scratchy, "Thank you."

Mom's grogginess eventually wore off as the evening went on. Around seven, after making sure Mom and Dad were settled, I said my goodbyes for the evening. I worked on Mom's "to do" list that evening and the following morning before heading back to the hospital to visit with them. After I arrived, I asked Mom how the night went and she said she hadn't slept very well.

"Were you in too much pain?" I asked, worried.

"No, your daddy's snoring kept me up," she replied, rolling her eyes.

I chuckled. "I should've stayed with you. But I know Dad wouldn't have let me even if I'd offered."

I urged Dad to get out of the hospital for a little while, to go home and take a shower or go for a jog if he felt like it, but he refused. I told him he might regret his decision if they ended up being cooped up there for longer than another day, but he was adamant that he was fine. I knew he just really didn't want to leave Mom's side.

After visiting for a couple of hours, I gently hugged Mom bye and squeezed Dad in a big bear hug, telling them not to hesitate if they needed anything and that I would be checking in each day to see how they were doing. Mom was tentatively scheduled to be released the next day if everything went well, and the ladies from the church where they attended had already arranged meals for the next week.

Our family celebrated Christmas a day early because we had to leave for Memphis on Christmas Day; Santa obliged our crazy schedule by coming early. Santa only brought a few toys because the girls had already received so much after Kate was diagnosed. We enjoyed our day together and the girls loved playing with their new toys.

The next morning, Christmas Day, we packed our bags and loaded the car for our monthly trip to Memphis. We pulled up at the Grizzlies just before dinner time. It was a ghost town and we were amazed at how quiet it was! We checked in and made our way up to our room. As we were unloading, one of the employees at the front desk came into our room hauling a huge bag of toys. The bag was taller than the girls were!

I laughed and told him, "Brandon and I were just talking in the car on the way up about how spoiled the girls are getting."

He simply smiled and shrugged. "Merry Christmas!" he called as he walked away.

The girls eagerly dug through the bag of toys. There were over thirty good-sized toys in the bag, ranging from dolls to a horse with a barn to

L. Erin Miller

a few electronic games. Brandon and I agreed that the girls could each pick two toys and then we would donate the rest to the homeless shelter. The girls made their selections and then we headed over to the hospital cafeteria for Christmas dinner.

As we bathed the girls for bed that night, I pointed to Kate's legs.

"Look at the bruises on her legs, Brandon! I've thought she's been looking pale the past few days and would probably need a blood transfusion, but I bet her platelets are low too. That's crazy though because they were awesome last week!"

Sure enough, the following morning Dr. Pui walked into the room, shaking his head. Kate's counts had come back and while her white blood cell count and ANC were not terrible, her platelets and hemoglobin were both critical.

"Her platelets and hemoglobin are low because of full doses of cyclo/ cytarabine that she had last week. We will need to do reduced doses of that treatment from now on, so that it does not bottom her counts out this low again," explained Dr. Pui.

Brandon expressed his concerned at Kate not getting the full dose of her chemo and Dr. Pui shook his head once again.

"It is more important to receive chemotherapy every week than to get full doses and end up missing a week of chemotherapy because counts are too low. Also, I do not feel comfortable doing lumbar puncture today with platelets and hemoglobin being so low. It increases risk for internal bleeding as well as risk for complications with anesthesia. However, I do not want to do any transfusions. She will start steroids this week, so it will naturally thicken blood and raise counts. I want her body to rebound itself rather than transfuse." He paused to check Kate's treatment plan. "Next week is off week and it will be last off week for rest of therapy. I want Kate to go ahead and get scheduled chemo for today which is pegaspargase, but can you come back to Memphis again next week for LPIT?"

We were thrown for a loop. Even though we had expected her hemoglobin and platelets to be low, we just assumed that she would have a blood and platelet transfusion and then have her LPIT later that day. We

181

repeated what Dr. Pui had just said back to him for clarification and he nodded that we had understood him correctly.

His request was definitely a hassle, but what were we going to do? Tell him no?

"Yes," I finally answered. "We can come back next week."

Justine, Dr. Pui's nurse, explained that we would need to go to the medicine room for Kate's chemo and that she would call procedures and let them know we would not be coming today. We shuffled our schedule around and I played with Jenna while Brandon and Kate hung out in the medicine room for Kate's two hours of pegaspargase.

Brandon and I were both irritated. We had not only just driven to Memphis for nothing, but we had also driven to Memphis *on Christmas Day* for nothing. The stress and emotional strain of Mom's diagnosis and surgery the previous week was still fresh. We were tired and frustrated and we took it out on each other. We were very snappy at each other as we got in the car and made our way back home. At some point, though, we just had to move on. Life certainly keeps moving, and the silent treatment only lasts until the next medication is scheduled. "Hey, it's time for Kate's second dose of DEX. Have you given it to her or do I need to?"

Kate began her week of steroids, and we were up with her several times a night as usual. We survived the week of hour-long screaming fits and nearly constant weeping, and then the girls and I geared up for our back-to-back trip to Memphis.

Having learned a valuable lesson the week before, I arranged with Dr. Pui's nurse practitioner, Martha, for Kate to have her counts checked and a therapy visit the afternoon before her lumbar puncture was scheduled. By doing this, if she needed to have a blood transfusion or platelet transfusion, we could get it done that evening and avoid the surprise right before procedures like we'd had the week before.

Judging by the paleness of Kate's face and the fact that her hemoglobin had not risen on its own since she'd been diagnosed, I knew Kate was going to need a blood transfusion.

L. Erin Miller

The girls and I arrived in Memphis in time for Kate's labs to be drawn in assessment triage. After Kate's labs came back, the nurse met us in the hall of A Clinic. "Kate's platelets have risen, but you were right about her hemoglobin," she confirmed with a smile. "Her hemoglobin is critical and I've already ordered a blood transfusion. Give the medicine room a few minutes and then they can get her going."

Once the blood was ready, I settled the girls down in one of the mini-sized hospital rooms and put in a movie. We spent an evening camped in front of the television, watching movies and eating cafeteria food while Kate received her transfusion.

Very early the next morning, New Year's Eve, I drove Jenna over to a friend's house. Jenna had made a buddy while we were visiting at Bartlett Church of Christ during our initial stay in Memphis. The mom was happy to watch Jenna for a few hours so I could focus on Kate's procedure. We agreed to meet at a nearby store after we finished that morning.

As usual, Kate had to be fasting and could not eat eight hours before her lumbar puncture was scheduled, which is a big deal to someone who had just finished a week of dexamethasone. I quickly began to understand why they normally do the LPIT *before* the patient starts steroids rather than after. Kate was hysterical in procedures that morning. She was a hot sobbing mess. As they prepped her for anesthesia, she was going so crazy that they had to slip some meds in her line to calm her down. It worked only marginally.

As the anesthesiologist began to push the anesthesia into her line, Kate suddenly choked. Her eyes flew open in panic and she grabbed at me, unable to catch her breath. I cupped her face in my hands and tried to whisper soothing words to her, frantically glancing out of the corners of my eyes at the faces of everyone around me. Inside my head, I was screaming, "Aren't you going to do something?!" But no one moved. I continued stroking her face, until at last, she caught her breath and closed her eyes to sleep.

"We'll take good care of her, Mom," the nurses and doctors gently reminded me, as they always did.

"I know you will," I replied, as I always did, although shakily this time.

After I slipped out the door, my eyes filled with tears and I leaned against the wall for support. Didn't this ever get any easier? Here we were, nine months into treatment, and I was still fighting back tears as I watched my baby put to sleep.

I didn't have my usual errands to run at the hospital because I had run them the week before, so I sat outside of recovery reading my Bible. I took a coffee break after twenty minutes and then resumed my vigil. It wasn't too much longer before a nurse stuck her head out the door and beckoned for me. I smiled that they knew I always waited there.

"She's waking up," she called to me, motioning for me to come.

I walked into recovery and a little beast was waiting for me when I came up to her hospital bed. If the week of steroids had made her cranky, the round of anesthesia took her crankiness to an entirely new level. She was screaming and throwing the mother of all fits. Kate screamed, eyes bulging and veins throbbing, as if possessed by a demon. She was irrational and nothing could be said or done to calm her down.

The nurse looked concerned, but I told her Kate was always emotional after anesthesia, so she let us go. I loaded my bucking bronco into the stroller, waved a hurried goodbye to the nurses in recovery, and then bolted for the door. Kate was still hysterical after we'd reached the car, complaining of severe stomach pain. I gave her some food to eat, thinking she would calm down after she ate, and then texted the mom watching Jenna before pulling out of St. Jude's parking lot.

The food did not calm Kate down or ease her stomach pain, however. I slipped her some ranitidine as we drove, thinking the empty stomach plus the lingering steroid might have caused acid reflux, but after a few minutes, the screaming continued. I gave her oxycodone in an attempt to ease her pain, but still the screaming continued.

By the time we reached our meeting place, Kate had reached a level of hysteria that I had never seen before. My friend pulled up next to us with Jenna. I told her we might need to go back to the hospital, but that I was going to call first to see what I needed to do. She offered to take Jenna inside the store to occupy her while I called and just to text her whenever I was ready. I agreed and, after giving Jenna a quick hug, I called A Clinic. I had to stay out of the car to hear what the nurse was saying because Kate's screams were ear-splitting. I explained what was going on and all the meds I had already given Kate.

"Give her another dose of her pain meds and wait thirty minutes. If she has not calmed down in thirty minutes, then come back up to the hospital," the nurse instructed.

I was doubtful, but obeyed. About fifteen minutes after giving Kate an extra dose of her pain meds, her hysteria slowed to sobs and then finally, she was quiet. She sat sucking her thumb, an exhausted look on her tear-streaked face.

I stroked her little arm and was relieved. I called my friend and told her she could bring Jenna back to the car. I was especially grateful for her help that day and even more grateful to be heading home, even if I was emotionally and physically drained.

Surprisingly, neither girl slept on the way home. Brandon welcomed us with open arms and helped us unload. The girls ate an early supper and were in bed for the night before seven, worn out from such a crazy trip.

After the girls went to bed, Brandon and I heated up a plate of leftovers and sat down to watch a football game. After a few bites, I suddenly began to sob, nearly choking on my food.

Brandon immediately put his arm around me. "What's wrong?" he asked.

Gut-wrenching sobs shook my entire body. "I'm just so ready for this year to be over with!" I wailed.

There was a hint of a smile on his face. "You're going to get your wish in about five hours," he observed.

I cried on his shoulder for a few minutes and, honestly, felt better afterward. We finished dinner and it wasn't long before we were both ready for bed. I knew when we woke up the next morning that the year

2014 would not magically make everything better. We still had almost two years of chemotherapy left with Kate. And Mom was only just beginning her battle.

But 2014 held the promise of being a better year. Kate would feel better more often. We would be another year closer to the end of her treatment. She would be another year closer to being healed.

But most of all, we would, Lord willing, welcome our baby in the summer of the upcoming year.

God is still so good.

As we reflect on the trials our family has battled in 2013, we realize that in spite of all the bad, we have seen much good. One positive thing we have gleaned from these trials is a closer relationship with God.

Job said, "But I know my living Redeemer, and He will stand on the dust at last. Even after my skin has been destroyed, yet I will see God in my flesh. I will see Him myself, my eyes will look at Him, and not as a stranger. My heart longs within me" (Job 19:25-27 HCSB).

Job declares that he knows God. God will not be a stranger. Through this trial we have come to know God better. From reading Deuteronomy 20:3-4 on the day you had surgery at the beginning of this journey, to prayers specifically answered time and time again, to a lessening of our burdens just when they seemed too hard to bear any longer, we know without a doubt that God is listening to us, watching over us, and loving us each step of the way. What a wonderful blessing it is to be a child of God!

We are also recognizing areas of weakness in our character and how, through leukemia, we are being afforded many an opportunity to improve. Through this trial, we are gaining wisdom, endurance, and trust in God. Oh, and patience. Lots and lots of patience.

Our character is being shaped and molded as God refines us through fiery trials.

One day, we will walk the street of gold, and when we greet God He won't be a stranger. We will know Him for the merciful and loving God He is and understand that He allows us to have trials to discipline us, to mold us, and to test our faithfulness.

So, Kate, when reading through the book of Job, don't despair in the first forty-one chapters. Always hold out to the end of the book, where in chapter 42, "the Lord increased all that Job had twofold" (Job 42:10 NASB), "the Lord blessed the latter days of Job more than his beginning" (Job 42:12), and "Job died, an old man, and full of days" (Job 42:17).

Although, we might just settle for no more chemo!

Love,

Mommy

> *"For you, O God, have tested us; you have tried us as silver is tried. You brought us into the net; you laid a crushing burden on our backs; you let men ride over our heads; we went through fire and through water; yet you have brought us out to a place of abundance"* (Psalms 66:10-12).
>
> *"And I will put this third into the fire, and refine them as one refines silver, and test them as gold is tested. They will call upon my name, and I will answer them. I will say, 'They are my people'; and they will say, 'The Lord is my God'"* (Zechariah 13:9).

Chapter 10: Home

April 4, 2014

Dear Kate,

After you were diagnosed last year and we spent about two months in Memphis, we couldn't wait to go home. Once we were sent home, it didn't take long to realize that home was not what it used to be. Our home life was consumed by rigid medication schedules, adherence to the low bacteria diet, side effects from chemotherapy, and hearts full of worry. Between our trips to Memphis every four weeks, the clinic in Huntsville every Tuesday, and your occasional weeklong PICU stays, our time at home was generally short-lived.

Home had changed for us. It had been tainted by cancer.

After the rain comes the rainbow. At the close of 2013, it was most assuredly time for a rainbow. That moment came just a few days into the New Year.

We had my sixteen-week OB/GYN appointment in early January and were getting a sneak peek to find out the gender of the baby. Overall, the pregnancy had gone well. My nausea was much less than it had been during my previous pregnancies, and I was sleeping well at night as long as it was not Kate's steroid week. My baby bump was very noticeable, and because we had not shared our news with the general public yet, I always wore a fuzzy fleece jacket to hide this telltale sign.

Brandon met the girls and me at the doctor's office and the four of us all crowded into the tiny ultrasound room once again. The girls both sat in his lap in the corner of the darkened room as the ultrasound tech squirted gel on the wand and began to move the wand across my ever-growing belly.

After a minute or two of searching, she began to focus on a few images. As she angled the wand for a better look and paused, I peeked at the screen. I could definitely see two legs. And then I was pretty sure of what I saw in between those two legs. I lifted my head a little and gave Brandon a big smile. A big smile spread across his face as well. He saw it too.

"Well, what do you think it is?" the ultrasound tech asked.

"A boy?" I asked, my excitement mounting.

"It's a boy!" she exclaimed.

I laughed and Brandon threw his arms up in the air in victory. "Yes!" he shouted. He hugged the girls who were sitting in his lap. "I'm so happy I could spike one of you!"

We all laughed and the ultrasound tech began to print out pictures for us to save and also to share with the grandparents. "Congratulations!" she called to us as we walked down the hall, jubilant at the news we'd received.

"Thank you, God, for our rainbow today," I thought as we walked.

We had waited longer to share our good news of this baby than we had with either of the girls. After this appointment, we felt we were finally at a point where we were ready to share it with the world. I had been so scared to feel true joy over this baby for most of the pregnancy because deep down I wondered how anything good could actually happen to our family at this point. I was too scared to tell others because I was afraid I would lose the baby. And I wasn't sure I could take much more sympathy from people.

Our joy now though was overflowing and abundant and couldn't be contained. We called our family and told them the good news—"It's a

'Bob'!" and then we shared our news with friends far and wide. Once again, not one person asked if we were crazy, but rather celebrated with us. And for that, we were thankful.

A little over a week had now passed since Mom's double mastectomy and she was recovering well. A couple of weeks after her surgery, her doctor ordered a PET scan to determine how much her cancer had spread. The PET scan came back showing that Mom had eight lesions on her skeletal system and one lesion on her liver as well. A biopsy of the largest lesion on her skeletal system showed that the lesions were cancer. Her cancer was Stage 4—incurable.

Mom began chemotherapy immediately after her appointment to receive her biopsy results. Her doctor sent her straight from his office for her first round of chemo. Mom named her port "Bob." I think she did that to lessen the blow for Kate when we didn't eventually name her baby brother that. She also ate a bag of cheese puffs as her chemo ran in honor of Kate.

In all, Mom was scheduled to have four rounds of chemotherapy staggered three weeks apart. She would also be on a hormone blocker because the tumor in her breast had been fed by estrogen. She would receive a monthly shot to strengthen her bones and take doses of dexamethasone with each round too. I told Dad we could take turns keeping Mom and Kate when they were on steroids.

Mom usually felt horrible the week or two after her chemotherapy and spent most of her days on the couch. She usually ran a fever for a few days and suffered greatly from a flu-like achiness. She told me after one treatment that she got into the shower and just cried—not for herself, but for Kate. Mom knew now exactly what Kate had been going through.

Overall, Mom had a great attitude about her battle. "If Kate can do it, I can do it," she reassured everyone. Even when faced with her mortality all too soon, Mom knew that she was in a win-win situation. Such is the hope of all Christians!

My sister Haley and her husband Bryan were able to fly to Birmingham for Martin Luther King, Jr. weekend, so Brandon, the girls, and I headed down to spend time with them as well. I cooked all day long the day before we left, so that we would have meals ready to eat while we were there and we could just enjoy being together as a family. Mom felt well, although she tired out quickly and slipped off to her bedroom to rest as needed. Bryan, Brandon, Haley, and I stayed up late playing card games, laughing and joking, and steadily eating our way through a plate of cookies.

Jenna made sure she got in on some cookie action as well. One night, we were all sitting around the dining room table after dinner and I was in the middle of telling Haley a story. Jenna crawled up on the bench next to me, grabbed my face, and tried to turn my face toward her, saying, "Hey. Mom. Look at me. Look. At. Me. Mom. Hey. Hey." This went on for over a minute until I finished telling my story and turned toward her. She put both hands on either side of my face, leaned in very close putting her nose to my nose, and with a very serious look stated slowly, "I. Need. A. Cookie."

Kate kept us laughing as well. We were explaining to Kate that Haley was Mommy's sister and that Daddy didn't have any sisters. He just had brothers. She leaned forward toward Brandon and asked in a hushed voice, "Did they take away your coat [of many colors] and throw you in a pit too?"

Haley, a fantastic photographer, also organized a photo shoot and had a friend come take pictures of our entire family, shooting the individual ones herself. The goal was to take these pictures before Mom's hair fell out. It was perfect timing because Mom's hair started coming out just a few days later.

It was wonderful to be all together again as a family, although the reason for it pretty much stank. Our family had to load up that Monday and go home because the girls and I had to leave for Memphis again the following day. I hugged my sister extra tight as we said goodbye and she rubbed my belly, telling "Bob" that she couldn't wait to meet him. I hugged my parents goodbye and we headed back to Huntsville.

Our trip to Memphis was, thankfully, uneventful and Kate was in unusually good spirits.

L. Erin Miller

When we arrived at registration that Wednesday morning, there were a couple of teenage boys in line behind us, heavily adorned with gold necklaces. Kate turned around and told them, "Hey, boys aren't supposed to wear necklaces!"

Later in procedures, Mr. Tony was hooking up Kate to her heart monitors, and after observing the tattoos on his arms she very gravely asked him, "Does your mommy know you colored all over your arms?" After she woke up in recovery, she warned him that he'd better ask his mommy next time before he colored on his arms!

Our last stop for the day was for chemo in the medicine room. The nurse was removing Kate's dressing from over her port and Kate cried, "Don't take my ranch dressing off! Don't take my ranch dressing off!"

It was refreshing that, even in the midst of cancer treatment, we could still laugh.

On week twenty-eight of continuation, Kate began a cycle of treatments that repeated every four weeks. She would be on this cycle for the next year. Before, there had been no pattern to her schedule of chemos. Now, however, there was a pattern and we were able to monitor and predict the rise and fall of her counts much better than before.

For the first week of the cycle, Kate would have her LPIT in Memphis as well as vincristine, the nerve-damaging chemotherapy. This week was also steroid week. For the second and third weeks, Kate would receive methotrexate, a five-minute push, and take her oral chemo 6mp as well. And for the fourth week, Kate would have cyclophosphamide and cytarabine, "count dropping" chemos. These were the chemos that had to be reduced after the first round due to the extreme plummet of her counts.

Even the reduced dose of cyclophosphamide proved to be nasty. It was still a thirty-minute infusion with four hours of fluids afterward to flush the chemo out of her bladder, but we found out that our time of fluids could be reduced if Kate would drink a certain amount of water. Our goal was usually for Kate to drink two bottles of water, which would shave about two hours off of our fluid time.

193

Kate was a pro at flushing chemo out by this point and could down two bottles of water in no time. I would set goals for her—"See if you can drink it down to here" or "Take ten sips"—and she also liked showing off for people. I would usually grab anyone who walked by and tell Kate, "Show Mrs. Lois how well you can drink." Kate was always happy to oblige if she had an audience. Of course, after she finished her last bottle, we would rush off to find one of her nurses and she would proudly show them the empty bottle.

The problem that naturally came from drinking a large amount of water, while fluid is also being flushed through the port, is that this little person has to go to the bathroom an exorbitant amount of times. Every ten minutes, I rushed Kate off to the bathroom, pushing her pole behind her. In fact, it was usually pretty difficult to make it the twenty-minute drive from clinic to home without having to stop to go to the bathroom too.

A difficulty that also arose after cyclo was that we had to continue flushing the chemo out of her bladder for the next twenty-four hours, which meant getting up every three hours during the night to take Kate to the bathroom and attempting to get her to drink as well.

Our routine a few times each night went a little like this:

I would creep into Kate's room and gently nudge her shoulder.

"Kate, wake up. It's time to go to the bathroom."

Nothing.

I would nudge harder.

"Kate, wake up honey. We need to go take a potty break."

Kate would stir.

Wait.

Then nothing again.

I would start shaking her shoulder vigorously.

"Kate, come on. It's time to get up."

And then the crying would start.

"Noooo! I don't want to!" Kate would wail over and over again.

The best approach to getting Kate out of bed and going to the bathroom was to wear her down by being persistent and unyielding, which took time because she is stubborn. I would tell her that Caroline, her nurse, said I had to take her to the bathroom every three hours and that Mommy had to obey Caroline. I would throw Dr. Pui under the bus as well, claiming it was his fault we were having to do this. She loved both Caroline and Dr. Pui unconditionally, so I didn't mind transferring the blame.

Eventually, although she screamed at the top of her lungs the entire time, she would comply. By comply, I mean I carried her to the bathroom, pulled her panties down, put her on the potty, wiped her bottom (with medical gloves on my hands to protect myself from any chemo in her urine), pulled her panties back up, flushed, and carried her back to her bedroom. She didn't have to wash her hands because she never even touched the toilet. Then I would urge her to drink a few sips of water.

Then we got to do it all over again at least two more times that night.

I hated cyclo nights!

With this pattern of chemos, however, we began to notice a pattern in her counts as well. Finding this pattern made it easier to know when we could most likely enjoy the freedom that comes with high counts and also know when we needed to rein back into our little bubble during the low counts.

We celebrated Kate's fourth birthday at the end of January. I filled the hallway outside Kate's room with pink and purple balloons and fixed fluffy mouth-watering birthday pancakes for the girls. After breakfast, the girls and I headed to my twenty-week baby appointment, which included a more in-depth ultrasound. Kate had just finished her steroids and was still pretty grouchy toward her sister. While lying on the reclined chair with my protruding belly, it was difficult to keep them separated in the tiny ultrasound room. Although I had explained Kate's situation to the ultrasound tech, it was still embarrassing as Kate screeched and ranted at poor Jenna.

Everything looked great with baby boy "Bob," and after meeting with my doctor we headed upstairs for Kate's day at the clinic. (Yes, you still have to get needles and chemo even if it's your birthday.)

After Kate was accessed and labs were drawn, we went to play in the back. The girls grabbed their weekly bag of cheese puffs and settled in to watch a movie while we waited on labs and chemo. Caroline came to find me an hour or two later with Kate's counts, wearing a grim expression on her face.

"Kate's ANC is sixty and her white blood cell count is four hundred," she reported.

My heart skipped a beat. "Four hundred?" I asked in shock. Her white blood cell count had never been that low before.

"Yes," she affirmed. "Kate will not get chemo today and you will need to take neutropenic precautions. Be sure to keep an eye out for fever and infection."

That evening, a friend who shares a birthday with Kate came over to bring a birthday cake for Kate. The cake was beautifully decorated with pink icing, flowers trailing down the side. Kate couldn't wait to have a piece! There was one problem though. The cake had not been covered up. One rule of the low bacteria diet is that the patient cannot eat any food that has been sitting out for more than an hour. We just smiled and told that dear friend thank you but didn't say anything to Kate just quite yet.

I made Kate's favorite cheesy potato soup for supper that night and as we ate, I noticed she was starting to shiver some with each bite. It was very cold outside that night, so I hoped that she was just chilled. Brandon kissed her forehead and said she felt fine. She was acting fine, so we continued on with our birthday celebration.

When it came time for dessert, I dug a bag of chocolate candy out of the pantry and talked them up enough to persuade Kate to eat the chocolate candy rather than the cake. She begrudgingly obliged and I poured her a generous bowl of the candy, while the rest of us ate her cake right in front of her. We're very sympathetic like that.

196

Kate continued to shiver after dinner, so we took her temperature. It registered right at 100. We are supposed to head to the emergency room when it reaches 100.4 so Brandon began to take her temperature every thirty minutes. Sometimes, her temperature would be normal, and other times it would be 100. It was getting very frustrating. We put on smiles as best as we could and continued with our celebration by opening gifts and cards from friends and family.

We debated on whether or not to put her to bed. Brandon wanted her to get a good night's rest to help her body fight off the fever, but I argued that her white blood cell count was 400! She had absolutely nothing with which to fight! In the end, we put her to bed.

As I tucked Kate in bed, I asked, "Did you have a good birthday?"

"Yes," Kate agreed. "Even though you wouldn't let me have any of *my* birthday cake," she added as she closed her eyes to sleep.

I smiled in the dark in spite of the worry in my heart. The teenage years were going to be tough with this one!

Brandon and I climbed in bed for the night, but I lay wide awake, too worried to sleep. It wasn't very long before we heard the creak of Kate's bedroom door opening and the pitter-patter of her little feet coming toward our bedroom.

"Mommy, I don't feel well," Kate whimpered when she reached our room.

Brandon turned on his lamp and we fumbled for the thermometer —100.6. It was time to call. Brandon called Dr. Russo and she instructed us to go to the emergency room. While Kate went to the bathroom, I angrily began shoving clothes into a bag, tears running down my cheeks.

"Don't act like that!" Brandon reprimanded me. "We expect our girls to not throw fits and you're in here throwing a fit."

"It's her birthday!" I growled through clenched teeth. "She's going to get admitted into the hospital on her birthday!"

"Do you think she cares that she's being admitted on her birthday? No, she doesn't. It only matters to you!"

I glowered at him. "Just let me throw my fit, okay?"

He sighed and went to get Kate ready. Kate naturally was very upset at having to go to the hospital, not because it was her birthday but because she knew she was going to have to get more needles.

The nurses in the emergency room accessed her port and drew a blood sample. Then they also drew blood from a vein in her arm to determine if there was an infection in her port. Kate screamed as we struggled to hold her down and I felt as if I were in a fog as it neared one in the morning. We were sent upstairs to PICU and I relayed all of Kate's medications, their doses, and their schedule to her nurse there, struggling to remember all of this tedious information this late at night. Whenever I gave Kate's birthday, each nurse would exclaim, "Oh, it was her birthday!" and I would give each a rueful smile.

Kate stayed for four days in PICU and her fever, which never registered above 99 at the hospital, was gone within twenty-four hours. Nothing ever grew on the blood cultures, so her fever was deemed to be "just a neutropenia fever" due to low counts. I stayed with her the first two days in the hospital and Brandon stayed with her the last two to give her poor pregnant mama a break. Sleeping while pregnant is uncomfortable. Sleeping on a pullout hospital couch while pregnant is a form of medieval torture.

After this hospital stay, Dr. Pui tweaked Kate's medications some more. He reduced the dosage of cyclo/cytarabine once again to keep her counts from dropping into neutropenia as they had around her birthday. He also reduced her oral chemo, 6mp, that she took two weeks out of every four. His last attempt to boost Kate's counts again was to take her off trimethoprim and sulfamethoxazole, the antibiotics she took to prevent pneumonia. This antibiotic was known to drop counts a little and we made the switch to a monthly one-hour infusion of pentamidine. This antibiotic wasn't as effective as trimethoprim and sulfamethoxazole, but would hopefully not suppress her counts. And so pentamidine was added to our repertoire of infusions.

The month of February is full of drudgery in our household. While Brandon's birthday and Valentine's Day are in this month, it is also the tail end of winter. It is dark and cold and we are just sick and tired of winter by this time. February, to the Miller family, is the pits. February is even more the pits when you have not been able to leave the house already for almost a year. The expression "cabin fever" had taken on an entirely new meaning.

We could not leave the house with Kate, so we tried to break up the monotony with fun activities—family bowling competitions in the kitchen, camping out upstairs in the playroom, art projects, and movie nights with homemade popcorn.

During the month of February, Kate had a particularly rough round of dexamethasone. The week of DEX also fell during the week of our gospel meeting where we worshiped. Brandon and I took turns taking Jenna to the meeting while the other stayed with Kate.

On the afternoon of my night to take Jenna, Kate awoke from her nap with terrible stomach pains. The steroids can cause extreme irritation of the stomach, so I knew that was probably the cause of her pain. I had already given Kate a dose of ranitidine for acid reflux that morning, and as her next dose wasn't due until bedtime I hurried to get supper ready so she could eat, hoping that food would help. I was in the kitchen cooking some macaroni and cheese for her when I heard piercing screams coming from her bedroom. I threw down the spoon and hurried to her bedroom. Kate lay on her bed, clutching her stomach.

"It hurts so badly," she cried.

I ran to her side and asked, "Do you need to go to the bathroom?" She shook her head no. "Do you feel like you're about to throw up?" She shook her head no again. "Baby, I'm almost done making your supper. Let me go finish so you can eat. I know it will help you feel better." I turned to leave the room, but she started screaming again.

"It hurts! It hurts!" She suddenly stopped screaming and looked around wildly, her breathing becoming more and more frantic as the pain mounted in her belly. She began screaming again, not able to bear the pain.

"Mommy?" I turned at the voice in the hall. Jenna, who had been taking her nap, stood there confused and scared in the hall.

"Hey, baby," I greeted her. I turned toward Kate. "I'll be right back."

I carried Jenna to my room and flipped on the television, finding some cartoons as quickly as I could. "Stay right here while I tend to Kate," I instructed her, but she was already engrossed in the show. Kate was still screaming and I ran back to her room, stopping only to grab a dose of her pain medication on the way.

I climbed into Kate's bed and pulled her into my lap, cradling her like a baby, and then slipped in a dose of her oxycodone. "Kate, the most important thing you need to do right now is calm down. You are hurting your stomach even worse by screaming like that."

Kate was sobbing as I rocked her. "I can't calm down. I can't!"

"Yes, you can. Just take deep breaths. Breathe with me," I instructed as I took slow deep breaths.

Kate calmed down momentarily as she breathed with me, but her face suddenly contorted and she clutched her stomach again. Screams erupted from her again and she cried, "Mommy, please make it go away! Mommy, please take me somewhere where I won't hurt anymore!"

I thought I was going to lose it. I wondered if I should take her to the emergency room, but I also knew my daughter. I knew that yes, her stomach probably did hurt. But I also knew that Kate was already an emotional kid and that the steroids just made her lose every ounce of control. I knew how hysterical she could get over the littlest thing and felt sure that if she would eat something, she would feel better.

"Kate, you're going to be okay. Let me go finish your supper and you can eat. You will feel so much better," I reassured her, forcing the tears back.

"Mommy, don't leave me! Don't leave me!" she screamed.

"Baby, let me go get you something to eat," I implored as I slid out of her bed.

"No! No, Mommy!" she cried.

I ran back to the kitchen and stirred the pot of boiling pasta, my tears falling hard and fast now. I could hear Kate talking to herself in her bedroom as I mixed the cheese sauce into the pasta.

"You can do this," she was telling herself. "You can do this. Just breathe. Be brave." And then she would scream again for a few seconds as the pain stabbed her stomach. Then I would hear her again. "Be brave, Kate. Breathe. Be brave. You can do this."

I was sobbing now.

Within a few minutes, Kate was eating a bowl of macaroni and cheese at the table. Brandon arrived home from work shortly after that and we all sat down to eat a quick meal before Jenna and I headed off to our gospel meeting. Kate was still having stomach pains, although not quite as severe, and Brandon was under strict instructions to call me if she took a turn for the worse again.

Jenna and I buckled ourselves into the car and as soon as we pulled out of our driveway, I began to weep. I cried all the way to the church building and then cried all the way home. Jenna and I came home to find Kate eating blueberry muffins, bananas, and crackers. She was feeling much better and my heart lightened at her smiling face!

At clinic the next morning, I relayed the previous evening's events to Dr. Russo who ordered an extra set of labs for Kate. Everything came back completely normal and we chalked up the episode to the evil DEX and to the dramatics of Kate.

We managed to make it through the rest of the cold winter months without any major illness other than a nasty cough that Kate battled off and on. We were thankful to reach March. Spring was in the air and we ventured out of our house a little more often! Plants began to grow, and so did Kate's hair! She had a lot of peach fuzz that everyone liked to rub, and I rejoiced at this sign of new life!

The end of March brought the one-year anniversary of Kate's diagnosis day. Brandon and I tried to decide what we should do that day. We weren't really sure what one does on the anniversary of the day that they were diagnosed with cancer, but we decided that you couldn't go wrong with ice cream. Kate's counts were good and so we all went for some ice cream before going to Bible class. Jenna's teacher delivered her back to us after class with special instructions: "No more ice cream for Jenna before Bible class." Jenna certainly didn't need any encouragement to be wild!

The week following Kate's one-year anniversary of her diagnosis was a special week because we headed south to put our toes in the beautiful white sand of Gulf Shores. Now that we could monitor the rise and fall of Kate's counts better, we tentatively reserved a week at Brandon's parents' condo.

We didn't breathe a word about this trip to the girls because we knew how things could change in an instant with Kate's health. We had Kate's clinic day moved up to Monday and Brandon took the girls so I could stay home and pack. When he texted me that her counts were normal, I whooped and started loading the car! After Kate received her push of methotrexate, she was de-accessed and Brandon and the girls headed home.

Once home, Brandon held out the papers with Kate's counts on them. "Your counts are good, so do you know where we get to go?"

Kate was lying on the floor in the kitchen and Jenna was sitting on top of her. "I can't guess because Jenna is sitting on top of me."

Brandon and I both laughed and he continued, "Where have you been asking to go for a while now?"

Kate abruptly sat up, knocking Jenna off her back. "The beach?" she asked.

"Yes! We are going to the beach!" Brandon exclaimed.

"And we're leaving right now!" I chimed in.

Both girls started jumping up and down and squealing, although I think Jenna was just jumping and squealing because Kate was.

Kate paused in the middle of her celebration. "Are we going to collect shells? And swim? And are we going to eat?"

We laughed again and I thought my heart would burst at their joyous celebration. Before too long, we had loaded the final things in the car and were on our way to Gulf Shores.

When we walked out on the beach the next morning, I thought my heart would burst again. The girls ran through the sand squealing and their innocent awe of the simple things in life humbled me. Brandon and I watched, both teary-eyed, as the girls ran toward the waves and raced back screaming as the waters chased after them. Oh, to have a carefree heart again!

Our plan was to stay until Saturday, but alas, Kate's health intervened. On Friday morning, Kate woke up in the wee hours of the morning, choking and unable to get her breath. She sounded very congested. Once she caught her breath, I brought her in the shower with me and turned it as hot as we could stand it. It wasn't too long before the steam had broken up most of the congestion that was giving her such a hard time.

Brandon and I debated what to do. I called the clinic as soon as it opened and explained Kate's situation to Dr. Cox. She cautioned there was a chance that Kate could start running a fever with the cough and that if she developed a fever, we would need to drive to the children's hospital in Mobile. As soon as Dr. Cox started talking about fevers and hospitals, we knew it was time to head home. We did not want to be stuck in the hospital six hours away from home with unfamiliar doctors and nurses.

We packed and loaded the van and headed north. We arrived home late that evening, and while we were glad to be home and in short range of the Affiliate Clinic we were disappointed that our trip had to end so abruptly.

Everything had changed so much—because of cancer.

Our lives over the past year have created a longing in me for a different home—a home where, as you begged me a couple of months ago, you wouldn't hurt anymore. I longed for a home where my heart would not be constantly consumed with worry. I longed for a home that would be constant, whose glory would never fade.

I was longing for my home in heaven.

One thing I have learned is that this world is not my home and it will never bring satisfaction to my soul while I'm here. When I was younger, I wasn't mentally ready to go to heaven. I had things I wanted to do here on earth—I wanted to go to college, get married, have kids, travel the world, and I was always looking forward to the next party or holiday around the corner. I figured that once I'd been filled with all this world had to offer, my desire and focus could be shifted more toward heaven. I was storing my treasures here on earth, rather than in heaven.

However, earth, as we have learned over these past few months, will never satisfy. While there are many wonderful things about our life here on earth, it will always disappoint and leave us feeling empty. And I'm sorry that it took you having cancer, Kate, for me to realize this. I pray that down the road, long after you have finished treatment, I will never forget this truth.

Heaven is our home. It will be perfection. There will be no tears and no suffering. We will be with our Creator and Maker, who we will praise all day long. What about that disappoints? What about that does not satisfy? What about that does not fill your cup?

Kate, as you grow up, cling to the knowledge that this world is temporary and hold fast to the hope of our home eternal, waiting, prepared for us!

Love,

Mommy

"For the Lord himself will descend from heaven with a cry of command, with the voice of an archangel, and with the sound of the trumpet of God. And the dead in Christ will rise first. Then we who are alive, who are left, will be caught up together with them in the clouds to meet the Lord in the air, and so we will always be with the Lord" (1 Thessalonians 4:16-17).

"He will wipe away every tear from their eyes, and death shall be no more, neither shall there be mourning, nor crying, nor pain anymore, for the former things have passed away" (Revelation 21:4).

Chapter 11: Like Your Daddy

June 20, 2014

Dear Kate,

Your daddy caught my eye almost fifteen years ago. We met at his aunt and uncle's Fourth of July celebration while I was in high school. Over the next few years, we saw each other randomly—at a wedding, on a rafting trip—and each time our paths crossed, he gained my attention more and more. I was impressed by his looks, intellect, kindness, and most importantly, his unquestionable dedication to God. Those were all qualities that I was looking for in a husband, and as we began dating, my love for him began to grow.

After dating for a year, your daddy proposed to me on the beach in Gulf Shores the summer of 2003, and we were married the following summer. Over the years, we have had our ups and downs. We have enjoyed traveling together, making memories, and building our lives together with God. But we have also had our difficult times through job changes, your daddy going back to school, and, of course, the Iron Bowl every year. Maybe I should just say football season in general?

Nothing has challenged our marriage more, though, than these past fifteen months.

S oon after the abrupt ending to our beach trip, our family members also celebrated the blessed day of remission! Three months post procedure, Papa Don had his PSA level checked and received news that it was zero. April 3, 2014 was now his remission day. A few weeks after her fourth and last round of chemotherapy, Mom had a PET scan. Her doctor warned her repeatedly that she would not yet be in remission but that he just hoped to find that her cancer was inactive. Mom's PET scan came back completely clear. What do doctors know anyway? April 7, 2014 was now her remission day, and we praised God for the wonderful news!

Kate's hair was now almost an inch long and Mom's hair was also beginning to grow back. Mom wore a turban while her hair was gone but did occasionally let the girls peep at her fuzz. One morning, after we'd spent the night with Mom and Dad, Kate crawled into bed with Nonna. Kate looked at Mom with her short spiky hair and asked, "Nonna, does P-Daddy know you look like a hedgehog?"

Kate was feeling better more often now, and we reveled in the tender heart our daughter was developing. Whenever she heard another kid crying, she wanted to stop and pray for them and often said, "God is awesome because He healed me!" She became my little encourager. At one of my OB/GYN appointments, I had to have two routine shots, and when I asked her if she thought I was going to cry, she reassured, "No, Mommy, you're going to be brave because I'm going to be right here with you."

Kate was not quite as magnanimous later with her sister's routine shots. I asked Kate if she was going to help Jenna be brave by holding her hand and she shook her head no.

"Well, what are you going to do to help when Jenna gets her shot?" I asked.

"I'm going to help by covering my ears," she replied.

The months of April and May were upon us and we enjoyed the freedom brought by the spring weather and fewer illnesses floating around. Flu and cold season had died down and Kate's counts were more consistently normal, so Brandon and I permitted Kate to go to Bible class without her mask. For the first time in almost a year, we sat together as a family for worship. When we brought Kate into the auditorium and settled down on the back row, Kate couldn't stop smiling.

"I'm so happy to be out here with everyone," Kate whispered to me before the worship service began. We felt the same way.

In the spring, Brandon, Jenna, and I made a trip to Atlanta to buy a minivan for our growing family. Kate's counts were too low to go, so my parents came up to keep her while we were gone. We did not want Kate to be too far from a hospital in case she ran a fever. We thoroughly enjoyed spending some time with Jenna who, we felt, sometimes got lost in the shuffle of her sister's healthcare.

But God had granted Jenna a big enough personality that she was far from going unnoticed.

My parents called Jenna a "happening waiting for an accident." If there was something to run into, she ran into it. If there was something to knock over, she knocked it over. If there was a big mud puddle, she splashed or sat in it. Jenna was even known to tackle a boy or two flat on their backs, all the while still loving dolls and princesses. She still truly believes in living life large.

Jenna liked to keep us on our toes too.

She loved our dog Lily and liked to pretend she was also a dog, just like Lily, whenever we played outside. Lily laid down and Jenna laid down. Lily rolled over and Jenna rolled over. Lily barked and Jenna barked. And when Lily went out to the yard and squatted and peed, Jenna, potty-trained and fully clothed, went out to the yard and squatted and peed too. It was really hard to keep a straight face at dinner when Brandon was talking to her, telling her it was okay to pretend to be a dog, but it was *not* okay to pee in the yard like a dog.

Once when the girls were chasing each other through the house, they got tangled up in each other and Kate tripped and fell. Jenna ran off, so we brought her back, telling her that if someone fell and got hurt, she needed to stop and make sure they were okay. Jenna started stroking Kate's head, comforting her in the sweetest voice, "Kate, I am so sorry. Are you okay?

You're not hurt. Everything will be all right." She paused and then added in the same sweet voice, "Now suck it up." And then she walked away.

May marked the end of the school year when teachers and students alike wind down in their studies and gear up for a summer of beautiful sunshine and fun. The yearbook sponsor from the middle school where my mom had taught contacted my dad and me asking for pictures of Mom. The 2013-2014 yearbook would be dedicated to her. We were happy to oblige.

But she also had a special request.

"I want to have a special yearbook dedication program for your mom, but I want it to be a surprise. I want your family to attend and would love if Kate would speak at the ceremony."

I told her I would be thirty-six weeks pregnant then and as long as I wasn't in labor and Kate's doctor approved, we would be there. Kate was excited and decided she wanted to sing a song for everyone. I prepared a short speech just in case.

At the clinic just a few days before the surprise dedication program, Kate's counts came back as low as ever with an ANC of 300. Kate would not be getting chemo that day and we were told to hold her nightly oral chemo as well.

My heart sank. There was no way I wanted to put Kate in an auditorium full of students with an ANC of 300. However, Dr. Cox received word from Dr. Pui in Memphis that he wanted Kate to come back Friday for a count check. If her counts were high enough, she could restart her nightly oral chemo over the weekend. He had never done that before, but I held to the hope that Kate's counts would rebound quickly.

And just because nothing can be normal in our family, I received a text from Mom late Thursday night, the night before the yearbook dedication program, that read, "Your dad fell down the back porch stairs this afternoon. We are at an urgent care. He is okay, but in a lot of pain."

I immediately tried to call to check on Dad, but also to figure out what to do about the program the next day. Mom, however, refused to let me talk to Dad. "He needs to rest," she explained. "We are going first thing in the morning to have an x-ray done. The doctor is pretty sure he broke a few ribs, but we'll see what the x-ray shows."

I hung up, wondering what to do, but decided to wait until the morning to see what the doctor said about Dad before deciding what to do about the program.

All four of us hurried to the clinic that Friday morning, had Kate's finger pricked to check her counts, and went ahead and left to make it to Birmingham on time. Kate's nurse reassured us that the clinic would call with her counts when they came back. We stopped to eat lunch on the way out of town and chose to sit in a booth out of the way to keep Kate as protected as possible.

Mom and Dad finally finished with his doctor's appointment and Mom texted me the results. Dad had broken three ribs, fractured his back, and was still in an incredible amount of pain.

I called Dad's cell, and thankfully he answered his phone.

"I'm so sorry, Dad," I began. "Are you okay?"

His voice was a little strained, but he answered that he was doing fine.

"Can Mom hear me?" I asked hesitantly.

"Yes," he replied.

Great, I thought. *How do I ask him what he wants to do?*

"The doctor commented that I'll be fine and everything can go on as planned in my life," he continued.

I smiled, knowing exactly what he meant. "Okay. I won't keep you, but I love you and we're praying for you."

"Love you too."

With that news, we continued to Birmingham. Now we just needed to hear from clinic!

We arrived at the school about thirty minutes before the program was scheduled to begin. We had still not heard anything about Kate's counts, so I called to see if they had come back before we went into the school.

Kate's nurse answered and said they were not back yet, but they would call as soon as they were.

The secretary of the school came to let us in a back door and she and a couple of teachers escorted us to a back room. We would wait there until it was time to go up onto the stage where Mom's family and friends would be seated. Kate had her mask on, but any time a student came within a hundred feet of us, one of the teachers put her arms up in front of Kate and barked at the student to find another route. We felt like celebrities!

When it was time for the program to begin, we came through the back door of the gym and made our way to the stage where a few other family members and friends, as well as former principals and coworkers were waiting. The band was playing and the gym was filled with students and teachers. Many students sat in the bleachers, but others, all wearing lime green T-shirts designed for the occasion, were standing, making a path for Mom. Each one held a pink rose to give to her as she passed. There was also a huge banner hanging on the back of the stage that had a quote from my mom emblazoned on it: "I am counting on you to be the generation that discovers a cure for cancer."

As we sat in our metal folding chairs, taking in our surroundings, an overwhelming surge of emotions filled me.

I looked at Brandon beside me and whispered, "I need a place to go to have a good cry."

He smiled. "This is amazing. I'm so glad we are part of this."

And then Mom came in. Under the impression that she needed to finish signing some paperwork for her retirement and that the secretary who had the papers was in the gym, she entered the gym with Dad tottering slowly behind her. A cheer rose from the crowd and Mom's hands flew up to her face when she realized what was going on. The band started to play a ballad and the tears started flowing. My mom was crying. Teachers were crying. Students were crying. And I was crying.

Mom made her way through the path of her students, stopping to receive her rose from each one. A teacher followed close behind, holding a bucket for mom to put her roses in when they got too heavy. Dad wasn't too far behind her. At one point, his face chalky, he reached and took the bucket of over one hundred roses from the lady because, as he told us later, he was worried it was getting too heavy for her.

I leaned over to Brandon and asked incredulously, "Did he just take that bucket from her?"

Brandon was already on his feet, hurrying to relieve my dad. But another teacher, who knew the predicament my father was in, took the bucket. Mom came around the corner to the stage and when she saw all her former principals, coworkers, friends, and family, she started weeping all over again. A teacher escorted her and Dad to their folding chairs next to us and urged them to be seated so the ceremony could begin. This was a little easier said than done for my poor dad.

The ceremony was wonderful. Coworkers and students spoke about Mom. One former assistant principal with a beautiful opera-trained voice sang "How Great Thou Art" acapella and another led the gymnasium in prayer for Mom. I thought about how people say God is not in our schools anymore, but He was there that day as He was praised in song, petitioned in prayer, and glorified for His power to heal!

Kate got up at her turn to speak and I walked to the microphone with her. I held the microphone to her and asked if she could say hi, and she burst into tears. (She later asked, "Why did I cry when I got on stage?" and her daddy explained, "That's called stage fright.") So much for her performance!

I squatted down next to Kate, praying her baby brother wouldn't drop out in the process, pulled her in next to me, and began reading the speech I had prepared just in case. When I finished, everyone cheered and clapped and probably offered a quick prayer that this very pregnant woman was able to get herself up off the floor. After a couple more speeches, the program was over.

As soon as it was over, a few students swarmed Kate and I mouthed to Brandon, "I want her out of here—*now*!" Brandon hurried Kate out of the gym. I followed soon behind with Jenna, and when I checked my phone I saw that I had a missed call. A voice mail said Kate's ANC was 1,000, and I breathed a sigh of relief. An ANC of 1,000 still wasn't normal, but it was much better than 300.

We left to head back to Mom and Dad's house. After Mom finished visiting with her coworkers and students, she and Dad came home. Dad entered the house stiffly, his face as pale as I'd ever seen it.

Brandon immediately went to help him. "What can I get you?" he asked.

Dad whispered shakily, "A cup of water."

Brandon fixed him a glass of water and Dad raised it to his mouth, his hand trembling. Mom helped him to his recliner and retrieved his pain medication. We threatened Kate and Jenna within an inch of their lives if they even thought of touching him.

Dad's recovery was long and slow. He opted to sleep in the recliner in the living room, finding the reclined position more comfortable than lying on his back. Mom said she heard him scream in pain during the night as his back would spasm and send shooting pains up his vertebrae. After a few weeks of resting and healing, though, he was a little more mobile.

Then the month of June rolled around. Baby month. The summer was heating up fast as it usually does in the South. And I was rotund. The Southern summer heat and rotund are not a good combination. I tried to pass the time by keeping very busy. We went swimming or to the park almost every day. I even took the girls to the zoo in Birmingham at thirty-eight weeks. I could have had Mom and Dad on standby that day, but I didn't dare tell them what I was doing because I knew I would get a nice long lecture.

A couple of weeks before my due date, we received a new twist at the clinic. We had been sailing smoothly the past couple of months, so apparently it was time to create some waves. Kate had been battling a cough off and on for months now, so Dr. Russo had ordered Kate's immune globulin levels checked. Kate's labs came back showing her immune globulins, one type of infection-fighting white blood cell, were nearly depleted. Dr. Russo explained Kate would need to start having an immune globulin infusion (IVIG) every four weeks or so to replace the immune globulins being wiped out by her prolonged chemotherapy. I asked how long the infusion would take and she replied five to six hours. My shoulders slumped.

As Kate's chemotherapy cyclophosphamide infused that morning, I spent a good deal of that time staring off into space, lost in thought. I thought we were getting into some easier territory with fewer surprises. Now, just a couple of weeks before I was about to add a newborn into the mix of our crazy lives, I found out we were adding a five- to six-hour infusion to one of our visits each month.

Kate was already receiving her long cyclo/cytarabine treatment that day, so Dr. Russo requested that we come back the following day for her IVIG. I was mentally trying to rework our plans when one of her nurses spoke up.

"Would you like to do her IVIG today?" Caroline asked.

I was confused. "Dr. Russo said it takes five to six hours. It's already two o'clock. We wouldn't have time."

"It only takes three hours to infuse," she corrected and then explained. "Doctors never give the infusions, so they don't really know how long they take. I'm willing to stay late if you want to get it done today."

I smiled appreciatively. "I would love to get it done today."

At thirty-eight weeks for me and at week forty-eight in treatment for Kate, we began adding a monthly IVIG to Kate's repertoire of infusions. We decided to keep it on her cyclo day, so we would have just one really long day and three shorter days each month.

For week forty-nine of continuation, Kate was due to be in Memphis for her monthly lumbar puncture and chemotherapy. I, now thirty-nine weeks pregnant, obviously did not need to take her to Memphis so we decided Brandon would take both girls while I stayed home to rest. Grammy went with him in case I went into labor and he needed to leave, and my parents came to stay with me. Mom made me sit on the couch from the moment Brandon walked out the door until he returned.

"Bob" stayed put and we were actually at the clinic on my due date. When we walked in, Laura and Caroline greeted us.

"Isn't your due date soon?" Caroline asked.

"It's today actually," I replied.

"Today?" she repeated in shock. She immediately led me to a bench and made me sit. She grabbed the arms of one side of the bench and motioned to Laura. "Grab the other side," she instructed, pretending to lift her end. She turned to me, "Don't you move a muscle!"

But my due date came and went as little man was content to stay put. And, for the time being, that was fine with me. We had just finished up a week of steroids and I had been up with Kate five to six times each night. I was exhausted and desperately wanted a night or two of rest before welcoming baby brother.

But again, nothing can go normally in our family.

The day after my due date, Wednesday, Jenna woke up with a terrible cough and was running a fever. I took her to see Dr. Klemm, her pediatrician, that afternoon. His nurse was surprised to see my rather large belly and was even more surprised to hear that I was past my due date.

When Dr. Klemm came into the exam room, he exclaimed, "I heard I'd better hurry in here before you went into labor!" He examined Jenna thoroughly and even though he determined it was just a virus, he said he decided he would go overkill for my sake and for Kate's. He put Jenna on an antibiotic and her fever broke that evening.

By Thursday evening, Jenna had been fever free for twenty-four hours and I was ready to get this baby out! As I headed out the door for a walk, I told Brandon, "I am walking until I go into labor." Four miles later, I was not in labor, but my feet were swollen and it was getting dark, so I headed home.

Brandon greeted me as I walked in the door, "Had the baby yet?"

I rolled my eyes at him, but around one in the morning I got up to go to the bathroom, and when I lay back down I felt a gentle pop. I thought, "Did my water just break?" I didn't really feel anything gushing and wasn't having any contractions, so I figured I would just go back to sleep.

L. Erin Miller

I woke up around three with a sharp contraction. When I got up to go to the bathroom again, I realized immediately that my water had most assuredly broken. I woke Brandon, who called our parents and then our neighbor to come sit with our sleeping girls so we could leave.

I felt very scattered as I tried to think of the last minute items I needed. With the girls, I had taken the time to make a list, but I had not taken the time to do so with baby number three. I had not packed a single thing until the day before my due date! I had, however, taken the time to type the list of Kate's medications, dosages, and schedule in case I went into labor during steroid week. That list was three pages long!

I was throwing the last few items in a bag when our neighbor arrived, excited at the news of baby boy's impending arrival. We left and arrived at the hospital around five in the morning. My contractions were still coming steadily, although I was easily able to breathe through them. We made our way to labor and delivery and I checked myself in at the front desk. While we waited, I tried to stay standing as long as possible, letting gravity be my friend. Within thirty minutes, a nurse had come to escort us to the delivery room.

She asked a few questions along the way as we walked, then gave me a gown to put on once we arrived in the delivery room. After I'd settled in bed, she gave me a few forms to fill out and I set the clipboard very awkwardly on top of my large belly. The contractions were coming on stronger now and I had to pause in order to breathe through them. When the nurse asked if I wanted an epidural, I vigorously nodded my head yes.

After she walked away, Brandon urged me, "You said you were not going to get an epidural. I really think you can do this naturally."

I shook my head emphatically. "I'm tired," I told him bluntly. "I've been up for a week with Kate because of steroids and then Jenna got sick. After the past year we've had, I just want something to be easy. I want to sit here calmly and visit with you and my parents. I want to sit here and push when they come and tell me it's time to push."

He shrugged his shoulders. "Whatever you want."

I had made up my mind. "That is what I want."

The nurse returned a few minutes later with the day shift nurse, Sarah, as well as the anesthesiologist who would be administering my epidural.

"My shift is about over and Sarah will be your nurse for the rest of your labor and delivery. I'll stay while the anesthesiologist places your epidural and then Sarah will take over."

I pulled myself up to sitting position and dangled my feet off the side of the bed. Getting into position for an epidural was one of the more challenging requests in life, but I hunched over as best as my large pregnant belly would allow and tried to stay still while I continued to breathe through my contractions. The anesthesiologist cleaned my back, quickly numbed the area, and then got ready to place the needle. I felt a big stick and drew in a sharp breath, but focused on staying absolutely still.

"I'm sorry," he muttered after a few moments. "It seems that there is a slight curve to your spine. I need to move the epidural up a little."

"Okay," I said begrudgingly as I braced for the stick of the needle again. I focused my mind on Kate and all the needles she'd had over the past year. It helped take my mind off the sting. He moved the needle up a little and I clenched my fists as I felt the stick again. I felt a slight tingle in my spine and he began to secure the needle with large amounts of tape.

I wrapped my hands around the bars of the side of the bed as another big contraction mounted. I breathed in and out, comforted with the knowledge that I only had to endure a couple more contractions before it kicked in. However, more contractions came and went, just as painful as the ones before. I glanced apprehensively at Sarah.

"Shouldn't I be feeling some relief by now?" I asked her.

"Sometimes it takes a few minutes," she reassured me.

A few more minutes went by and the contractions were stronger than ever.

"When I had Jenna, they had to give me another bolus of anesthesia, so maybe that would help," I explained to Sarah in between contractions.

Sarah administered another bolus through my line and we waited a few more minutes. Nothing. By this time, I was in incredible pain. I began to moan and yell with each contraction and had very little rest in between each. Dr. Callison, my doctor, entered the room.

"That sounds like a mama without an epidural," she commented and then looked at Sarah, confused.

"Her epidural does not seem to be working," Sarah explained.

Dr. Callison checked me and I was eight centimeters already. "There might be time to try another epidural. Do you want to try again?" she asked me.

I nodded my head vigorously and Sarah paged the anesthesiologist once more. Dr. Callison was leaving to check on another patient, but before she left she gave instructions to Sarah.

"I don't want you to leave her side. This is her third, and when he comes it could be quick."

Sarah smiled reassuringly. "I'm not going anywhere."

The anesthesiologist returned around seven and I was in the throes of labor by this point. My parents arrived outside the delivery room at the same time, and Brandon left momentarily to speak to them. He stuck his head back in and asked if it was okay for them to come in and I shook my head no. I couldn't focus on anything else—even my sweet parents. All my energy had to go into delivering this baby.

The anesthesiologist conferred with Sarah and then pulled out an alcohol wipe. He rubbed it on my arm and asked, "Feel that?" I nodded my head. He rubbed it on my right leg. "Does that feel the same as your arm?" I nodded my head again. He rubbed it on my left leg. "Does that feel the same?" And once again, I nodded my head.

His shoulders drooped. "I'm sorry," he began.

As soon as I realized he was of no use to me, I rolled over and clutched the side of the bed with one hand, waved him off with the other, and moaned through yet another contraction.

Brandon was holding my hand and encouraging me to breathe. Sarah realized that I was having this baby naturally and she switched into coaching mode.

"All right," she instructed, after checking my cervix once more. I was nine centimeters. "Here comes another big contraction. Let's breathe." She breathed with me. I was always right with her at the beginning, but my breathing turned to yelling at the climax of each contraction. I endured the worst contractions of all for the next forty-five minutes. There was absolutely no break between them. Once one contraction began to ease off slightly, another one reared its ugly head. The pain became so bad that I knew I was about to throw up. Sarah grabbed an emesis basin just as I hurled.

"I'm so tired," I pitifully wailed, wiping my mouth with the edge of the covers. "I don't want to do this anymore!" Sarah and Brandon exchanged a small smile with each other.

Suddenly, my contractions became much more bearable. They still hurt a good deal, but I was able to breathe through each one with more control. I also began to feel a lot of pressure with each contraction now and Sarah checked me a couple of times before finally announcing, "It's time to push!"

Another nurse came in the room to assist and she and Sarah both began to prep the bed for delivery by removing the end of it and pulling the stirrups up. I looked at Brandon.

"You're gonna do great," he encouraged me.

Sarah got me to focus my attention on her. "You can do this. When you push with each contraction, you may feel the urge to scream. Don't. Use all of that energy to push the baby out. Understand?"

I nodded my head.

"Great! Let's do a test push. Here comes a contraction. Ready and push," Sarah coached.

I bore down with all my might and Sarah counted to ten for me and then instructed me to stop. She whipped her phone out of her pocket and called Dr. Callison.

"Erin is pushing. You need to come, but you can walk," she instructed. She hung up and focused back on me again.

"All right, let's push again!"

I pushed for a couple more contractions. Anytime a sound began to escape my mouth, both nurses shushed me, encouraging me to use that energy to push. I realized that the harder I pushed, the sooner this baby would come out so I pushed with every ounce of strength in me.

Sarah suddenly pulled out her phone again and called Dr. Callison. "Run!"

A minute later, Dr. Callison popped into the room and the attending nurse suited her up. She assumed her position and was ready to coach me through the next contraction. Sarah stood on one side while Brandon remained vigilant on the other.

As I pushed through the next contraction, though, I was suddenly pulled out of my intense focus by a steady smacking on my left shoulder. *What is Brandon doing?* I thought. *Stop it!*

Thump, thump, thump.

I let go of the side rail for just a second to knock his hand off my shoulder. He must have thought I was just grabbing out at him in pain because he immediately resumed his smacking.

Thump, thump, thump.

Surely he is not going to make me actually open my mouth to ask him to stop! I was furious with him.

Thump, thump, thump.

It took every ounce of energy I had to formulate the word, but I slapped his hand away again and growled, "Stop."

He stopped. "I was just giving you encouraging pats. Like they do in sports!"

"Stop," I growled again.

Brandon wisely stopped and I clenched my teeth for yet another contraction.

"You got it, Erin! Push! This is it!" Dr. Callison cried.

Out came our sweet baby boy's head, and with one more push he was here! Friday, June 20 at 8:44 in the morning! His cries filled the room, and I smiled weakly in relief. Brandon leaned over to kiss me on my forehead. "You did it!" he exclaimed.

The nurses quickly cleaned him and placed that precious little man on my chest. I cradled him close to me, whispering soothing words until it was time for him to get evaluated.

The verdict soon came in on how much "Bob" weighed. He was a whopping nine pounds fourteen ounces and twenty-one inches long! When Dr. Callison left, she hugged me. "There aren't many people who could have done that. Congratulations." I tiredly thanked her as she left the room.

Brandon was able to give him his first bath right there in the delivery room. After he was clean, Brandon brought him to my side and held him near me. "What do you want to name him?" he asked.

I replied, "At this moment, I really couldn't care less what we name him!" Brandon laughed. He pulled out a list we had made of our top five baby names and consulted it. The middle name was already set in stone. He would share the middle name "Keith" with his daddy.

"How about Elijah?" he asked.

I nodded my head in agreement. "Elijah Keith Miller."

As I unwrapped Elijah to nurse him and he snuggled against me, I realized this was the sweetest feeling in the entire world. I stroked his soft skin and soaked up every one of his features from his precious head down to the tips of his baby toes.

Elijah was a solid baby. He did not have any fat rolls like his big sister Jenna had as a newborn even though he weighed over half a pound more than her. He had the most kissable little red lips and the cutest little button nose. He was perfect. He was our baby boy, a reminder of the abundant blessings of God and a ray of sunshine during what had been such a dark time. We thanked God for a healthy baby and for blessing us with this bundle of joy. I vowed to myself right then that I would raise our son to love God with all of his heart. I vowed to raise him to be a leader, to be kind and caring, to be confident, and to be a hard worker.

I vowed then and there to raise him to be just like his daddy.

Although I would most assuredly teach our son not to smack his wife on the shoulder while she was in labor!

My love for your daddy has deepened since this journey into the world of cancer began. The patience and strength he has shown for our family have been unfailing. Your daddy is quick to keep me grounded when I start straying. His prayers to God for your healing have never wavered.

And who would've thought my love would have deepened for him when I saw him sling your pink and purple princess backpack over his shoulder and walk through the hospital halls? Or that my love would've deepened when Jenna and I came back from Bible study one night to the Ronald McDonald House to find that he had helped you decorate your cardboard partition with butterfly stickers and spell out words with pink and green letters?

I thought once before that God began preparing us for this journey three years ago when your daddy had to begin traveling so much and was able to accumulate so much leave. But I was wrong. God began preparing us for this journey on the day we met so many years ago.

God knew your daddy would need me and that I would need your daddy.

My prayer for you and your sister is that, one day, you will be as blessed as I was to find such a loving, caring, and godly man as your daddy. Set your bar high and never settle. You are worth it!

Love,

Mommy

> *"I found him whom my soul loves"*
> *(Song of Solomon 3:4a).*

Chapter 12: Doubly Blessed

October 1, 2014

Dear Kate,

Our beginning as a family of five was crazy, as was fitting for our family. The past year had obviously been crazy, and I had hoped for a smooth transition as we welcomed our baby boy into our family. But you, unfortunately, had other plans, and this hormonal, postpartum mommy was discouraged and devastated at the events that played out over the week.

However, as always, the clouds were soon to pass.

We arrived home from the hospital Sunday afternoon, ready to begin our journey as a family of five. But our journey did not begin as planned.

In the wee hours of the following morning, I was awakened by a strangled scream coming from Kate's room. I flew out of bed, knowing exactly what was happening. My heart pounded as I raced to the other side of the house. Kate sat in bed, choking and coughing, unable to breathe. Tears were streaming down her face as she struggled to get a breath and I focused on calming her down. Once she had calmed down, I escorted her into a steamy shower to help break up the congestion, and she coughed up most of it in just a few minutes. I checked her temperature and it was normal, so I propped her up in her bed and tucked her back in for the night.

Tuesday morning was a repeat of the same scenario. Kate woke up strangling on her congestion. Elijah had a rough night as well, so by the start of the day I had only snatched a couple hours of broken sleep. There was no going back to bed because it was Tuesday, Kate's clinic day, and Elijah had his newborn checkup that morning too. My parents had come to help for the week, so Mom and Brandon took Kate for chemotherapy, and I took Elijah for his newborn checkup. Dad stayed home with Jenna, who was still coughing severely.

Elijah looked great at his newborn appointment. He had surpassed his birth weight already and was doing well nursing. Dr. Klemm asked if I was getting any sleep and I could only smile ruefully at him.

My phone rang as I pulled into the driveway of our home an hour or so later. It was Brandon.

"How are her counts?" I asked as soon as I answered.

"They are okay," he replied hesitantly. "But Dr. Russo was concerned about Kate's cough so she ordered a respiratory panel for Kate as well as a chest x-ray. The results have already come back and Kate has parainfluenza as well as pneumonia."

His words hit me like a ton of bricks. "Pneumonia?" I repeated back in shock.

"Yes," he confirmed. "Dr. Russo says her pneumonia is viral. If it were bacterial, she would have a fever. And her counts are good, so she says Kate does not have to be admitted." He paused. "But I did ask her about you and Elijah and she believes, while she hates to break up the family right now, that you and Elijah will need to leave the house. You need to stay well so you can take care of him and it is very important that he does not get this."

Tears were already filling my eyes. "Is she concerned about Kate?"

226

"She admitted it's never good for a cancer patient to get pneumonia, but that Kate's is mild."

My postpartum, sleep-deprived, hormonal self couldn't hold back the flood any longer. I sobbed as Brandon tried to reassure me.

"She's going to be fine," he repeated again and again.

"But what if…(sob)…what if…(sob)… Elijah gets pneumonia and has to go…(sob)…in NICU and then Kate…(sob)….gets worse and has to go in…(sob)…PICU and…?" My voice trailed off as a new wave of tears swept over me.

Brandon was calm. "We'll deal with that problem if it comes. For right now, you need to figure out where you want to go and start packing for you and Elijah. Dr. Russo warned to be prepared to stay a week or so. Kate will not be getting chemotherapy today, so we will be heading home pretty soon. They do want to see her at the clinic tomorrow though to see how she's doing."

"Okay," I sobbed. "I love you."

"I love you, too." His voice was tender. "Hey, she's going to be okay."

"I know," I cried and hung up. I sat in the garage, trying to compose myself before walking in to see Dad and Jenna. After a few minutes, I gave up on composing myself and just went inside.

I explained the situation to Dad through my tears. I decided that Elijah and I would go back to Birmingham with him, as he had been planning to go home that evening anyway. Mom planned to stay with Brandon to help tend to Kate and Jenna, and she would keep Jenna at home during Kate's follow-up clinic appointment the next morning.

I began packing a suitcase for the both of us and tried to think of everything I might need to take. It was overwhelming—the nursing pillow, a box of diapers, nursing pads, breast pump, and on and on the list went. Brandon, Mom, and Kate arrived while I was packing and we were careful that Kate went straight to her room until Dad, Elijah, and I were safely loaded in the car. I cried as we pulled out of the driveway.

In the end, my few days away were probably the best thing for me. Before we left, I was not getting any sleep and was exhausted. At my parents' home, I slept in every morning and took naps during the day. I was able to go for walks, although I probably set a record for the world's slowest pace ever. I was also able to sit and just love my baby.

While I was resting and recovering, Brandon was left behind in the trenches. I was disappointed for him. He had taken the week off to be with his family and spend some time with his new son, and he wasn't even getting to be with him at all. Mom came back down to Birmingham on Thursday, exhausted from tending to two sick girls.

But then Friday afternoon, Brandon called to say that Kate's cough was remarkably better and that it would be safe for us to come home.

I couldn't wait! While I enjoyed my time with my parents, I was ready to be a family again. Elijah and I arrived after the girls were in bed. Brandon helped us get settled and we headed to bed.

Around four in the morning, I was nursing Elijah and could hear Kate coughing in the room beside his. *She sounds terrible*, I thought to myself, surprised.

She continued to cough off and on. After I finished nursing Elijah, I put him to bed and went back to bed myself. It was hard to sleep as I listened to Kate coughing. The next morning, she still sounded awful.

"Kate sounds worse," Brandon observed with a frown. "Her cough was almost completely gone yesterday afternoon."

Kate was very lethargic that Saturday morning, and when she woke up from her nap that afternoon she was very weepy. I knew what that might mean and reached for a thermometer.

101.

"Brandon, her temp is 101!" I exclaimed.

"Are you serious?" he asked, shoulders slumping.

We immediately began the scramble to call her doctor and get her and Brandon ready to go to the emergency room. They were out the door in no time and Jenna, Elijah, and I settled in for the evening. I fixed supper for Jenna and soon got both of them in bed. Brandon texted that the doctor said Kate's pneumonia had gone from viral to bacterial, hence the delayed fever. Her counts were good, but they wanted to keep her overnight to monitor her. Her doctor was also going to start her on an antibiotic now that the pneumonia was bacterial.

I was a blubbery mess.

Kate ended up being able to come home Sunday around lunch, with strict instructions to keep her away from Elijah. Brandon was due to head back to work on Monday, and although he offered to stay home an extra day to help juggle the madness that our family had become, I assured him I could handle it.

Jenna was better and was allowed out of her room, Kate was confined to her room, and we confined Elijah to his room to minimize his exposure. I wanted to make sure each kid got equal Mommy time that day, so I bounced back and forth among all three, scouring myself with anti-bacterial soap in between. I would nurse Elijah, get him tucked back in his crib, and then go play with Jenna for fifteen minutes. After fifteen minutes, I would change shirts in the hall outside Kate's room and put a mask on over my face. I would play with her for fifteen minutes, and after I left her room I would change out of my germy shirt, take off my mask, and go wash my hands and arms. I would usually spend the next thirty minutes moving laundry through and preparing a meal or snack before starting my routine all over again. It was crazy, but at the end of the day everyone was happy.

Kate was thrilled at first to be confined to her room. She had her own bin of toys, got to eat all of her meals there, and even got to watch a cartoon or two on my tablet. This excitement waned a little the second day and was completely gone by the time she got home from the clinic the third day. Mom had taken her that day and reported that Dr. Russo said Kate was doing much better. We had wanted to know how much longer she had to stay in her room and she speculated that Kate could be free to come out in the next day or two. Kate's cough was almost completely gone by the next day so we let her out of her room, although we did not let her anywhere near Elijah. This broke her heart, though, because she adored her baby brother.

When both girls were completely well, we allowed Kate to finally hold Elijah. She couldn't take her eyes off him. At dinner, our family was sitting at the kitchen table while Elijah snoozed in his bouncer on the floor next to Kate as she watched him sleep. He was making all the typical sleeping baby faces and noises and at one point made several crying faces in a row and whimpered. Kate informed us that he was having a bad dream and Brandon asked what he was dreaming about.

"I think he's dreaming about when the mean king said to throw all the baby boys in the river."

Steroid week was looming again after Independence Day, and I absolutely dreaded the thought of being up with Kate *and* Elijah each night. But Kate threw us for a loop! While she did have a huge fit or two in which she screamed in her room for over an hour straight, she did much better overall at handling her emotions. Elijah seemed to have a calming effect on her and kept her grounded. Sometimes when she started to throw a tantrum, I told her I was taking Elijah out of the room because I didn't want him to see her act like that. Or I told her she was scaring Elijah, and she stopped!

Kate also didn't wake up quite as much during the night to eat or go to the bathroom. In fact, one night she slept a few hours straight! I glanced at the clock when I woke up the next morning and my mouth fell open in shock. Immediately following the shock was sheer panic that something was wrong, and I hurried to check on Kate!

In August, Mom, the kids, and I drove to Memphis for week fifty-seven of treatment. (We now only had to travel to Memphis for Kate's LPIT every eight weeks rather than four.) I was traveling with two cancer patients, my wild two-year-old, and a newborn who hadn't pooped in three days. I wasn't sure who I should be the most concerned about, but my guess would be Jenna!

Mom stayed with a young couple from Bartlett Church of Christ while the kids and I hunkered down for the night at the Grizzlies. Elijah was one unhappy little fellow and screamed for almost an hour as I scurried to set up his playpen, bathe the girls, get all of Kate's meds administered, and get everything ready to go for the morning.

Kate's appointments the next morning went well, and Mom and I stayed busy juggling the three kids. The car ride home went pretty well until we got just outside of Huntsville. Even though we'd stopped just a couple of hours before to nurse Elijah, he was hungry again. We were only twenty minutes from home and I was determined to make it home, so we pushed on. Mom tried to appease him with his pacifier, but to no avail. It was around this time that Kate started feeling sick at her stomach in the backseat and began to gag and heave. I tossed Mom the emesis bag that I kept in the console, which she held in front of Kate while also holding the pacifier in Elijah's mouth. I grabbed Kate's bag of medications next to me, measured out a dose of diphenhydramine, and passed it back to Mom, all while driving seventy miles per hour down the interstate.

I often refer to our family as a three-ring circus; this moment perfectly demonstrated the reference! We made it home and were glad that it was another eight weeks before we had to report to Memphis again.

The week after our Memphis trip and steroids, we had a new beginning for our family. Kate started preschool! We received permission first from Dr. Pui before signing her up and were thankful to find a preschool that would work with our crazy schedule. Kate went on Wednesdays and Thursdays, and because clinic was on Tuesdays we knew exactly what her counts were each week before sending her to preschool. The preschool was great about not charging us for times she missed, such as steroid week, weeks we were in Memphis, weeks that her counts might be too low, or weeks that she might be in PICU.

I was excited for Kate's first day, but a little apprehensive about how she would behave. We had toured the preschool to help her ease into this new situation with confidence, but I was still uncertain as to how she would feel about being away from Mommy. She and I talked a lot about it and she declared she was ready!

We pulled into the parking lot and after unloading Jenna, Kate, and Elijah, we walked to Kate's classroom. I smiled as we walked in, helped her get settled, and gave her a quick hug goodbye. Kate was all smiles. As we walked out the door, Jenna began to cry.

"My Kate! Mommy, don't leave her! That's my Kate!" she wailed, tears streaming down.

I wrapped her in a big hug. "You're going to make me cry!" I jokingly scolded her. "We'll be back in a little while to pick her up, but we've got some fun things to do first!"

We stayed busy all morning, running errands. When we arrived to pick Kate up, she was just as happy as she could be. I couldn't wait to hear about Kate's first day and hammered her with question after question as we drove home. Even though she had thoroughly enjoyed herself at preschool, she was very brief with each reply and took a good nap that afternoon, worn out from all her morning activities.

I was worn out as well. Being up at night nursing a newborn for the past couple of months and then getting all four of us fed, dressed, and out the door three days a week—once for clinic, twice for preschool—was exhausting. I couldn't even fathom how someone did that five days a week for school!

I was glad Kate enjoyed preschool, but it was always hectic getting the four of us out the door on Wednesday and Thursday mornings at such an early hour. We were usually rushed as I hurried all three babies to the van.

One morning, after making sure all three kids were buckled in safely, I backed the van out of the garage. Jenna suddenly began complaining.

"My straps are too tight!" she whined.

I waved off her complaints, knowing she was strapped safely and that we really didn't have time to stop and adjust them.

"I'll loosen them when we get there if they are still bothering you," I promised. Jenna continued to cry and whine, so I quickly came up with a plan. "You want your straps loosened?" I asked.

Jenna nodded her head.

I reached up and pushed a random button on the ceiling of the van and made a buzzing noise.

"Is that better?" I asked.

Jenna shook her head no.

I reached up and pushed the button again, buzzing a little louder this time.

"Is it better now?"

Jenna thought for a second and then nodded her head yes as a huge smile broke across her face.

"Good!" I exclaimed, snickering under my breath.

The very next morning, Jenna complained again about her straps being too tight.

"Mom," Kate called out. "Push the button."

"Huh?" I was confused.

"You know, the button that loosens Jenna's straps."

"Oh, right! *That* button."

The weeks blurred together into an endless stream of nursing, preparing meals, nursing, clinic, preschool, and more nursing. Kate was still going through the same cycle of treatments—Vincristine and steroids one week, a week of methotrexate and pentamidine, one quick week of just methotrexate, and one week of cyclo/cytarabine that also included her immune globulin transfusion (IVIG).

Taking all three kids to clinic was a challenge. While we had many offers for help, I wanted to be the one taking care of my kids and also wanted to keep us all together as a family. The eight-hour-long cyclo/cytarabine and IVIG days were hardest, but we survived. Elijah cried a lot when he was awake and I thought, *These poor kids. They have to come get chemotherapy and listen to a baby scream.* The nurses, volunteers, and Ms. Beth were always willing to lend a hand though. Even the physical therapist and music therapist jumped in to help change a diaper, get the girls set up with lunch, or walk a fussy baby. I was and will always be extremely thankful for all these special ladies and their kind hearts and helpful hands.

At the end of August, we reached week sixty of continuation! Week sixty was a big deal to us because it marked the halfway point! On the way to clinic, we blasted rock music in the van and sang at the top of our lungs. We also picked up cupcakes to share with the nurses.

As elated as I was to reach that halfway point, the next day brought the overwhelming feeling that we had to do it all over again. Granted, her chemotherapy now would be nothing like what we saw the first year and a half, but I felt like we'd been doing this forever and we still had forever to go.

Would we ever reach the end? I remembered when Brandon and I ran the Country Music Marathon in Nashville the year before Kate was born. Just before the halfway point, those running the full marathon split off from those running the half marathon. As the half marathoners split off to the right, so close to finishing their race, it was so tempting to follow! We'd already run almost thirteen miles. Wasn't that far enough? Couldn't we just go ahead and be done? Sheer determination to finish the race was the only thing that kept us running to the left. Halfway there. We would be done before we knew it.

And sheer determination to finish would carry us through the next sixty weeks of treatment too.

September brought Jenna's third birthday. She wanted nothing more than a princess birthday party. I was happy to oblige for this sweet, but somewhat wild, child of mine. I decorated the dining room like a ballroom with tulle swags sweeping from the chandelier to the walls. A blue tablecloth adorned the table along with white pumpkins with signs reading "Bibbidi," "Bobbidi," and "Boo." I found glass slippers at the discount wedding section of the craft store, which served as a perfect decoration in between each pumpkin. Jenna's birthday gift was a princess dress to wear to her party that night. She was excited, to say the least!

We had just invited family for dinner. Jenna tromped around in her dress, tripping every few minutes and popping back up with an "I'm okay!" After one fall, P-Daddy helped her out of her dress in the backyard, thinking she had on clothes underneath…only to find that she most decidedly did not have on any clothes underneath her dress! He delivered the dress to me inside.

"Dad!" I exclaimed. "Is she running around in the backyard naked?" He nodded and laughed as I ran to retrieve our daughter.

As I snuggled next to Jenna in her bed that evening, I reflected on all that Jenna—not Kate—had been through in the past year. Her compassionate and mothering nature had blossomed. Jenna held emesis bags for Kate whenever she felt sick at her stomach. She lay down to rest right beside her sister in the driveway whenever Kate became too tired to play. She tucked her into bed and told her that she loved her. Jenna was a constant, a forever friend. She was her sister.

Mom, the kids, and I headed for Memphis for another visit at the very end of September. Kate's appointments went smoothly once again and we headed back to Huntsville, stopping to pick up lunch on our way out of town, as had become our ritual. We arrived home around five that evening, which was the earliest we'd made it home in a while! We pulled into the driveway and were surprised to find Brandon already home. We began unloading a few things out of the van, and I grabbed the nursing pillow so I could nurse Elijah, who had been letting everyone in the van know he was very hungry for the past thirty minutes.

Brandon, however, herded all of us into the office, saying that we had to watch this really cool video that my sister Haley and her husband Bryan had sent. Normally Brandon is a no-nonsense guy when it comes to getting out the door on time for something and we only had a little over an hour to eat and get ready before heading to Bible class. This meant every move and every breath for the next hour had to be focused if we were to get out the door on time, so he piqued my curiosity with this change in behavior.

The girls gathered in front of the computer screen while Mom sat in the chair and I stood in the background. Brandon started a video, which began with a shot of Haley and Bryan holding a basket of eggs they'd collected from their chickens. They began showing the different colored eggs they'd received from their different types of chickens and we smiled at their little collection. Then Haley pulled out a white egg and casually commented, "Hmm, this one actually has some writing on it." The screen showed a close-up of the egg Haley was holding and on that little white egg, written in black marker, were the words, "Hatching April 2015." Mom and I squealed in excitement, Kate and Jenna immediately covered their ears, and Elijah started to cry because of all the racket. Brandon had to take him out of the room so that we could hear.

In the midst of the squealing, celebrating, and crying, the video continued. We couldn't hear what they were saying, but we saw Haley hold up another white egg that had "Me too" written on it. Mom and I looked at each other in confusion, suddenly growing absolutely quiet.

"Wait, what?" I exclaimed.

The video continued into another scene in which Bryan was sweating bullets about expecting twins. He ranted that he had sent in letters of resignation to the employers of all the grandparents so they could move immediately out to Colorado. He lamented about all the diapers and formula they would go through, and while Mom and I laughed at Bryan's antics we were still confused. We never knew when to take Bryan seriously.

Toward the end of Bryan's monologue, Mom leaned over and whispered incredulously, "Are they expecting twins?" and I exclaimed, "I don't know!"

Music began playing and the video showed Bryan and Haley hugging and then they held out the ultrasound toward the camera. I leaned forward to take a closer look at the ultrasound and couldn't believe my eyes.

"It is! Is it? Is it?" I wondered, my voice getting more and more high pitched with every word.

Suddenly the final words of the song played "And everything will change" and a black screen displayed the words: "The Allen Twins, Coming April 2015."

Mom and I both squealed "twins" and Mom fell back into the chair, laughing and crying as I ran whooping around the office.

I thought later how, while our family had certainly been burdened with many trials in 2013, God was showering us with abundant blessings that year. And for that, we were thankful.

Doubly thankful!

A few months ago, our family was split apart by pneumonia and I felt my spirits sink to a new low. Soon after, we reached the exciting halfway point of continuation, but in the weeks that followed came the overwhelming feeling that this journey was never going to end.

The turning point came as I realized that the only thing that was going to carry me through this slump was to completely place all my hope and trust in God. Every care in my heart was handed over to Him. And He so willingly bore every burden I handed Him. Over and over again, I reminded myself that God was faithful. He would see us through. He's already seen us through so much, hasn't He, little girl?

Gradually, the darkness left the depths of my heart. We celebrated Jenna's birthday. We enjoyed a week just soaking up the sun at the beach. And pretty soon, we are going to welcome twins to our family!

God is faithful, Kate. Always.

Love,

Mommy

> *"Come to Me, all who labor and are heavy laden, and I will give you rest. Take my yoke upon you, and learn from Me, for I am gentle and lowly in heart, and you will find rest for your souls"*
> (Matthew 11:28-29)
>
> *"My soul is bereft of peace; I have forgotten what happiness is; so I say, 'My endurance has perished; so has my hope from the Lord.'...But this I call to mind, and therefore I have hope: The steadfast love of the Lord never ceases; his mercies never come to an end; they are new every morning; great is your faithfulness. 'The Lord is my portion,' says my soul, 'therefore I will hope in him'"*
> (Lamentations 3:17-18, 21-24).

Chapter 13: If He Does Not

January 21, 2015

Dear Kate,

It has almost been two years since you were diagnosed with cancer. Sometimes, I can't believe it has been that long. Other times, I feel like we have been living this life forever.

Earlier I thought that everything would be smooth sailing by this point in treatment. I thought we would be breezing in and out of clinic each week. I assumed our lives would have returned to normal with the chemotherapy only a nuisance and a side show. I thought that things would be easier in time.

The thing about cancer treatment, though, is that it is never easy. Easier? Maybe. But never ever easy.

And these past few months have shown us that.

We'd enjoyed being "PICU free" for the past four months, but inevitably, as October rolled on, Kate's old cough flared up again. She woke with pink eye one Tuesday morning and Dr. Russo started her on eye drops at the clinic, but then the next night I was awakened by an all-too-familiar sound.

I was in Kate's room in a matter of seconds. I sat down, pulled her up to a sitting position, and got her attention. "Just breathe," I told her calmly. "You need to calm down. Getting upset is only going to make it worse. Breathe in…and breathe out." I breathed deeply, trying to get her to follow my example. After a couple of minutes, she had regained her breath enough to calm down, but she still struggled. Each breath was ragged and her cough was deep and congested.

I kissed her forehead to check her temperature. She felt slightly warm, but not hot, so I carried her into the shower. I turned the water on as hot as she could stand it, closed the doors, and let the steam work its magic. "All right," I instructed. "Blow your nose into the shower and start coughing."

Kate obliged, but after a few minutes, her cough did not improve. After getting her dried off and redressed, I gave her some cold medicine from her medicine bin. I lay down in bed with her to wait and see if it helped. It didn't.

Then I noticed she was shivering. I took her temperature and she had a low grade fever. It was not necessarily high enough for us to have to call, but she was still struggling to breathe and I didn't want to just sit around waiting for the inevitable. I wasn't going to waste another minute.

Brandon packed a bag and then called Kate's doctor to let her know what was going on. I packed a bag for Kate. She was distraught at the idea of being admitted to the hospital, but I reassured her that we had to get her better and going to the hospital was the only way to do that. My heart hurt for Kate, but it also hurt for Brandon. I used to be the one to stay with Kate when she got sick, but now that I was nursing, the burden fell on him. He had to miss work and it was always hard for him to catch up again later. But he never complained.

Brandon called later that morning to report that Kate's chest x-ray showed she had pneumonia again. Her counts were a little low, so Dr. Russo wanted her on antibiotics and admitted her to PICU to monitor her until her cough improved and her counts were trending upward. Kate and Brandon ended up spending four days in PICU and were finally able to come home Saturday. Kate's counts and cough were much better and the antibiotics for the pneumonia had cleared up her pink eye as well.

In October, I took my mom on a trip for her sixtieth birthday. Brandon had generously consented that our gift would be a trip to a southeastern destination of her choice. We decided to go to Asheville, North Carolina because my sister Haley, a photographer, was shooting a wedding there the weekend we were taking our trip.

As excited as I was to go on this trip with my mom, the few days leading up to the trip were nerve wracking. Brandon was out of town on business and Kate started coughing again. I was terrified that she would wake up choking again and that I would have to haul three kids to the emergency room in the middle of the night. I would lie in my bed at night, listening to her cough on the other side of the house, and my mind would be spiraling out of control with fear and worry.

Brandon's business trip was scheduled through most of our trip and my dad was going to keep the girls. I was worried that Kate would get sick while neither of her parents were there. Worry, worry, worry. That is all I did for the few days before we left.

Mom, Elijah, and I took our trip and had a fantastic time. We ate at some neat restaurants, enjoyed the gorgeous fall foliage, and had a great day with Haley. She was showing and just glowing. She loved finally getting to meet Elijah and snuggled with him throughout the day.

And Kate stayed absolutely well while I was gone.

As we neared the end of October, Kate reached week sixty-eight of continuation, which was her last round of cyclophosphamide and cytarabine, both count-dropper chemos. These were also the chemos that required her to drink a lot of fluid afterward and for which we had to wake her up throughout the night to go to the bathroom. That night, as I coaxed Kate out of bed and carried her, screaming and crying, down the hall to the bathroom, I whispered over and over again, "This is the last night I have to wake you up to do this…ever!"

Week sixty-nine, the following week, held the promise of a reduced dose of Kate's steroid, dexamethasone. We hoped that maybe the half dose of DEX she would now be taking might prove to be a little easier on her, but Kate had just as hard a time with the reduced dose as she did with the full one. We were disappointed that we couldn't tell a difference in her behavior or eating habits on the half dose.

Oddly enough, Kate began having "itchy spells" during her steroid weeks. She never developed a rash or had hives; she just itched obsessively and no amount of lotion would ease her itchiness. Brandon was getting her out of the bathtub one night and commented that she had a long claw mark on her backside from scratching.

I asked Kate, "Do you have a scratch on your bottom?"

She replied, wailing, "Yes! And I have a crack in my bottom too!"

Halloween rolled around on day five of DEX, so she was plenty miserable by the time we attempted to trick-or-treat that night. Jenna was a beautiful princess, Elijah was a very unhappy mouse, and Kate was a steroid-raging blue butterfly. Unfortunately, the weather was horrible that night too. It was incredibly windy and cold, so we loaded up the kids in the van and drove from house to house.

Kate did well overall, but after just a few houses she announced that she was done. "I have enough candy. I don't need any more. Besides, I would rather just hand out candy to other people." Brandon and I exchanged a smile. It wasn't too hard to convince me to go home. Elijah was about to blow a gasket and the warmth of our cozy home was calling my name.

Brandon drove Kate, Elijah, and me home and then he and Jenna left to go to a few more houses. I fed Elijah some rice cereal and Kate hovered by the front door with our basket of candy, ready for the first sound of the doorbell. It wasn't long before the bell rang and I let Kate answer the door.

"Trick or treat!" the group called.

"Hi!" Kate said as she began doling out candy into the opened bags. "What do we have here? Someone dressed like a blue puppy? Puppies aren't supposed to be blue! Oh, I like your princess costume. Purple is my favorite color." She continued to chat with each person as they filed up to our door, one at a time, to receive their candy. "Happy Halloween!" she called out before she shut the door once again.

"That was fun!" she exclaimed, turning to me. I had been lurking in the dining room, keeping an eye on her, and chuckled a little at her little old lady ways.

The first part of November flew by uneventfully, which is really saying something in the life of a cancer patient. Kate loved going to preschool each week and only had to miss it occasionally when her counts were too low or if she were sick and in PICU, as had been the case in October.

With November came the colder weather and the abundance of germs that tag along with it. Anytime someone coughed around Kate, I had a little nervous twitch in my eye. I frequently had to resist the urge to spray disinfectant on the other kids around my daughter.

Kate was still doing her fair share of coughing too. Her steroid weeks and IVIG weeks seemed to help her cough improve. Briefly. And then the cough came raging back again. For the first time, I fully understood the meaning of the expression of "one's soul being vexed." Kate's cough vexed my soul. It kept me awake at night, worrying, as I listened. I felt like I was going crazy. And it wasn't even officially winter yet!

Kate was due in Memphis the day before Thanksgiving. On Thanksgiving Day, we drove to Birmingham to spend the day with my family. Kate was on steroids once again, but only on the second day, so she did pretty well. She still didn't feel one hundred percent and did slip off after lunch for a nap, but being around her extended family was a good distraction for her.

Thanksgiving with Brandon's family, on day four of DEX, did not go as well. The Miller family always goes to Brandon's grandmother's house in Athens, Alabama on the Saturday after Thanksgiving. While cramming over thirty people into a small house was fun when we first got married, it was not as enjoyable once we had kids. We had tried to persuade Kate to stay home, but she really wanted to see her cousins. She did well for a little while, but things started to spiral downward after lunch.

Kate desperately needed a nap, but there was nowhere to go and certainly no place that was quiet. The whole family always goes on a hike on Brandon's grandmother's land after lunch, and while I offered to stay at the house with her, Kate did not want to be left behind. However, she whimpered and cried almost the entire time we were hiking.

We lingered for just a little longer after the hike and then loaded everyone into the van. As soon as we got into the van, Kate burst into tears and cried her little heart out. She felt so awful, bless her heart, but hadn't wanted to miss out on anything. All three kids fell asleep as we went home and I sat, numbly looking out the window and reflecting on how miserable the day had been. After a little while, Brandon and I made eye contact and we just had to laugh.

Around the middle of December, both Kate and Jenna started coughing a little. Kate's preschool teacher told me that croup was going around in Kate's class. I commented that Kate had a cough too, but that she had had a cough off and on for months. The fact that Jenna was coughing now caused more concern.

Kate's preschool class had a Christmas program on the last day before Christmas break and Jenna, Elijah, and I beamed at her as she sang a few Christmas songs in the gym with her classmates. She looked so pretty up there in her little red dress and pixie "haircut," as everyone who didn't know better called it.

A few days later, Kate woke up with a fever, and her cough was worse than ever. Brandon took her to the emergency room, but fortunately her counts were good so she was sent home on an antibiotic. We were so thankful to have avoided a week in PICU! I called Memphis first thing Monday morning with a couple of questions, one of which was seeking advice on winter protocol.

Last winter, Kate's counts had been terrible so there was no question as to whether or not we would go out in public with her. This winter, however, even though her counts were better, her immune system was not. She was going to catch whatever was kindly passed along to her. Dr. Pui's nurse Justine recommended that we pull Kate out of preschool for the winter. The strain of flu that was prevalent this winter was not one of the strains covered in the two flu shots Kate had received, and there could be grave repercussions if Kate caught the flu. She also recommended that we not only skip out on preschool but that we keep Kate out of public completely for the rest of winter.

I was a little disheartened at first, but honestly it was welcome news. We were tired from constantly being on the go. It had become hard to enjoy anything. Now we had an excuse to just say no.

Kate was upset for a little bit about not going back to preschool. We sat down and talked with her about how things were going to change for a few months. We explained that we would be staying home during the winter months to help keep her safe and healthy. We would take her to worship services, but one of us would sit in the back room with her the way we used to do. We explained that if she wanted to go to Bible class, she would have to wear her mask. Kate wasn't too fond of that rule because she'd grown used to not wearing her mask, so we didn't push her to go to class. Brandon and I knew dividing and conquering with three kids was going to be a challenge, but we also knew this was the best decision.

At clinic the following week, Dr. Russo ordered a CT scan of Kate's sinus cavity because Kate had been getting sick so often. The results were sad. Kate had a severe sinus infection. It was so severe that her right sinus cavity was one hundred percent filled with infection. The left sinus cavity wasn't too far behind it. Dr. Russo put Kate on two different strong antibiotics for three weeks to help clear up the sinus infection. She proposed that if Kate was still coughing after the three weeks of antibiotics, we would look into surgery to drain the remaining infection.

Kate began the three weeks of antibiotics right away. Both Kate and Jenna's coughing stayed strong for a week but gradually began to fade. Even though we'd attempted to keep the girls away from Elijah, he started with a cough as well, although it was not anywhere near as severe as the girls' coughs had been. We celebrated Christmas with each set of grandparents but stayed away from extended family.

Kate was on steroids again for Christmas Day. She felt pretty poorly, but was still excited to see her presents under the tree. It was a nice, quiet, and relaxing day, which was just what Kate needed as she finished up her steroids.

We were excited to ring in 2015 as it would be the year that, Lord willing, Kate finished her treatment for leukemia!

We couldn't start a new year in treatment for cancer without a problem though. Around the first week in January, Mary, Kate's physical therapist at clinic, approached me after completing a session with Kate.

"I've been noticing that Kate is walking on her tiptoes some." I nodded. "I decided to measure the range of motion in her feet and it looks like she has regressed some. As you know, the chemo vincristine causes damage to the nerve endings in the patient's feet and hands. Many patients do not fully extend their legs because it is painful and that eventually causes some problems as their calf muscles get knotted up. If this problem isn't corrected, patients often have to have surgery to lengthen the leg muscles."

My heart skipped a beat.

"To fight this regression, I want you to start doing physical therapy with Kate three times a day—just some leg stretches to help stretch those calf muscles back out again. If that doesn't help, we may need to start Kate in leg braces at night to force those muscles to stretch back out."

"Leg braces?" I repeated, trying to imagine Kate's reaction to having braces strapped on her at night. She would throw a fit! I was sure of that! And so we added physical therapy three times a day at home to our crazy routine.

Mary worked with Kate at clinic on strengthening her leg and arm muscles. Kate couldn't wait to play with Ms. Mary every week. To strengthen her legs, Mary had Kate practice alternating legs going up and down stairs. She also had her squat to pick up toys and do "shuttle runs" in the back hall of the clinic. To strengthen her hands and arms, Mary gave Kate playdough with beads embedded in it for Kate to dig out. She also had her draw and write to practice her fine motor skills.

One afternoon, Kate and Mary played a game with Kate's favorite tiny dinosaur models and cones. Mary was pretending to do magic by putting a dinosaur in her hands, covering it up with a cone, saying some magic words, and making it disappear. (She would sneakily push the dinosaur into the top of the cone until it stuck.) They had my attention and I was curious to see Kate's reaction.

All week long at dinner, Brandon had regaled the kids with a similar magic trick. He would take a toy, say a few magic words, and say, "Hey, what's that over there?" When the kids turned their heads to look, he hid the toy in his lap. Kate was absolutely amazed with her daddy's talent and tried to perform the magic trick herself. She had chanted a few magic words and then pointed, asking, "Hey, what's that over there?" Kate was so disappointed each time when she looked back to see that the toy was still sitting in front of her.

So now, Kate was incredibly impressed that Ms. Mary could do magic as well! Mary let Kate try, and Kate eagerly agreed. Kate recited the magic words as she waved her hands over the cone concealing the dinosaur. She finished her chant with the grand command, "Make this dinosaur disappear!"

Mary quickly pushed the dinosaur into the top of the cone as Kate lifted the cone. When Kate saw the dinosaur was gone, she gasped.

"I did it," she whispered in disbelief. "I did it," she stated again. She suddenly stood up and started jumping up and down, shouting, "I did it! I did it!"

Mary and I were crying with laughter. We never did let her in on the secret.

Around the first week in January, Kate finished her three weeks of antibiotics for her sinus infection but was still coughing. I braced myself for Dr. Russo's decision. I had researched the surgery and found that it involved breaking through the cartilage in Kate's mouth to tunnel into her sinus cavity and drain the infection. Even though she would be asleep, it sounded very painful.

At our clinic visit, Dr. Russo listened to Kate's chest and cough and speculated that infection still lingered in her sinuses. She decided to e-mail Dr. Pui with her request to drain the remaining infection in Kate's sinus cavity. A few hours later, Dr. Russo found us in the back and relayed that Dr. Pui had replied and that he was vehemently against creating an open wound in the mouth of a cancer patient. She added that he did a very good job conveying his tone through his e-mail. I had to smile.

Dr. Russo decided to refer Kate to a pulmonologist instead. She hoped another doctor could shed some light on Kate's mysterious cough and snorting. We were scheduled to see one in Huntsville at the end of the month.

The following week, Jenna woke up with a fever. This was the second time Jenna had been sick in a short period of time, and I was a little concerned. With the exception of everything going on with Kate, our family very rarely got sick. We quarantined Jenna to her room and her fever came and went for two or three days with no other symptoms. I didn't want to take her to her pediatrician just to be told that she had a virus and it had to run its course, so I just kept an eye on her.

Jenna's fever was gone after a few days, but she stayed very pale and fatigued. I figured she was tired because she'd been sick or may have even been going through a growth spurt and was simply pale because it was January.

Suddenly I realized those were the same words I had uttered before Kate was diagnosed and felt sick to my stomach. I rationalized for a day or two that Jenna didn't have any bruises and if it was leukemia, Jenna would have bruises. Jenna, our bull in a china shop, would have lots of bruises! However, I couldn't shake the nagging feeling I felt. The final straw was after Kate took a picture of me and Jenna with our faces squished side by side. I have a pretty fair complexion, but Jenna's face was ghastly white compared to mine. That was it! I was calling her pediatrician.

The nurse was very kind and agreed to squeeze her in right at closing time. We met Brandon a couple of hours later in the pediatrician's parking lot. He planned to take her in while I sat in the car with Kate and Elijah. We certainly did not need to take Kate into a doctor's office in the middle of winter! After I nursed Elijah, I drove down to a nearby restaurant and planned to go through the drive thru to pick up supper.

I waited on pins and needles for news from Brandon. He had texted me once already saying that they had drawn blood and were waiting on the results. Jenna hadn't even cried when they had pricked her finger!

248

I texted Brandon to ask him what he would like me to order for him and pulled into a parking space to wait on his reply. I waited for about five minutes before giving up and going on through the drive thru. After picking up our food, I pulled back into a parking space and handed Kate's food back to her so we could go ahead and eat while we waited. I kept checking my phone to see if he had replied and even texted him again, asking if everything was okay. There was no reply.

The silence was excruciating.

My stomach was in knots and my mind was racing. I just knew that he was sitting there in the pediatrician's office while the doctor sat on a stool and told him that our daughter had leukemia. The doctor was explaining that he wanted Jenna at the emergency room immediately and that St. Jude would take over her care. I just knew Brandon was trying to take it all in before calling me to let me know the bad news. I prayed and prayed for everything to be okay.

Twenty minutes went by and then my phone rang. It was Brandon.

My voice was shaking when I answered, "Hello?"

"Everything was fine," were the first words out of his mouth.

Relief flooded through my veins as tears filled my eyes.

"Dr. Klemm was very thorough in checking Jenna. He explained the likelihood of Jenna having cancer as well was slim to none, but he knew that none of us would sleep well tonight if he didn't check her counts. Her counts were perfect. He speculates that the lingering fatigue and paleness is just a lasting effect from the virus she had last week. But Jenna looked great."

"Thank you," I whispered to Brandon, to Dr. Klemm, and to God as I wiped away my tears.

Was it always going to be this way? Would every fever, complaint of not feeling well, or extra bruise or two send me into a frantic state, thinking the worst? The thought of life forever being this way was overwhelming. I wasn't sure I could handle it.

Later that night as we lay in bed, Brandon gently explained to me that I couldn't overreact like that again. He reminded me how unlikely the chances were for Jenna to have leukemia as well.

"I know," I argued defensively. "But do you know how many families I've met along the way where that was the case? I met one mom whose son was in the hospital undergoing treatment while her daughter was an outpatient undergoing treatment too. I met another whose three kids, ages five, three, and one, were all waiting for bone marrow transplants. It's not that rare in the world our family lives in!"

"You're right," he consented, "but we have to trust that God is in control and we can't let our worries consume us. You're going to drive yourself crazy with worrying."

"You're right," I admitted. "You're exactly right. I am driving myself crazy with worry. I just can't help it after all that our family has been through. I try to rein my mind back in whenever it starts heading down those dark roads, but it inevitably takes off again. Being the middle of winter doesn't help anything either. I'm just ready for spring to come again." Tears welled in my eyes again.

"It will," he reassured me, leaning over to kiss me good night. "It will. Spring will come again."

Kate's pulmonology appointment was the next week and we would leave straight from her appointment for Memphis. My plan was to stop in Florence on the way to drop off Jenna with Grammy.

I'm not sure what I was thinking, but I took all three kids to Kate's appointment with me. I guess I thought it would be a quick visit because it was just a consultation, and if I had all the kids we could just leave right after her appointment was over. I loaded our luggage into the van and we made it on time to Kate's morning appointment in downtown Huntsville.

We met with a couple of different nurses who were very friendly and asked a lot of questions about Kate and her cough. Kate did a breathing test, which looked good, and then we were sent to wait in a tiny exam room. The four of us ended up being there for almost two hours. Jenna liked to jump on the rolling chair and sling herself from one side of the tiny room to another. Elijah was getting fussy, so I fed him some baby food, which appeased him for a little while. Kate entertained herself with a few toys that I kept stashed in the diaper bag. A nurse would come in for a few minutes to ask questions, and then we'd sit for another thirty minutes before someone else would come in. The wait was driving me crazy!

Finally, the pulmonologist came in to meet us. He was an outdoorsy looking older man who was friendly enough, but very brief. He listened to Kate's lungs and asked a few questions regarding trademark signs of asthma.

"Does she wheeze? Or does exercise trigger a coughing fit?"

I answered no to every question, but he decided that he wanted to treat her for asthma and begin her on an inhaler. I really didn't like putting her on medication as part of a trial-and-error approach, but I wanted to cooperate on the off chance that this would solve her problem. I agreed to start her on an inhaler twice a day.

Then he mentioned in passing that if it was not asthma, we might be looking at a case of interstitial lung disease. I wasn't sure what that was, but I thought anything that had the word "disease" in it could not be good. I told myself I wasn't going to worry about whatever he had mentioned. We were going to take this one step at a time and asthma was the first step, but I couldn't shake the sick feeling in my stomach.

A nurse came in to demonstrate how to use an inhaler with an air chamber; we scheduled a follow up visit for March, and were out the door. Poor Elijah had fallen asleep in my arms and didn't blink an eye when I transferred him into his car seat.

We met Grammy for lunch along the way in Florence and sat in a corner booth to keep Kate from being exposed to too many people. After we finished eating lunch, I transferred all of Jenna's belongings into Grammy's car, hugged her tightly, and told her I would see her the next day. Kate, Elijah, and I continued on our way to Memphis and arrived in town just in time for dinner. Tri Delta Place (the new name for the Grizzlies House) was full and we were sent to a nearby hotel for the night.

Elijah was desperately ready to nurse, so we hurried over to unload the van and get settled in our room at the hotel. After he was content, we headed back to St. Jude's cafeteria to eat before it closed at seven. After dinner, we boomeranged back to the hotel to bathe and get ready for bed. I nursed Elijah in a quiet corner of the room while Kate watched a show about blizzards, which was the only thing mildly appropriate for an almost five-year-old at nine o'clock at night. Kate learned all about getting stuck on a mountaintop during a blizzard and frostbite. The picture of the man's blackened amputated fingers was a nice image to have on our minds before we went to bed. After tucking Elijah into his playpen, I tucked Kate into bed, read her a book, and sang to her. She was soon fast asleep.

With both babies asleep, I pulled out the tablet to research the three words that had been plaguing me all day—interstitial lung disease. My resolve not to worry about it had diminished entirely. After scanning the list of websites that popped up, I chose one to research. What I read brought me to tears.

Symptoms of interstitial lung disease included a chronic cough. One of the causes of the disease was chemotherapy, namely cyclophosphamide and methotrexate, two chemos Kate had received for over a year now. While the spread of the disease could be slowed by certain medications, the end result of interstitial lung disease was death.

I lay in that hotel bed, tears streaming down my face, trying my best to control the sobs that racked my chest.

"After all this," I thought, "and it's not even going to be the cancer that kills her. Just some dumb side effect." I cried and prayed for a while as I read through the other information on the page. Eventually, the tears slowed and I reined my emotions back in. It was time to pull it together.

"Okay," I told myself. "I am going to read back through the website again and think rationally." Once I had calmed down, in my heart of hearts, I just couldn't and didn't believe that she had interstitial lung disease.

I started back at the beginning and read through the symptoms of interstitial lung disease one more time. Yes, Kate did have a chronic cough. However another symptom listed was that those suffering from the disease would easily get out of breath when exercising or sometimes even with minimal exertion. Kate most definitely did not get out of breath when exercising and she stayed pretty active! I clung to this glimmer of hope. I continued reading through the list of treatments for the disease and found that the second hope I could cling to was that she could have a lung transplant.

It's all about hope, I reminded myself. You've got to have hope.

I abandoned my research for sleep, was joined later by a certain little bed buddy, and then rose early to get us over to the hospital for the usual routine. Kate was accessed, and after we were called back for her therapy visit with Dr. Pui, I posed a few questions about Kate's cough and included the input from the pulmonologist.

Martha May, Dr. Pui's nurse practitioner, consented to beginning Kate on inhalers and also wanted to add montelukast sodium to see if that would help her snorting if she had a post nasal drip. She was very encouraging when I mentioned interstitial lung disease and observed that Kate looked and sounded as healthy as a horse. She also explained that the disease was very rare and only caused by high doses of cyclophosphamide and methotrexate. Kate had been given only one high dose of cyclophosphamide during induction and four high doses of methotrexate during consolidation. The rest of the cyclos that she'd received since then were half doses and Kate had not even been able to receive all of that due to her oversensitivity to it.

I felt better. Not completely better, but better.

While Martha and I were talking, Dr. Pui looked over Kate's counts. He was not satisfied with how high and how normal they had been lately. He thought for a minute and then decided he wanted to increase Kate's 6mp, her nightly oral chemo.

"Her counts are too high and we must do something. I also want to increase her dose of methotrexate. Because we are doing an increased dose, it will need to be administered over a two-hour infusion rather than the five minute push. It is better for her brain this way."

My heart sank a little. A two-hour infusion? I tried to wrap my head around adding two hours to our clinic days every week so that Kate could receive her chemo. Adding two hours to each visit with three kids in tow was a very big deal.

But what could I say? "Um, no, that is really inconvenient for me." So I just nodded my head and tried to remember the new dosage of 6mp and the new instructions for her methotrexate infusion.

We were finishing our visit with Dr. Pui when we heard a commotion in the hall. Suddenly, a dozen nurses crowded outside our door with a handful of bright birthday balloons, a banner signed by each nurse and doctor in A Clinic, and handfuls and handfuls of confetti. They burst into song, wishing Kate a happy early birthday. She would turn five the next week. Kate was beaming as they sang.

I was beaming too. I loved how, in the midst of all this cancer and chemo, there was hope and joy.

The winter thus far has brought nothing but anxiety and worry along with it. You have battled pneumonia, a severe sinus infection, and a chronic cough. We had to pull you from preschool and are now riding out the rest of winter within the walls of our home. Our clinic days are about to lengthen by a couple of hours each week, and the days in between are consumed by medications, inhalers, and physical therapy. Right now, the words "interstitial lung disease" are plaguing my heart.

The past few months have been discouraging. It seemed as though bad news was constantly waiting for us around every corner. It has been easy to lose my focus on the One who is capable of seeing us through these trials.

In the end, it all boils down to trusting in God and recognizing that He is in control. We have to trust that He will have completely healed you at the end of your treatment. We have to trust that you will not suffer any major side effects from your chemotherapy in the years to come. We have to trust that you will remain cancer free for the rest of your life. We have to trust in His perfect plan for our family and for you.

And if not? What if God's will is different from our will? What if His answer to our prayers is "No"?

I consider Shadrach, Meshach, and Abednego in Daniel 3:16-17 who, when faced with being thrown in the fiery furnace, answered the king, "O Nebuchadnezzar, we do not need to give you an answer concerning this matter. If it be so, our God whom we serve is able to deliver us from the furnace of blazing fire; and He will deliver us out of your hand, O king" (NASB).

What an insurmountable amount of faith it took for these three men to express such confidence and supreme trust in God Almighty when faced with death!

However, what these three men say in the very next verse, Daniel 3:18, took an even greater amount of faith in God: "But even if He does not, let it be known to you, O king, that we are not going to serve your gods or worship the golden image that you have set up" (KJV).

The magnitude of their faith can be summed up in four simple words: "if He does not." In these few words, they recognize that it may not be God's will to save them and that saving them may not be part of God's plan. But to these three, this doesn't change anything. They will praise Him, no matter what!

And so we pray for a faith like Shadrach, Meshach, and Abednego—a faith that puts complete trust in the Father and humbly submits to His will, whatever it may be.

We will praise Him through the ups and downs, through the joys and disappointments, through chemotherapy and after chemotherapy.

Won't we, my sweet Kate?

Love,

Mommy

> *"But you, O Lord, are a God merciful and gracious, slow to anger and abounding in steadfast love and faithfulness"* (Psalms 86:15).
>
> *"Whether it is good or bad, we will obey the voice of the Lord our God to whom we are sending you, that it may be well with us when we obey the voice of the Lord our God"* (Jeremiah 42:6).

Chapter 14: A Momentary Light Affliction

March 26, 2015

Dear Kate,

Happy Diagnosis Day! Well, that doesn't sound right. Merry Diagnosis Day? Congratulations on your Diagnosis Day? Those don't sound right either.

I'm really not sure how we should greet you on the anniversary of the day that you were diagnosed with cancer. This is the day that your life changed forever. This is the day that marked the beginning of an incredibly difficult journey for you and our family. This is the day that hundreds of people hit their knees and pleaded with God to save your life.

This is the day that the Lord our God manifested the greatness of His power as He began your earthly healing.

And while this earthly healing has most certainly not been smooth sailing, God has never failed us once.

So what do we tell you on the anniversary of your Diagnosis Day?

Really, three words will suffice.

God. Is. Good.

*A*t clinic the Tuesday after our trip to Memphis, we reached a huge milestone that Kate's nurses had promised would come one day, although I hadn't really believed them. Kate used to scream at the top of her lungs whenever the needle was pushed through the skin in her chest into her port. Her goal was to make sure everyone within a two-mile radius knew she was getting her port accessed. For two years, I had worked with Kate on facing her fear of the needle. We made charts, practiced breathing to calm down, and more.

Then suddenly, just before her fifth birthday, Kate didn't cry. As her nurse Jessica prepped her port with alcohol, Kate took a deep breath, clenched her fists, and squeezed her eyes shut tight when the needle was pushed into her chest. My mouth fell open in surprise.

"Kate Miller!" I exclaimed. "You did it! You didn't even cry!" Jessica and I celebrated with a lot of cheers and hugs.

As she drew blood, Jessica talked with Kate about how brave she had been and what tricks she noticed her doing.

"Kate, I noticed that when you got your needle, you squeezed your fists tight and took a deep breath."

Kate nodded her head in agreement. "I do that when I poop too."

We howled with laughter.

"You squeeze your fists and hold your breath?" Jessica asked, still giggling.

"Yes, like this." Kate started to demonstrate and then suddenly stopped, a sheepish grin spreading across her face. "Well, I better not do that right now!"

Kate's nurses and I giggled about that the rest of the day. We also bragged about how she'd gotten her needle without making a peep.

While I was proud and rejoiced at how far she had come, this moment was also a little bittersweet. She was growing up in ways she shouldn't have to.

Kate was learning compassion—because she daily watched children suffering from cancer. She was developing patience—because she had to wait for doctor's appointments for hours on end. She was mastering contentment—because she missed out on birthday parties and holidays that are normally part of childhood. She was gaining bravery—because she had to overcome her fear of being stuck in the chest with a needle every week.

As we reached this milestone with Kate, we also reached the time when Kate began asking questions. Because she was diagnosed with cancer when she was three, she took the diagnosis in stride, not knowing that this life was any different than any other kid. In fact, when Jenna turned three, Kate told her, "Now you are going to start getting needles every week, Jenna!"

But now, Kate was older and she realized something was different about her life.

One night at bedtime, Kate asked, "Mom, why do I have to get chemo?"

I took a deep breath. We had been waiting for this moment for almost two years. At the very beginning when we had tried to talk to Kate about leukemia, she was disinterested. We had decided then that we would not press the issue and Kate would let us know when she was ready to talk. She was ready.

"Well, Kate, you know how we talk about germs and call them bad bugs. When you were three years old, you were diagnosed with leukemia. Leukemia is a bad bug called cancer that gets in your blood. It attacked your platelets and hemoglobin, which are the good cells in your blood."

Kate began to cry softly.

"Oh no, honey! But do you remember how we celebrate your Remission Day?"

Kate nodded through her tears.

"That's because God healed you! The chemo you have been taking got rid of that bad bug a long time ago and now you get chemo just to make sure that bad bug stays gone. But God has healed you and leukemia is not something you have to fear."

Kate calmed down at that answer and I wrapped her up into my arms. I knew the talk had gone well, but my heart ached. No parent should ever have to explain to their little girl about the cancer that had attacked her little body and how her childhood had been forever changed by this monster of a disease.

Kate's counts were normal the week of her birthday, so we were able to press forward with the party we had planned. She wanted a unicorn birthday party and so she got a unicorn birthday party! We had the party the next day on Wednesday, her actual birthday, and kept our guest count low. We invited her grandmothers and aunts and then I told Kate she could invite two friends. She chose her cousin and another friend from church.

"Can I invite one more girl from Bible class?" she asked hesitantly.

My smile faltered a little. "Well, baby, we need to keep your party pretty small, so let's just stick with the two girls. Okay?"

"Okay," she replied, but I could hear a little disappointment in her voice.

The disappointment was forgotten once her party started! After two months of being cooped up in the house, Kate absolutely loved playing with her friends. The girls decorated unicorn horns, played "pin the tail on the unicorn," and devoured pizza and cake. After everything Kate had been through in the past two years, I was happy to see her celebrate another year of life, another year of the blessing of family, and another year as a testimony to the power of God.

The day after Kate's birthday was absolutely beautiful and surprisingly warm for January, so I took the girls and Elijah to the Huntsville Botanical Gardens for the morning. We had a picnic lunch on a luscious green lawn. After lunch, the girls took off their shoes and raced and rolled in the grass, soaking up the warm rays of sunshine. Elijah lay on the blanket, kicking his legs and squealing, enjoying the warmth of the sun just as much as his sisters. It was so refreshing to have that brief taste of spring in January.

And then the real world came crashing back down on us.

The next afternoon, Kate woke from her nap with a fever of 101.6. Brandon took her straight to the emergency room. Her bloodwork showed that she was neutropenic, so she was admitted to PICU. Fortunately, after beginning antibiotics, her fever was gone in a matter of hours. By the next day, her counts were slightly higher, so Dr. Cox took pity on Kate and Brandon and let them come home. We were happy for a shortened PICU stay and renewed our efforts to keep Kate better quarantined for the remainder of winter.

February marked the beginning of a special training for Brandon and me! We had signed up to run the St. Jude Half Marathon in Nashville at the end of April in honor of Kate. We also had signed up to raise money for St. Jude, and before training even started we had surpassed our goals and raised over $5,500 for our beloved hospital!

Finding time to train for a half marathon proved to be tricky as I worked around Elijah's nursing schedule, the yucky winter weather, and Brandon's business trips.

As crazy as us signing up for a half marathon might have sounded, it did us a world of good. Exercise, obviously, helped boost our mood and improve our health. It also gave me a chance to just let my mind wander and pound my frustrations out on the pavement. This race had so much meaning to us now. We had run it a few times in the past before kids came along, but now we had a personal connection to it and all that it represented. We were running with purpose. We were running for a cure for our daughter!

Our training in February started off with running three to five miles a few times a week and then our distance would increase slowly over the next twelve weeks until the race. I gradually began to see my last remaining pounds of baby weight drop off and enjoyed being able to fit in my regular clothes more easily!

Kate joined in on getting healthy as well. Her doctors at the Affiliate Clinic had been working to improve the selection of snacks offered to the patients and many of the girls' favorite treats disappeared from the snack basket. On one of our visits to Memphis, I let the girls pick out some snacks in the cafeteria. Kate reached out for a treat and then suddenly snatched her hand back.

"Kate, if you want the treat, I will buy it for you," I offered.

"No, Mommy," Kate refused. "My doctors said these are not healthy for you and I am going to obey my doctors."

Kate tried to persuade Jenna to join in on the family's exercise and eating habits as well. At dinner one night, Kate admonished Jenna to eat her edamame. Jenna folded her arms across her chest and shook her head no, a stubborn look on her face.

"Jenna, God gave you the edamame. You need to be thankful to Him for giving you this food!" Kate chastised her sister.

"I am *not* thankful to God for edamame!" Jenna exclaimed.

"Ooo, Jenna! God's gonna *strike* you!" Kate zapped her hand toward Jenna in imitation of a lightning bolt.

February came to a close and the first of March stood ready to welcome us. Spring was on the horizon. I could feel it in the air. The promise of warmer weather was just around the corner!

Kate's medication schedule was now mind-boggling, especially during steroid week—DEX three times a day, ranitidine twice a day, gabapentin three times a day, montelukast sodium once a day, allergy medicine twice a day, inhaler twice a day, her 6mp at night with fasting for two hours before she could take it, and her pain medicine as needed. I also did physical therapy for her legs three times a day.

One night, Kate and I were at a standstill at her bedtime. Kate had been asking for her pain medicine every night to help ease her leg pain. If it was the week of steroids and her vincristine treatment, I would gladly have given her the medicine. Without her oxycodone, the pain was too much for her to bear. However, as she became further removed from that week of treatment and had not complained of leg pain all day, I began to wonder if she was just asking out of habit. I started an experiment to see if she really needed her pain medication and I filled her syringe with water instead.

The first few times she had taken her "medicine" she said that it tasted funny. I just smiled and answered, "It does?" However that night, she asked, "Mom, is this water?"

"It's H_2O," I replied.

Kate furrowed her eyebrows and paused for a second before asking, "Is that how you spell water?"

Kate's cough continued into the month of March. I knew the next path the pulmonologist wanted to take—a CT scan to determine if she had interstitial lung disease. Kate was due in Memphis again mid-March and I had a list of questions to ask about Kate's cough. As soon as we were settled in the exam room for Kate's therapy visit, I began firing questions at Justine.

"So after two months of an inhaler and montelukast sodium, Kate still has her cough. She has an appointment with her pulmonologist back in Huntsville tomorrow morning. He wants to do a CT scan to determine if she has interstitial lung disease or not. Is exposing her to more radiation worth the risk if it is not likely that she has interstitial lung disease?"

Justine smiled. "If you ask Dr. Pui that, he is going to say that he is not a lung doctor. He will tell you he treats cancer and to let the pulmonologist do what the pulmonologist wants to do, but I can tell you this—a CT scan will not expose her to that much radiation."

I ran through my list of other cough-related questions and then posed the next one with bated breath.

"We have been keeping Kate out of public for a few months now, but spring and warmer weather are just around the corner. Is it safe to let her out yet?"

Justine emphatically shook her head no, and my hopes were dashed. "No, the flu is still going strong. I have two patients in ICU right now with it. The strain this winter hit hard and heavy and is lasting a lot longer than normal. I would wait a little longer," she advised.

We were disappointed, but we were certainly going to heed her advice. What was another month anyhow after spending most of the past two years in isolation?

After a few more questions, Dr. Pui entered the room and addressed me as he examined Kate. He was still dissatisfied with Kate's counts and wanted to continue her increased doses of methotrexate, which meant continuing the two-hour infusion of methotrexate.

"With an increased dose, the two-hour infusion is better for the brain," he reminded me and I nodded in agreement.

Kate had been receiving the two-hour infusion for a couple of months and our clinic visits were now ranging anywhere from six to eight hours. Tuesdays were long and draining. As soon as I got all three kids loaded back in the van and sat down, I was exhausted. Brandon might add that I was also irritable.

I had also found that other doctors, pharmacists, and nurses didn't necessarily agree that the methotrexate infusion had to be two hours. In fact, most believed that a five-minute push would suffice. But Dr. Pui's words were like gold to me and I was sticking by my man. I knew his notions were sometimes a bit old fashioned, that he was ultra conservative, and that he was probably tough to work with, but in my mind he had earned every right to be that way. I had so much respect for him that if he said that he wanted me to dye my hair purple and to run around the hospital clucking like a chicken, I would have done it.

The biggest problem we faced, though, because of the increased dosage of methotrexate, was that it was sending Kate's liver enzymes insanely high. She now had her liver enzyme levels checked every week before her chemo was given. She'd had to miss her chemo because her levels were too high. Dr. Pui voiced concern over her liver enzyme levels, but decided we would continue with the increased dosage of methotrexate and continue to monitor her levels.

The next morning back at home, Grammy came to keep Elijah and Jenna so that I could take Kate to her appointment with the pulmonologist. I was not about to sit in that little exam room for two hours with all three kids again! As I listened to Kate cough most of the way there, my stomach was in knots as to what her doctor would say.

We settled in an exam room, and it wasn't long before a nurse came in to evaluate Kate and her cough. A few minutes later, the pulmonologist joined us.

"So how is Miss Kate's cough?" he asked.

Kate coughed on cue. "It's still here, even after the two months of an inhaler," I admitted.

He frowned for a moment before speaking. "Well, it looks like what we're dealing with here is interstitial lung disease."

My heart tightened in my chest and I listened in silence as he continued to talk. He explained in detail about how chemotherapy can cause a scarring of the lungs and that the first thing he wanted to do was order a CT scan. His voice sounded fuzzy to my numbed ears and my eyes glazed over as I dwelled on the words "interstitial lung disease." But I snapped back to reality when he mentioned a lung biopsy and hope for an eventual lung transplant.

And I found my voice.

"I disagree with you," I began hesitantly, but my confidence was mounting with each word I spoke. "I researched interstitial lung disease and, while she does have a chronic cough, she does not ever get out of breath at rest or even when she is exercising. She can even ride her scooter for over a mile without getting winded! Yes, she has had cyclophosphamide and methotrexate, chemos that I read caused this disease, but it is the high doses of these chemos that cause the scarring of the lungs. She only had one high dose cyclo and four high dose methotrexates. I discussed this with her St. Jude doctor at clinic and she thinks it is highly unlikely that Kate has this lung disease." By the conclusion of my speech, my heart was pounding in my chest.

"What I need to do is to talk with Dr. Russo first," he determined, "and then we'll go from there." He stood and walked out of the room, leaving behind a five-year-old cancer patient who had been through too much in her short little life and a teary-eyed mother who was desperately trying to stay composed in front of her daughter.

It wasn't long before the pulmonologist came back in the room.

"Well, I've spoken with Dr. Russo," he informed me, "and she agrees that it is highly unlikely that Kate has this disease. However, we need to rule it out for sure. I am ordering a CT scan of Kate's lungs, and Dr. Russo wants to add a scan of her sinus cavity to be sure her sinus infection from the winter is completely clear. My nurse will set up the appointment for you before you leave."

He pulled out his stethoscope and, sitting on the stool, rolled himself forward to listen to Kate's lungs. He was quiet as he listened. "Well, I don't really hear the crackly sound that is an indicator of the lung disease. But let's go forward with the CT scan just to be sure." He stood and, before he left the room again, proposed that we start Kate on a different inhaler with a slightly different focus than the first one she had been on.

"I will check with her doctor to make sure that's okay," I replied, still numb from everything that had just transpired.

The pulmonologist nodded before he left the room, and his nurse soon came in with Kate's new inhaler as well as Kate's appointment for her CT scan. I was surprised to find out that it was scheduled for that very afternoon at two! I had prayed for so long for answers regarding Kate's cough, and we were finally about to get them. I called to see if my mother-in-law could stay a few extra hours that afternoon while Kate had her CT scan, and she readily agreed.

Kate needed to fast for two hours before the scan, so we hurried home to eat lunch. I also needed to squeeze in four miles in training that day while Grammy was there to tend to the kids, so after I fixed Kate a quick lunch, I changed and took off down the road.

As I ran, my mind had a chance to think about all that had just transpired. The longer I ran, the more furious I got with the pulmonologist. *Why in the world did he so confidently say that she must have interstitial lung disease?!* I ranted in my head. *He never even asked me once if Kate exhibited the symptoms of this disease. Nor did he even bother consulting her doctor about what chemotherapy Kate has had! And he listened to her lungs at the end of the appointment and decided he really didn't hear the crackly sound that is characteristic to the disease! Does he not know the worry he has caused us over the past few months?*

Normally, running was a fantastic release for all my frustrations and I felt at peace with the world afterward, but by the time I completed this run I was mad. I hurried inside to get a quick bite to eat, shower, and give Kate her dose of steroids and other medications before loading her back into the van to go to the hospital.

As we drove, I explained to Kate that they were going to take some pictures of her lungs. I also explained there would be a lot of sick people in the hospital, so she would need to wear her mask.

We had to wait for a little while in the waiting room before we were called back. Finally, a nurse came to take us back, escorted us into an exam room, and asked Kate to take off her shirt so she could access her port. I was unaware her port was going to be accessed for her scan and felt awful that I had not prepared Kate for that. Kate began to cry.

"Kate's doctor ordered a CT scan with contrast. Her port will need to be accessed so we can push the contrast in," her nurse explained to me. Kate continued to cry and I tried to explain that she'd had anesthesia the day before, was on steroids, and was exhausted. I also asked if she could leave her shirt on if we held it up and the nurse agreed.

The child life specialist in radiology headed off to get a tablet and moments later, Kate was calmly playing a game. She got her port accessed like a champ and we went to have her CT scan. I reminded Kate that she'd had a CT scan before and asked if she remembered the hamster that had drunk too much coffee and was running circles in its wheel around her head. She laughed and said she did remember.

Kate lay down on the machine's table and I donned a lead vest to wear while the scan was being done. The lab technician adjusted Kate into position and I held her hand as the table slid backward into the machine. The scan was loud and sounded like a helicopter that was about to take off. Kate's little hand tightened around mine and I reminded her to be really still, and to watch for the hamster running around her head.

The table slid in and out of the machine as it scanned her sinus cavity and then her lungs. At one point, the tech came over and hooked a syringe of contrast to Kate's line.

"This feels a little funny," she explained. "It doesn't hurt. It just feels like something warm is spreading all over your body." And she began to push.

Kate's lower lip began to tremble and she bit it to keep herself from crying. "That doesn't feel very comfy," she commented with a tremor in her voice.

"You're doing great," I reassured her. "She's almost done." I was so proud of her.

The tech finished the push a minute later and explained what was going to happen next. "The machine is going to tell you to breathe in, hold your breath for five seconds, and then to breathe out. Just do what the machine tells you to do."

The table slid Kate back into the tunnel and a woman's voice gave instructions as the machine scanned Kate's lungs again. I held Kate's hand again and demonstrated what she needed to be doing as the instructions were given. I wasn't sure if Kate was doing it or not, but when the tech came back into the room, she relayed that Kate did great.

"I have never had a kid that young that was able to do that," she complimented Kate.

Once the scan was over and Kate was de-accessed, we were free to go. The tech planned to send the results to Dr. Russo and to Kate's pulmonologist in a couple of hours, but it might be the next day before we found out the results because it was already late in the afternoon.

But Dr. Russo called early that evening. "I have wonderful news!" she exclaimed. "Kate's sinus cavity and her lungs were both crystal clear. She looks perfect."

L. Erin Miller

I breathed a sigh of relief and praised God for such wonderful news! I was so thankful that Dr. Russo called me as soon as she received the scans. As a pediatric oncologist, she knew how awful it was to wait for life-changing news regarding your child.

After I got off the phone with Dr. Russo, I immediately called Brandon and then texted our parents the good news.

It was a few days before the pulmonologist called with the results.

The following week brought "Diagnosis Day," and we recognized this day with a trip to the doughnut shop. Several brightly colored helium balloons were floating around the shop, their ribbons dangling, enticing kids to grab one. Kate and Jenna picked out the last two pink balloons in the bunch and brought them happily back to our table.

A few minutes later, another family with young children walked in and their kids' eyes lit up at the sight of the balloons. The daughter walked over and was crestfallen when she noticed there were not any pink balloons.

The little girl went to sit with her family at a nearby table and a minute later, Kate whispered to me. "Mommy, that girl wanted a pink balloon. I want to give her my pink balloon."

Touched, I commended her. "That is very sweet of you, Kate."

She sat nervously for a minute. "Mommy, will you go give her my balloon?"

Choosing my words carefully, I replied, "No. If you want to give her your balloon, you can walk over and give it to her." I paused, observing the indecision on her face. "But you don't *have* to give her your balloon."

Kate sat for another minute before abruptly standing up, taking hold of the pink balloon, and walking over to the girl. She shyly mumbled, "Here," and handed her the balloon. "You can have this." Then she quickly came back to our table, sat down, and resumed eating her doughnut.

I waited a minute. Then I leaned over and kissed her on the head. "I'm proud of you."

269

Kate smiled.

It had been two years since we began this long journey. The past winter had been very trying on our spirits with all that came with it—pneumonia, sinusitis, isolation, coughing, incredibly long clinic days, more coughing, Kate's loss of the range of motion in her feet, the interstitial lung disease scare, and more coughing.

As dreary as the winter had been and as dark as many moments in our journey had been, Kate was developing a beautiful heart, a heart that could turn the darkest and dreariest of times into a warm and sunny day.

In the wee hours of one morning during DEX week, I was in such despair with you, Kate. I had been up most of the night with you all week and was exhausted. I had just left you screaming hysterically in your room, having already tried everything under the sun to calm you down. Nothing had worked. My efforts only seemed to escalate your hysteria.

Once back in my room, I fell into bed and pounded my pillow in frustration. There were times when I felt like I was acing this whole "momcologist" thing. But for every time when I felt like I'd handled a problem with you well, there were ten other times when I felt like I'd utterly failed and reacted the wrong way. This was one of those times.

Knowing I would not be able to go back to sleep, I reached for my Bible. I flipped to 2 Corinthians, the book we were studying in my Bible class, to read ahead for the next lesson. The focus for the study was chapter 4, and through these verses God spoke to me:

"We are afflicted in every way, but not crushed; perplexed, but not driven to despair; persecuted, but not forsaken; struck down, but not destroyed" (2 Corinthians 4:8-9).

"Therefore we do not lose heart, but though our outer man is decaying, yet our inner man is being renewed day by day. For

momentary, light affliction is producing for us an eternal weight of glory far beyond all comparison, while we look not at the things which are seen, but at the things which are not seen; for the things which are seen are temporal, but the things which are not seen are eternal." (2 Corinthians 4:16-18 NASB).

While Paul was speaking of trials related to being a Christian, the message was clear.

This affliction is light and momentary and we will not be destroyed by it. God promises us that! What was being developed in us was worth far more than gold.

In these verses, God reminded me to keep my focus on the things that are unseen, knowing that in the end it will truly be worth it all.

Love,

Mommy

> *"For I consider that the sufferings of this present time are not worth comparing with the glory that is to be revealed to us"* (Romans 8:18).
>
> *"And after you have suffered a little while, the God of all grace, who has called you to his eternal glory in Christ, will himself restore, confirm, strengthen, and establish you"* (1 Peter 5:10).

Chapter 15: Choosing Joy

May 11, 2015

Dear Kate,

I'm not going to lie. This past winter was rough. It was mentally and emotionally draining. Of course, our family was functioning under extreme circumstances with a cancer patient and a baby under the same roof, but much of the strain during the winter was brought on by my constant worrying.

I had to yank my mind back repeatedly from wandering down dark roads. There were moments when I felt like the world was falling apart around me, and no matter how hard I tried I couldn't do anything to change it. The feeling of insignificance and insufficiency was overwhelming, and sometimes I felt like I'd lost my joy.

I n the midst of all the stress that winter and early spring brought, God granted our family a blessing—a double blessing! On March 31, Lorelai Mae and Madeleine Rose, our beautiful twin nieces, were born! Mom had been in Colorado the month of February and most of March to help Haley during her last few weeks of pregnancy. My dad had flown out the week of his spring break to visit as well. Haley was scheduled for a C-section because Lorelai, Baby A, was breech, and everything worked out so that both Mom and Dad were able to be there for the birth of the babies.

The twins were born on a Tuesday so, obviously, we were at the clinic. I checked my phone every few minutes, waiting anxiously for news of their arrival. Finally, my dad sent me a picture of a beautiful baby girl. A minute later, he sent a picture of another gorgeous baby girl. I was in love!

My nieces were just precious and my heart tugged within me. Everything had been so crazy and busy lately, I had not thought much about not being in Colorado for their births. While I was joyful for their safe arrival, I was also sad that I couldn't be there for such a wonderful moment. I knew it was not possible at this point because of Kate and even more so because I planned to nurse Elijah until his first birthday, but I hoped to be able to see those sweet babies—and my sister—soon.

Brandon and I were in the peak of our training for the half marathon, which was rapidly approaching. We were running anywhere from eighteen to twenty miles each week, saving our long runs for Saturday mornings. The weather was getting consistently warmer and flu season was coming to a close, so we opened the barn door for Kate and let her back into civilization again. She was absolutely overjoyed to be able to go back to Bible class and to sit with us in the auditorium once again!

We reached the last Saturday in April, and the long-awaited race weekend had finally arrived! I held my breath all week over Kate's cough and prayed she would not get sick before the race. Her getting sick would add complications on so many different levels, and I didn't even want to think about what we would do in that event. Fortunately, her cough maintained itself, no better but no worse either, and we loaded the van for a crazy weekend.

Grammy was going along as our babysitter, so she rode with us and P-Daddy followed behind us in his car. He was going to run the race as well. He was actually the first in our family to ever run the original Country Music Marathon and, while he'd been in retirement from long-distance running for a few years, he decided to dust off his running shoes for his granddaughter.

After checking in at the expo and picking up our race gear, we headed back to check in at the hotel. Because Brandon and I had signed up to be

Gold Heroes for St. Jude, we were each given a free hotel room. Brandon, Elijah, and I were going to sleep in one while the girls camped out in the other with Grammy. After we unloaded, Brandon took the girls swimming at the indoor pool. The pool, after all, was the only reason the girls had wanted to go on this trip in the first place.

All week, the weather had been looking stormy for race day, but we woke Saturday morning to overcast skies and an e-mail announcing, "The race is on!" After we ate a small breakfast, I pumped some milk for Elijah, and we were off!

Our hotel was half a block from the starting line, so we walked over and surveyed the massive crowd of runners. Brandon's corral was a few up from mine as his pace was a good bit faster. He offered to run with me this year because it was for Kate, but I waived his offer.

"You have trained so hard for this and I want you to beat your goal. I'm perfectly fine to run by myself," I reassured him. Inwardly, I smiled. Brandon was very competitive and I didn't quite have the speed he had. Never before had he wanted to run with me, but after the past two years I understood his desire to cross the finish line of today's race side by side. Nevertheless, I wanted him to run his race and urged him to his corral.

We said a prayer together before waving goodbye with a promise to see each other at the finish line. I worked my way through the crowd and found a spot to stand in my corral. The gun finally sounded for the first corral, the elite runners, to begin, and over the next thirty minutes our corral moved forward until it was finally our turn.

"Runners, get ready, get set, gooooo!" the announcer yelled. I wondered if he was getting tired of saying that so enthusiastically for all sixty corrals. Surely it was hard to be that perky that early in the morning.

The race started downhill toward the river, but all too soon turned and headed back up into town. I tried to take in the scenery and soak up the energy of the bands and cheerleaders I passed along the way as I ran. At every mile marker, I reached my hand into my pocket and pulled out a picture.

It was a picture of Kate taken the summer after she was diagnosed. She was squatting down with a huge grin on her face. She had on a blue jean dress and a pink headband with a pink flower on her precious little bald head. That was about the only time she ever let me put a headband on her head.

On the back of that picture, I had made a list of things to meditate and pray about for each mile. As I ran, I thanked God for seeing Kate safely thus far through treatment. I thanked Him for Kate's doctors and nurses. I even thanked Him for steroids and their conquering power over cancer. (I can't believe I was thankful for steroids!)

As I ran, I thought about all that Kate had been through, all the chemotherapy and the harsh side effects. I thought about her hair loss, her severe leg pain, her screaming with pain in her stomach. I thought about the words "potential infertility" and the damage her chemo had posed to her organs.

In our training schedule, Brandon and I had only trained up to ten miles in preparation for the race. We would finish the last three miles on inspiration, so as I ran the last three miles I prayed for Kate's future. I prayed for week 120, the end of her treatment. I prayed for the day, many years down the road, that we would hear the words "medically cured" for Kate. And as I ran the last mile, I prayed for the cure to be discovered for this horrible monster called cancer.

The course was hilly and I was tired, but that little face smiling at me urged me forward. That little face told me I could do it and it told me to never give up. As I crested the final hill and looked down toward the stadium, I surged forward. I was going to finish strong.

As I ran down the hill toward the finish line, I reached down in my pocket, pulled out that picture, and held it high and proud. I wanted everyone I passed to know who I was running for. I was running for my daughter Kate—my hero.

I crossed the finish line, picture held high, and laughed in relief and slight delirium. Oh, how my hips hurt! I weaved my way in and out of the crowd of finishers, ducked my head to receive my medal, and then headed straight for the snacks! I loaded my arms with fruit, granola bars, drinks, and anything else I thought the kids might devour. I found my little fan club waiting at the family reunion area under the big letter "M" for our last name.

"Mommy!" Kate and Jenna squealed in unison as they ran toward me. I gingerly stooped to give them both hugs.

Brandon greeted me with a smile. "Congratulations! How do you feel?"

"My lower half is beat. I am pretty sure that every organ and joint that was not back in place from childbirth is now officially back in place though."

I noticed Kate had Brandon's medal around her neck and I lifted mine off as well. But instead of giving it to Kate, I approached Jenna. She, after all, was my hero, too.

"Jenna," I began, "this is Mommy's medal for running a really long way for a really long time. I would like you to have it." I held out my medal to her.

Jenna started to take the medal and then became distracted by the goodies I had just put down. "Can I have that granola bar?" she asked.

So much for that sentimental moment with my three-year-old.

We bumped into Dad on our way back to the hotel and congratulated him on finishing the race. He said he hit the first hill and declared, "I'm sixty-two years old. I am not putting myself through this misery!" From then on, he walked up every hill and ran down the other side. We were thrilled to run the race and raise money for St. Jude, but we were also very thrilled that the race was over!

The first Sunday in May, Brandon preached during the evening service where we worshiped. He had e-mailed the elders, the overseers of the congregation, a couple of months before and asked to share our story and the lessons we had learned over the past couple of years. That Sunday was perfect for his sermon because Kate's Remission Day was coming up that week.

The girls sat next to me that Sunday night and one of our elders' wives held Elijah to help me out because my extra set of hands was in the pulpit.

"I want to thank the elders for letting me speak tonight," Brandon began. "I have two goals with tonight's lesson—the first is to share with you the journey that our family has been on the past two years and the lessons we've learned along the way. And the other goal is not to cry."

The audience chuckled and he continued. Brandon mentioned a few of the holidays we celebrate during the first week of May such as May Day and Cinco De Mayo. "But our family celebrates another holiday in the first week of May—May 7th. For us, May 7th is Remission Day."

Brandon shared the story of how Kate was diagnosed and highlighted the journey our little girl had traveled over the past two years. I don't think a single person moved a muscle, and the auditorium was absolutely quiet. This was probably the first time most of them had ever heard the details of the beginning of Kate's story.

Brandon went on to share that we had seen firsthand how God healed the sick. God, with His mighty power, allowed Kate to be brought into remission. Brandon also discussed how we witnessed the abundant love of our fellow brethren as they gave to us in our time of need. The church of Christ on Hughes Road at Gooch Lane had opened their checkbooks and their hearts and given freely. He urged them to hold fast to that spirit of love and generosity.

"And finally, the most obvious lesson we have learned from our experience is that there is no sickness in heaven.

"Dealing with cancer is not fun. Kate had a port implanted in her chest three days after she was diagnosed. To access that port, they have to stick a three-quarter-inch needle in her chest. Kate used to absolutely hate that process. She would kick and scream and several of us had to hold her down so the nurses could put her needle in. And I can't say I blamed her because if I saw a needle that long coming toward my chest, I would probably act the exact same way.

"Kate was poked and prodded. She had masks put on her and she would cry with her discomfort. It was very difficult to see our daughter go through that.

"But you know, when we get to heaven, all that will be gone. There will be no more chemo, no more ports, no more needles, no more masks, no more waiting outside the operating room, no more nausea, no more soreness, no more mood swings from steroids, and no more cancer."

Now our congregation is normally a very reserved and quiet group—remember, this is Huntsville, and most of our men are engineers—but at this last declaration from Brandon, a mighty "Amen" came out from the crowd. A few tears fell from my already brimming eyes.

Brandon continued. "It is summed up most beautifully in Revelation 21:4—'He will wipe away every tear from their eyes, and death shall be no more, neither shall there be mourning, nor crying, nor pain anymore, for the former things have passed away.' We so look forward to that day. I've always looked forward to heaven, but I especially look forward to it after March 26, 2013."

I was so proud of my husband. He has always been an exceptional man, but the integrity and the strong foundation he has shown over the past two years have endeared my heart to him even more.

The next day, Monday, Brandon took the girls to clinic. Our clinic visit was scheduled a day early because we were going to the beach that afternoon. Elijah stayed home to help me pack and we were on the road by midafternoon, arriving in Gulf Shores late that night.

The girls couldn't wait to get out on the beach the next morning. It had not been twenty-four hours since Kate's port had been de-accessed, so we decided to hike a trail along the bay and then visited our favorite kid-friendly restaurant for lunch. We ate by the water, and then I took the kids out to the restaurant's sand pit to play while Brandon paid for our meal. There was a small "Fountain of Youth" with buckets next to the sand pit and I instructed Kate to be sure to stay away from the water. I was sure to tell her sister not to dump any water on her also!

There were a couple of kids playing in the water, and both had a mischievous gleam in their eyes as they scooped up a bucketful of water and scampered toward Kate and Jenna. Kate looked at me, worried, and I mouthed to her, "Just tell them that you can't get wet."

I didn't think the kids were really going to dump water on the girls, but the mischievous gleam in their eyes was a little unnerving. One of the boys came near Kate with a bucket of water and she stopped him, hand held out.

"Do not pour water on me," she told him firmly. "Do you know why? 'Cause I have a port."

I smiled. The boy shrugged and ran off to play elsewhere.

Then May 7th rolled around. Remission Day. That morning, we sang "Happy Remission Day" to Kate, spent the day on the beach, and went out for dinner that afternoon. After eating, we stopped to listen to a live band playing at the restaurant, and a waitress stopped to talk to the girls while we were sitting.

Kate told her, "It's my 'Mission Day!"

The waitress looked at me, confused, and I explained that it was her Remission Day. She had been free from cancer for two years now.

The waitress smiled and turned back to Kate. "Well, then I guess I should tell you happy birthday! Because today is the day your life began again."

Oh, how right that waitress was!

After we listened to the band, we drove up the road to finish the day with ice cream. While we waited in line to order, I read off a few items from the menu to the girls.

"You could get a cone, a milkshake, a sundae…"

Kate interrupted, "Ooo! I'll have a sundae!"

Jenna chimed in too, "Mmm! And I'll have a Monday!"

Swimming in the ocean, dinner, a band, and ice cream? That wasn't too shabby of a Remission Day.

The rest of our trip flew by in a blur and, of course, none of us were ready to come home. However, once again we had a certain little kid who was due for chemo. And she was not just due for chemo but a lumbar puncture in Memphis the very next day!

And so we bid farewell to the ocean and headed back to reality once again.

With spring has come the hope for better days. Also with the blossoming of spring comes the realization of how close we are to the end of our cancer journey.

I wonder, though, after you are finished with chemo, how will we choose to remember this journey?

And that's the wonderful thing about it—it's our choice. It is our choice as to how we approach every trial in life, and we must realize that our choice determines whether or not we are glorifying God.

So how will we choose to remember this journey, Kate? Will we remember the bad? Of course!

As your parents, we will never forget the horror of the day you were diagnosed with leukemia. We will never forget the sound of your screams and cries as needles were repeatedly pushed into you and as you writhed in pain from your medications and chemotherapy. We will never forget sweeping up the wisps of blonde hair as they fell from your head. And we will never ever forget the fear of the unknown.

While these memories will forever be seared in our minds, we needn't dwell on these thoughts. Rather than letting our fears consume us, we must choose to concentrate on the many blessings this journey has brought along with it.

We count it a blessing to have met so many wonderful people on this journey. The friendships we have forged with your nurses, doctors, and other cancer families are ones that will last a lifetime. We will focus on the blessings of our family and our brothers and sisters in Christ who so generously and selflessly helped us during our time of need. We will choose to be thankful for the characteristics that are being refined within us from our journey.

But most of all, we choose to praise God for a better understanding of His love for us and for giving us a greater desire for a home in heaven with Him.

So Kate, when facing the troubles and trials that come in this life, remember this:

You can choose fear. Or you can choose faith.

You can choose worry. Or you can choose trust.

You can choose despair. Or you can choose hope.

You can choose self-pity. Or you can choose perspective.

You can choose tears. Or you can choose laughter.

You can choose to complain. Or you can choose thankfulness.

You can choose anger. Or you can choose love.

You can choose bitterness. Or you can choose joy.

My prayer is that you will always choose faith, trust, hope, perspective, laughter, thankfulness, love, and joy. Always.

Love,

Mommy

> *"Do not be anxious about anything, but in everything by prayer and supplication with thanksgiving let your requests be made known to God. And the peace of God, which surpasses all understanding, will guard your hearts and your minds in Christ Jesus. Finally, brothers, whatever is true, whatever is honorable, whatever is just, whatever is pure, whatever is lovely, whatever is commendable, if there is any excellence, if there is anything worthy of praise, think about these things"* (Philippians 4:6-8).

Chapter 16: Making Memories

August 9, 2015

Dear Kate,

Along this journey that is coming to a close, we have lost so much. We lost our ignorance of the terror that is childhood cancer. And believe me, ignorance was bliss! We lost our innocence as we were hurriedly ushered into this world of fear and worry. The world no longer has a rose-tinted hue and we certainly have lost some of our carefree nature that characterized our youth. Yes, much has been lost since March 26, 2013.

But what we have gained is even greater! We have gained a closer relationship with God as we have leaned on Him to see us through this trial. We have grown closer as a family as we have learned to deal with one another during stressful situations.

As we have grown closer, we have learned to treasure every moment we have—being extra aware that every moment and every memory we have is a blessing and a gift from God.

We arrived home from the beach late Monday afternoon. I unpacked, repacked, and the kids and I were back on the road again the following morning, Memphis bound. This was the first time I was traveling with all three kids by myself. My mother-in-law was on a Mediterranean cruise and my mom had just gotten back from Colorado the day before. In fact, I did not even tell my mom that I was going by myself because I knew she would try to help us and end up wearing herself out.

We stayed at a nearby hotel because the Tri Delta Place was full. Beverly Molloy, our friend from Bartlett Church of Christ, and her daughter, Zoe, met us at the hospital that morning, giving me two extra sets of hands.

At Kate's visit with Dr. Pui, he was once again dissatisfied with her counts. "It looks like she's not even on chemotherapy!" he exclaimed. We discussed a few options to achieve lower counts, but in the end he decided to keep things the way they were. She was so far into treatment, he didn't really see the benefit of changing things around now.

As Justine walked us over to procedures for Kate's LPIT, she and I discussed the end of treatment and she mentioned that after treatment, Kate could resume taking vitamins.

Something inside me jolted. "She's been taking a whole-food-based gummy, but it is explicitly advertised as not being a vitamin," I quickly reassured her.

"I would take her off of those," Justine instructed me without a moment's hesitation.

I stubbornly continued. "Are you familiar with this company, though? These gummies are flash-dried fruits and vegetables. It is not a vitamin."

She shook her head slowly. "I would still take Kate off of them."

"Okay," I hesitantly agreed and opened my mouth to ask more questions, but we had arrived at procedures and the team was waiting for us. I didn't think too much more about our conversation and decided I would just ask more questions about it at the clinic the following week.

The rest of the visit went well, but as we were packing up to go I could tell a huge post-anesthesia meltdown was building up in Kate. Beverly and her daughter helped get everyone loaded into the van, and after many hugs and goodbyes we were off! I was so grateful for their help that day.

Kate began her next to last week of steroids on this Memphis trip and did pretty well overall. On that Saturday, her fourth day of DEX, we even took her out in public! My dad was retiring after forty years of teaching and coaching, and Mom had planned a huge surprise retirement party for him at their local high school. Many of his former players and coaches as well as friends and family were gathered in the auditorium when Dad, under the impression that he was borrowing some tables for a party, walked out onto the stage. Everyone stood and cheered for him and his hand covered his mouth when he realized what was going on. Kate and Jenna squealed "P-Daddy" from their seats and waved excitedly at him.

Mom had arranged for a guest speaker from each school in which Dad had taught, and for the next hour or so we were entertained with funny coaching stories about Dad. You can only imagine what it's like when a bunch of coaches get together to reminisce. I spoke as well, and after my speech we watched a photo montage, then walked to the lunchroom for a reception. I quickly found Brandon and the kids, who had snuck out of the auditorium about halfway into the speeches. The food was delicious, the decorations were beautiful, and I enjoyed seeing some old familiar faces, but Kate was not going to last much longer. She'd given us all she could give and it was time to go.

The following week at clinic, Kate's nurse Laura was asking the usual questions in the exam room about Kate's week when I asked the question that had been bugging me since I had talked with Justine in Memphis.

"Laura," I began, "Dr. Pui's nurse and I were talking on the way to procedures last week about a gummy that Kate had been taking and she recommended that Kate stop taking it right away. Why is that?"

"Well," Laura replied, "vitamins contain a concentrated dose of folic acid. The goal of Kate's weekly chemo methotrexate is to break that down. So, in a sense, the vitamins rescue the folate that the methotrexate is trying to break down."

"But it is emphasized that this gummy is not a vitamin," I countered.

Laura shook her head. "It still contains a concentrated amount of folic acid."

As she spoke, a light bulb suddenly went off in my head. "Kate has been taking this gummy since October. Do you think that is why Kate's counts have been so high over the past six or seven months?"

Laura hesitated. "It very well could be. We won't know though until we see what her counts do now that she is off them." I felt sick at the possibility that I had jeopardized my daughter's treatment for cancer, but pushed the thought from my mind for the next two weeks. In a couple of weeks, we would know.

During those two weeks, Kate had another appointment with her pulmonologist to investigate her prolonged cough one more time. The inhalers had done nothing to ease her cough and the doctor decided his last ditch effort was to do a throat swab. Kate had had respiratory panels done before in which a nurse stuck a swab (as well as her arm all the way to her elbow) up Kate's nose and she was terrified of this swab coming toward her face. She refused to open her mouth for it and screamed, mouth shut, for a few minutes as we coaxed her to open it. When she finally opened her mouth to take a deep breath, the nurse shoved the swab in and the job was done.

Two days later, we received the results of the throat swab. Kate tested positive for three different viruses. I asked if it was possible that she had just been getting one virus on top of another all winter long and was told, yes, it was possible.

The following week was week 100, and I held my breath to see what Kate's counts would be. They had been significantly lower last week, which was her usual trend after steroids, but this week we would know more certainly. Sure enough, when Kate's nurse practitioner, Heidi, came to report her counts to me, her white blood cell count and ANC were low for the second week in a row. For the second week in a row, they were exactly where Dr. Pui had been wanting them to be for the last six months.

I called out a thank you to Heidi as she walked away, but felt like I was about to cry. I was absolutely sick to my stomach, knowing that

I had been inhibiting Kate's chemo for the past six months with a silly little gummy. I thought of all the hours and hours we'd been spending at clinic getting outrageously increased dosages of methotrexate. I thought of Kate's elevated liver enzymes. I thought of how I had likely increased her chances to relapse because, for the past six months, she'd been having ineffective chemotherapy. Guilt and sorrow just washed over me.

Kate's nurses were sitting in their office in the back and I interrupted them with my worries. They were each wonderful and offered encouragement, hugs, and hope, which is most assuredly part of the job description of a nurse.

Dr. Cox approached and counseled me as well. "The thing with cancer and chemotherapy is that you just never know," she shared. "I had a patient years ago who had been diagnosed with Acute Myeloid Leukemia (AML). She received two treatments, had a severe allergic reaction to the chemotherapy, and was no longer able to receive any more chemo. And she is still in remission to this day! You just never know," she comforted me.

The staff also tried to reassure me that they, in part, were to blame for not thoroughly investigating the cause of her high counts. Even though I obviously felt the full weight of the guilt, I knew deep down there was really no one to blame. It was just an unfortunate situation and I hated that it involved our daughter.

For the rest of the day, tears sat at the edge of my eyelids but never fell. I tried to cry, just to release the pent-up emotions inside and to ease the sick feeling in the pit of my stomach. But try as I might, none would fall.

Strangely enough, pressure washing was very therapeutic. For the next week during naptime, I was outside pressure washing the driveway. After dinner, Brandon tended to the kids and I pressure washed some more. Mom and Dad came up to spend a day and watched the kids while I pressure washed the back deck. If any good thing could have come from the news of the past week, it was that the outside of our house never looked so good!

By the next week, I had mostly moved on. What else could I do?

The next week was a huge milestone that our family had been longing for since the day Kate started dexamethasone—week 101. Finally,

Kate would receive her last vincristine, the chemotherapy that causes neuropathy. Also, on this week, Kate would begin her last week of her steroids! To celebrate, we picked up some cupcakes to take to Kate's nurses.

When we arrived at clinic carrying a couple of boxes of cupcakes, Caroline said, "Thank you for the cupcakes, but I'll be celebrating *next* week when Kate is *through* with steroids!"

I smiled. "We'll just have to bring cupcakes then too."

Caroline laughed. "I like the way you think," she replied.

And so we began our last steroid week ever, Lord willing. I felt as if Kate could have blown up the house and I would have giggled, patted her on the head, and told her to try to be more careful next time. We were so carefree and just plain ecstatic to be closing in on this huge milestone that no tantrum could make our smiles falter.

On Saturday, Kate's final day of steroids, we had a family reunion that morning, some visiting with some old family friends that afternoon, and a wedding for Brandon's cousin that evening. Kate did well at the reunion and at our visit with our friends. She ate the entire time, but she did great. By the time we got to the wedding, however, Kate was going downhill fast. I sensed a huge meltdown coming as she began whimpering and crying and I tried to head it off with her pain meds. By the time the wedding started, she was feeling much better.

The wedding was beautiful and the reception was set up inside a barn at the back of the property. Our entire family was there—aunts, uncles, cousins, and grandparents. We enjoyed visiting with them as we all sat under the darkening sky. After Kate finished eating dinner, I checked the time. It was time for her final dose of steroids. I pulled out the syringe, filled it, and looked around the table for something to mix it with but found nothing at hand.

Kate gave me a thumbs up. "Let's do this."

"Straight up?" I asked her, eyebrows raised, and she nodded.

She gave everyone watching a huge grin and swallowed her liquid steroid, gagging only a little at its foul taste. Our whole table cheered. I had wondered if I might cry when she took her last dose, remembering all that she had been through—all that we had been through—on this terrible drug, but there was no room for tears now, only happiness.

I had been pretty sure, when Kate took her last dose of steroids, that fireworks would explode overhead, that a chorus of angels would come down from heaven singing praises, or that a band might march by. But it was nothing like that. It was even better than I had imagined because we were surrounded by our family.

The rest of the month of June was a blur, and it wasn't long before we were full speed into July. The week after the Fourth of July, I spent the afternoon after Kate's clinic visit scrambling to tie up some loose ends and pack my bags because I was flying out the next morning for Colorado. I had officially weaned Elijah and I was finally going to get to see my beautiful nieces!

The twins were now three months old and their little cheeks were filling out, perfect for lots of squishing. There is nothing more precious than the feel of a baby snuggled up against your chest. And in this case, I had two! To watch them take each little breath, to stroke their velvety skin, to watch their long eyelashes resting on their cheeks. It was pure bliss.

Our time together flew by, as it always does. It wasn't long before Haley and the sleeping twins were driving me to the airport and we were saying goodbye. I was sad to leave my sister and nieces but couldn't wait to see my crew back in sweet home Alabama. My flight arrived around nine that Monday night, and I walked out of the terminal to see the most beautiful sight in the world—my family.

Brandon stood there with the girls and Elijah. Both Kate and Jenna squealed at the top of their lungs when they saw me and threw their arms open wide for hugs. They smothered me with kisses, stroked my hair, and told me over and over again that they missed me and loved me. I felt like a rock star. Elijah was slightly indifferent at my return but leaned in for the obligatory hug. I remembered how the girls acted when they were little after I'd been away for a while and his lack of excitement didn't surprise me. We stayed up late that night giggling and playing, but we had to go to the clinic the next day, so eventually the reunion had to come to an end and we went to bed.

At the end of July, I started homeschooling Kate for kindergarten. Brandon and I had debated all summer about whether or not we would start her in school. We knew if we did, we would expose her to a plethora of germs. She would already be missing a fair amount of school from being at the clinic one day every week, spending time in Memphis for the end of treatment, having surgery to have her port removed, and eventually going on her Make-A-Wish trip. And when she got sick, she would miss even more school. Homeschooling would give Kate a chance to build her strength and immune system back up. We also wanted to reclaim some time together as a family and enjoy life without cancer.

So I, a former elementary school teacher, spent weeks preparing a yearly overview, designing my weekly lesson plans, and dusting off my files stored in the attic. All summer, the girls begged to start school, and I held them off until the end of July. I figured with all we had going on and coming up, it would be good to get a head start. We spent each morning playing outside before it got too hot, and then when Elijah went down for his morning nap around ten the girls and I went upstairs to the playroom to start school. Jenna joined us as well, and I modified the lessons to do preschool with her.

It was hard to get our lessons done on Tuesdays because we were at the clinic most of the day. On some days I took our work with us, but the clinic was too distracting to get anything accomplished. Sometimes, we just did our work when we got home. Other times, we doubled up on our work the next day or did school on Saturday morning. The flexibility homeschooling provided was exactly what we needed!

One morning during school, the girls and I noticed a burning smell. I immediately set out to find its source. I checked the attic, every electrical outlet, the major appliances, and even the heating and air unit outside. I never could find the source of the smell. For days we continued to smell that mysterious smell, but only when we were in the playroom.

Finally, on our way downstairs after finishing school one morning, Kate asked, "What's that in the light on the wall?"

I looked in the light that hung on the side of the wall in the stairwell, and there in that light fixture—with a hole burned through the side—was one of Jenna's socks!

Jenna had a habit of leaving her socks wherever she took them off and they often accumulated in the playroom upstairs. When I told her the week before to pick up all her socks in the playroom and put them in the laundry basket, she collected all her socks and apparently threw them down the stairs—and one had landed in the light on the wall! We only smelled it when we were upstairs because we turned on the light in the stairwell while we were doing school! We now refer to this as "the burning sock incident." I saved the sock in Jenna's box where I keep special memories.

At the beginning of August, we made a trip to Atlanta for a long weekend to visit Brandon's youngest brother and his family. They had just moved to Atlanta over the summer and we were excited to go visit. We drove over on a Friday and decided to spend Saturday at Stone Mountain.

Stone Mountain was amazing! It had changed a lot since I was a little girl. Kate and Jenna joined the adults on a treetops ropes obstacle course, and although it took an hour they made it. There were a few tears, but with a lot of encouragement and cheerleading they made it! The worker at the end of the course commented they'd never had a three-year-old complete that course before. Granted, not many three-year-olds are as tall as Jenna and meet the height requirement to even do it. Jenna also almost made it to the top of the rock climbing wall after she finished the ropes course. We rode the Summit Skyride to the top of the mountain, watched a 3D movie, rode the train, played minigolf, went to the petting zoo, and utterly wore ourselves out.

We capped off the day by staying late for the fireworks and laser show. We all piled onto a blanket on the lawn in front of Stone Mountain as the music blared over the loudspeakers. We were amazed. Kate, especially, was beside herself with joy. She was enthralled by the laser light show as she watched the stories play out on the side of the mountain in front of us. As the show came to its climax, fireworks were blasting, the laser lights were flashing crazily, and "The Star Spangled Banner" was blaring. Kate got caught up in the moment. She scrambled to her feet and began jumping up and down, shouting, "Yeah! Yeah!"

I thought my heart would burst in that moment. Her joy was so innocent and heartfelt, completely unrestrained. In that moment, I thanked God for the blessing of making yet another precious memory with our daughter.

Over the past few months, I have been humbled and amazed at how normal our lives have seemed. While we spent most of the past two years of treatment in Memphis, within the walls of our home, or in the hospital, these last few months have afforded us more freedom as your health has remained more stable. As we flitted to reunions, weddings, retirement parties, and even to Atlanta, we could almost forget that you were a cancer patient undergoing treatment for leukemia. (Almost.)

With each and every event we attended, we were blessed with the opportunity to make another memory. They were not necessarily all grand and majestic. Some were as simple as watching you and your sister run across the sand to the ocean and crying out in delight as the water splashed your faces. And some were as uneventful as when all five of us were piled into bed together at night to read books before bedtime.

We bottled away each and every memory bestowed upon us, knowing just how blessed we were to have them. We knew all too well how fleeting life could be, as you came all too close to losing yours, little girl. We knew to cherish every memory that God grants us.

Love,

Mommy

L. Erin Miller

*"A glad heart makes a cheerful face, but
by sorrow of heart the spirit is crushed"*
(Proverbs 15:13).

*"And whatever you do, in word or deed, do
everything in the name of the Lord Jesus, giving
thanks to God the Father through him"*
(Colossians 3:17).

Chapter 17: Far More Important

October 7, 2015

Dear Kate,

After two and a half years of treatment for cancer, I have come to a conclusion: None of this has mattered.

Cancer doesn't matter.

Chemotherapy doesn't matter.

A cure doesn't matter.

September came in full throttle and included another family trip to the beach for a week. We arrived home late at night. Brandon and I quietly carried three sleeping babies to bed and tucked each one in with a kiss goodnight. We unloaded the van, pulled out a few necessities from our luggage, and went to bed ourselves.

Around midnight, however, we were awakened by screams coming from the other side of the house. I threw the covers off and sprinted to Kate's room and was surprised to discover the screams were coming from Jenna's room instead. I opened the door, flicked on the light, and stared horrified at the scene before me.

Jenna had thrown up everywhere and was sitting in bed, crying in the middle of all that mess. My heart sank and I immediately began to reassure her that everything was okay.

"Gross." Brandon had followed to see what was wrong and was standing in the doorway.

Brandon offered to be in charge of cleaning up Jenna and helped her out of bed and in to the bathroom. I heard the shower start running as I stared at the scene before me, wondering where I should start.

I stripped all the linens off the bed and dragged them to the utility sink in the laundry room where I began washing each sheet out, one at a time.

"Ugh. This is good motivation to not have any more kids," I muttered to myself as I washed out her pajamas.

By the time I'd finished thoroughly cleaning up the room, Brandon had washed and dried Jenna's hair. We got her tucked into bed again before heading back to bed ourselves. Brandon had to leave for a business trip in just a few hours and I dreaded the idea of being at home by myself with the stomach bug looming.

Jenna did fine the rest of the night, but was still queasy the next day. Elijah started that day with the worst diarrhea I had ever seen. Kate was due at clinic the next day and I knew I could not take Jenna or Elijah there. I called my dad to see if he could come up and keep the two sick kids while I took Kate. Dad immediately agreed, but Mom voiced her concern that they were supposed to leave for their New England trip in a few days and was worried Dad would get sick.

"You know I wouldn't ask unless I was desperate," I lamented. I knew what I was asking and hated to expose Dad to this horrible stomach bug, but I knew I couldn't get any cancer patients at clinic sick. Nor did Kate need to be in the small isolation room with her sister and brother.

Dad came up and kept Jenna and Elijah the next day while I carried Kate to the clinic for week 116. While we were there, Kate began complaining of her stomach bothering her. My heart was tight in my chest as we drove home and I hoped we hadn't just carried a stomach virus into the clinic.

When Kate and I arrived home, Jenna was doing much better, but poor Elijah hardly moved. He felt awful and just lay on me the rest of the day.

Brandon came home from his business trip late Wednesday night. That was good timing, as I came down with the stomach bug Thursday morning and Jenna got sick again as well, even though it had been four days since she'd thrown up. Brandon stayed home from work and took over taking care of the kids while I was in bed.

By the weekend, Jenna, Elijah, and I were all on the mend. We were holding our breath to see if Kate would get it.

Kate's cough had flared up significantly during the week. It was sounding more and more croupy with each passing day. She had still complained off and on that her tummy was bothering her, but had not thrown up or had any diarrhea by the weekend, so we hoped we were in the clear.

On Saturday night, we went to a party for the young families at our preacher's house. We ate dinner and the kids loved jumping in the moon bounce they had rented. Kate was very weepy and moody, did not eat much of her food, and was coughing horrendously. When we got home that night, she had a huge coughing episode and coughed up gunk into the toilet. Brandon and I exchanged concerned glances and then, after calming down a very upset Kate, helped her get ready for bed.

We decided to keep her home from worship on Sunday because her cough was wretched. We were glad we did because during the night Sunday night, I was awakened once again by screams from the other side of the house. The stomach bug had finally hit Kate.

Kate nibbled throughout the day on Monday, kept everything down, and was able to get week 117 of chemo on Tuesday. I prayed that Kate was in the clear, and although her appetite had not returned she had not thrown up any more. However, that changed Wednesday night.

Kate threw up during the night Wednesday. And then she threw up again during the night Thursday. And then every night after that until the following Tuesday. It was always in the middle of the night when Kate got sick. There's nothing like that adrenaline rush of hearing your child screaming for you from the other side of the house, shooting out of bed, running to the other side of the house, and helping your poor baby get to the toilet just in time before she threw up. It always took me a couple of hours to go back to sleep after Kate threw up because it took that long for my nerves to settle back down. The longer Kate's stomach bug went on, the longer I stayed up worrying.

Tuesday arrived again. Clinic day. Week 118 of chemo. I had called clinic every day to keep Dr. Cox apprised of the situation. We had gone into clinic a couple of times the week before for them to monitor Kate, but her counts were always decent and she was never dehydrated, so we were just trying to wait out this stomach bug.

When we got there, we crowded into the isolation room as we waited for a few tests to be run. Dr. Russo ordered an ultrasound of Kate's stomach and an extensive battery of tests on Kate's bloodwork. While we were going through a checklist of the tests that morning, Kate announced urgently that she needed to go to the bathroom.

I took her then, and then took her about five more times in the next hour. I felt relief flooding through me. The stomach bug was finally working its way out!

Kate's ultrasound of her stomach came back normal, but did show Kate's spleen was enlarged, likely from the stomach virus. Kate's counts came back normal as well, but significantly lower than the week before. A red flag waved in the back of my mind and I talked to Dr. Russo about Kate's dropping counts. She reassured me that the virus was the culprit of the lowering counts.

We ended up being there for almost eight hours that day, and Kate was wilting fast by the last hour. I could look at her eyes and tell she felt awful. She received her chemo as well as an early infusion of her IVIG, moved up a week to try to help her fight this virus, and then we headed home.

Kate nibbled on some graham crackers and applesauce, the only things she seemed to be able to keep down, and begrudgingly drank the water I handed her every ten minutes. The light had gone from her eyes and as I tucked her into bed that night and leaned in to kiss her goodnight, I froze. I grabbed a thermometer from her bathroom closet and inserted it under her tongue.

101.

My heart sank to the floor. I found Brandon down the hall giving Elijah a bath.

"Kate has a fever," I told him. I saw his shoulders slump from behind. "I'll go call Dr. Cox."

Dr. Cox instructed us to go to the emergency room, but reassured us that we would not have to stay because Kate's bloodwork from that day had been normal. I grabbed Kate's backpack and headed back to Kate's room to get her ready to go. She cried as I pulled out some clothes and shoes for her to put on.

"I'm so tired," she sobbed. "I just want to go to bed."

"I know, baby girl, but we have got to get this fever checked out," I told her, wanting to sob along with her. How I had hoped we would have no more emergency room visits during therapy! We were so close to the end!

As Kate and I walked inside the emergency room twenty minutes later, I slipped her mask over her face. I saw a couple of kids seated with their parents in the lobby, and the kids had buckets in front of them. I cringed and was glad Kate had her mask on!

The room with a private bathroom that St. Jude patients are typically put in was occupied, so we were taken to a spacious room in front of the nurses' station. Kate settled into the bed while I sat in the chair next to her.

Our nurse walked into the room a few minutes later, pretending to limp like a gangster, and drawled, "What up, Kate?"

Kate and I both raised an eyebrow at her.

Fortunately, a wonderful child life specialist joined us as we prepared to get Kate accessed. I explained that anticipation was Kate's worst enemy when getting a needle. I told her nurse there was no need to count nor to try to calm Kate down if she got upset. The best thing was to do what she needed to do as quickly as she could do it.

I stood in front of Kate as they got ready to access her port. She was crying and very unsure about her nurse. The child life specialist calmly talked to Kate while her nurse rubbed alcohol on Kate's chest. A second nurse came in.

The first nurse picked up Kate's needle and access line and asked Kate if she was ready. Kate shook her head no and the nurse began counting. "Ready, 1...2... Are you ready, Kate? 1...2..." A look of terror was spreading across Kate's face and she began leaning away as the nurse stood poised with Kate's needle in front of her.

I was screaming inside my head at the nurse. *She had not listened to anything I'd said!*

The nurse suddenly tried to push the needle into Kate's chest. And she missed Kate's port. Kate screamed in pain and the nurse pulled the needle out, shaking her head in frustration.

"Kate, do you want to sit in my lap?" I interjected, as fury coursed through my veins.

Kate nodded through her tears and I climbed onto the hospital bed with her, wrapping my arms around her and holding her tight while the nurse prepared to access her again.

Kate continued to scream and I whispered repeatedly in her ear, "Feel me breathe? I want you to breathe in and out, just like I am doing. Breathe with me...in...and out." I took deep breaths, Kate's chest rising with mine, as I tried to soothe her.

The nurse was talking very loudly to Kate, a hint of exasperation in her voice, and I just wanted her to be quiet so Kate could focus on my words and calm down.

Kate calmed down a little and the nurse was able to get the needle in Kate's port. I sighed in relief, but knew one more needle still lay ahead.

The nurse drew blood from Kate's port into a couple of vials and then both nurses moved to the side to draw blood from her arm. One nurse held her arm tight while the other prepped Kate's arm. Kate renewed her efforts to get away with newfound zeal. I tightened my grip and repeatedly whispered in her ear how important it was to stay still.

Kate screamed suddenly and I guessed the needle was in. My eyes met the eyes of the child life specialist and she nodded her head in affirmation as the nurse drew a vial of blood, only to shake her head no a few seconds later.

Her vein blew, she mouthed at me.

The second nurse sighed. "We'll just have to try again."

The first nurse shook her head emphatically. "I'm done. We are not sticking her again."

The other nurse argued, "But she said she wanted us to run another test and we need another vial of blood to do that."

The first nurse, who I was growing to dislike more and more by the minute, shook her head again. "That's just too bad. I'm going to tell her we're not going to do it. You know she listens to me anyway."

Assuming the "her" they were referring to was a doctor and perhaps one of Kate's St. Jude doctors, I decided it was time to speak up.

"Listen," I interrupted. "If you are supposed to run another test, I want you to get the blood you need—even if that means having to stick her again."

The nurses looked embarrassed, as if they'd forgotten that I was in the room, sitting right there, and listening to every word they were saying. The first nurse tried to reassure me that they had everything they needed, but the second nurse had a look of doubt on her face.

Kate announced suddenly that she needed to go to the bathroom. Unfortunately, we were sharing a bathroom with all the other kids in the emergency room that night. I strapped Kate's mask on before we left her room and after she went to the bathroom, I made sure she washed her hands really well and then opened the door for her as we left. We made many more trips to the bathroom as the evening wore on and as the stomach bug continued to make its way through Kate's system.

The doctor in the ER that night came by to examine Kate and ordered a chest x-ray, just to rule out the possibility of pneumonia because Kate's cough sounded so rough. She also ordered two rounds of the usual antibiotics Kate received whenever she had a fever.

Our nurse came by and escorted us to have the chest x-ray done. Afterward, as she guided us back to the room, she mentioned that they were almost ready for us upstairs.

"We're being admitted?" I asked confused.

"Yes. Were you not expecting to be admitted?"

"No, I spoke with Dr. Cox earlier and she said that because Kate's counts were normal at the clinic today, she could get her antibiotics and we could go home."

The nurse left our room to see what we were supposed to do and Kate and I settled back in her room. She came back a few minutes later with a few medications in her hand, informed us we were not being admitted, and then launched into a long ramble about why she thought we would be going to PICU.

Suddenly, the other nurse came sprinting into Kate's room, her hand clutched over her heart.

"Those are not for her!" she gasped, pointing at the medications in the other nurse's hands.

The nurse looked confused and then looked down at the medications she was holding. "I know they aren't for her. I was just stopping by to tell them something before I took the meds to the next patient."

Relief crossed the face of the nurse and her hand dropped down. They left the room conferring together and I sat back down, praying to God that we would leave without any mishaps.

One more mishap was bound to happen though. We were getting ready to be discharged when the nurse realized she had never started Kate's second antibiotic. This added another half hour to our stay. Finally, around one in the morning, we were done. I was so glad to walk out those doors and leave the emergency room behind, hopefully for a long time.

Kate slept late the next morning and woke up feeling fantastic. After being sick for so long, it was wonderfully refreshing to see her smiling and wanting to eat!

Heidi, the nurse practitioner at the clinic, called to check on Kate a little later that morning and I asked her if we needed to hold Kate's oral chemotherapy for the evening as she had not been fever free for twenty-four hours yet.

"I wanted to talk to you about that. We received an e-mail from Dr. Pui this morning and he wants to stop Kate's chemo."

"Okay," I agreed. "Does he want me to start her back once she's been fever free for twenty-four hours?"

"Well, from what I understand, he says Kate is done with chemo."

I was confused. "Done? As in completely done?"

Heidi laughed. "Yes, I believe completely done."

I was at a loss for words. My mind was completely blown by this news. "Kate is really doing much better today. We only have two more weeks left. Maybe I'll call Martha and talk to her about Kate getting her last two rounds of chemo." I couldn't believe I was arguing for my child to get chemotherapy!

Heidi consented that would be fine and to keep her updated if anything changed. I agreed before saying goodbye and hanging up.

I immediately called Martha and left a message for her, explaining what I was calling about, and then began to fix lunch for myself and the kids. I was quiet throughout lunch, my mind reeling at the news, and working to formulate a plan to propose to Martha. While we ate, my phone rang.

303

It was Memphis.

I took a deep breath and answered to hear the kind voice of Martha on the other line.

"Hey, Erin. It's Martha. I got your message and I think it's just fine for Kate to be done with chemotherapy. I agree with Dr. Pui completely."

"Well," I argued, "she's doing so much better today. She does not have a fever, her appetite has returned, and she seems to be feeling great. Could we…?" I started to ask.

"Listen," Martha stopped me. "Kate's ten days of the stomach bug, prolonged cough, elevated liver enzymes, and enlarged spleen are her body's way of trying to tell us that she has had enough. Missing the last two weeks of chemo is not going to change a single thing."

"But," I faintly protested as the tears welled up in my eyes.

"We don't need to push her any more. It's time now for her body to start healing." Martha was gentle, but firm.

Sobs welled in my chest. "So she's done?" I asked one more time, my voice cracking.

"She is done." Martha confirmed.

I couldn't hold back my sobs any longer. I wept. The years of worry and pain and fatigue and schedules and medications and prayers and more spilled forth in my tears.

"I'm so sorry," I managed to choke out to Martha who sat patiently on the other line.

"Don't you apologize," Martha scolded me. "This is completely normal after all that Kate and your family has been through. I would be worried if you weren't crying! "

I looked up through my tears to see three curious little faces staring at me in concern. I smiled feebly back at them. I thanked Martha, placing the phone down on the table.

I walked around to where Kate sat and squatted down next to her chair. I took her little hand in mine as I spoke.

"That was Martha May," I explained, tears still streaming down my face. "She called to say that you are done with chemo. No more chemo." A new wave of sobs erupted from my chest and Kate began to cry too and jumped into my arms.

Elijah took one look at us, crying next to him, and began bawling. Jenna saw her whole family falling apart and immediately erupted into loud wailing too. I had to laugh.

"It's okay, it's okay," I tried to reassure them.

"Then why are you crying, Mommy?" Jenna asked through her alligator tears.

"These are happy tears, baby," I explained. I took some deep breaths and announced, "We need to call Daddy and tell him the good news!"

We called Brandon at work and I let Kate share the news with him. Brandon was surprised and happy, and had a lot of questions about what had transpired that morning.

After talking to him for a bit, we began calling all our immediate family. Kate excitedly shared her good news with her family members. My favorite phone call was to her Aunt Haley. Kate started the conversation with, "My name is Kate. And I am done with chemo."

When Brandon came home that afternoon, he arrived with balloons and cupcakes and lots of hugs for his little survivor.

At the close of the day, once the elation of the news of the day had ended, a small feeling of disappointment settled in our stomachs. Yes, we were absolutely thrilled that Kate was done with chemo, but we were disappointed that she had not been able to finish the full 120 weeks of treatment. For two and a half years, we had longed for the last day of her chemo, but the day before when she had received her chemo through her port at the clinic and when we gave Kate her oral chemo at bedtime, we had not realized those would be her last. We didn't get to savor that moment and felt slightly robbed of the anticipated triumph for which we had waited so long.

But again, at the close of the day, she was done. She had survived and life could go on.

Cancer, chemotherapy, and a cure don't matter one bit if we fail to teach you to love God and obey Him. This is the ultimate purpose in life. It is the sum of our being. It is the only thing that matters.

Far more important than vincristine, dexamethasone, cyclophosphamide, cytarabine, doxorubicine, daunorubicin, pegaspargase, prednisone, and methotrexate is that we teach you how amazing and wonderful God is and how deserving He is of our praise and adoration.

Far more important than two and a half years of chemotherapy is that we teach you the importance of reading God's Word to discover His will for us and obey the commands and examples set for us in the Bible.

Far more important than finding a cure for cancer is that we teach you the cure for sin through obedience and the waters of baptism.

Far more important than a life after cancer is that we teach you about our home in heaven where there will be no more sickness, death, cancer, or needles. Your daddy and I must continually strive to foster in you a desire to go to heaven and to live in such a way that you can spend an eternity there!

These are the things that matter!

Love,

Mommy

L. Erin Miller

> *"The end of the matter; all has been heard. Fear God and keep his commandments, for this is the whole duty of man"* (Ecclesiastes 12:13).

Chapter 18: The Thief

October 15, 2015

Dear Kate,

God is good, God is love, God is light, and God is joy. We, as His followers, are called to do what is good, to love others, to be lights to the world, and to be joyful.

We are to be joyful through the good and even the bad. Our eyes are focused on our goal—heaven—and the joy of our purpose carries us through every trial.

But sometimes, it's really hard to be joyful. And that's because the Devil is really good at what he does.

The Devil is evil. The Devil is hate. The Devil is darkness.

And the Devil is a thief.

On the Wednesday that Martha called to tell us Kate was done with chemo, Kate had felt better than she had in almost two weeks. She had eaten normally and kept her food down. We were so thankful that the stomach bug had moved on and she was getting better.

However, on Thursday Kate wilted again. She complained of her stomach hurting and did not want to eat. I assumed she had overdone it the day before and did not push her to eat. The next morning after Brandon left for work, I was awakened to the sound of Kate screaming from the other side of the house. My heart plummeted as I flung myself out of bed and hurtled to her room, just in time to see Kate beginning to heave in her bed. I hurriedly pulled her from her bed and ran her to the toilet just before she threw up. I was distraught. What in the world was going on?

Once the clinic opened that day, I called to let them know that Kate was sick again and they wanted us to come in to check her out. We spent the morning in the isolation room. Everything checked out fine, although her counts were much lower than they had been on Tuesday. I once again voiced concern over her counts dropping and was assured again that a prolonged virus like this could most certainly cause Kate's counts to drop. Yet I still had an unsettled feeling in my stomach.

Kate continued to drink well when prompted by me but still did not want to eat. She managed to keep a few nibbles down for the next couple of days. My heart tugged within me every time she walked by. She had now lost eight pounds and her pants hung limply around her waist. I felt encouraged that she went a couple of days without throwing up and prayed the sickness on Friday was just a fluke.

Brandon and I had been asleep for an hour Sunday night when, around midnight, I heard Kate screaming. I bolted to her room to find her already in the bathroom, throwing up. We went through the very familiar post-vomit routine of gargling water, brushing teeth, washing her face with a cold washcloth, and getting tucked back into bed. And then I crawled back into bed with Brandon and sobbed. He wrapped his arms around me and I cried for the next half hour. I was worried to death. In my mind, I kept thinking she had survived leukemia but was going to die of a stomach bug.

As the first rays of light filtered through the blinds of the window, I fell back asleep for an hour or so until our early bird Jenna entered the room. The night had been so long and I dreaded what the day would bring. I talked on the phone with Heidi once more and we formed a game plan for our clinic visit the next day.

Meanwhile, it was Columbus Day and a friend was getting married. Brandon stayed home with Kate and Elijah while Jenna was my date to the wedding. Jenna had been asking for almost three weeks to go to the playground or to go to an indoor trampoline park and kept getting told no. "Kate is too sick," was always my answer, so today I was so thankful to get to spend some time with her.

Everyone at the wedding asked how Kate was doing and I had to answer honestly. "She's not doing well at all." I tried to smile like everything was under control, but inside I was afraid.

After the wedding, Jenna and I went to eat lunch and then it was time to go home. That evening, Brandon and I got the kids in bed and we, having been up most of the night, were not far behind them. It wasn't long, though, before we heard the sound of footsteps outside our bedroom door.

Kate peeked her head into the room, tears streaming down her face, clutching her stomach. "I'm hurting so badly," she cried.

Brandon motioned for her to come join us in bed and we made a special spot for her in between us. She lay propped up on her pillow for a long time, trying to breathe through her pain. I lay awake listening to her breathe, until finally her breathing became long and slow and I was sure she was asleep.

I drifted off and was awakened an hour later by Kate moaning next to me.

"My stomach hurts so badly," she whimpered.

"Do you feel like you need to throw up?" I asked her.

She shook her head no.

"Do you need to go to the bathroom?" I prompted.

"Maybe," she admitted.

Brandon helped her up from the bed and as they walked to the bathroom, Kate started crying. "I'm about to throw up!"

He hurried her into the bathroom, shutting the door behind them, and I heard her wailing combined with the sound of her throwing up. I climbed out of bed to see if I could help Brandon and my mouth dropped when I opened the bathroom door.

There was a long messy trail of diarrhea and vomit all the way to the toilet. Kate sat on the toilet while Brandon held a trash can in front of her as she continued to throw up.

After she finished, she looked at the scene before her and wailed pitifully, "What have I done?"

My heart hurt for our poor sweet girl who was suffering so much. "You don't worry about that. I'll take care of it," I reassured her. I grabbed her soiled panties and tossed them into a garbage bag.

"Aren't you going to wash them?" Kate asked.

"Nope! I think in this case, it is perfectly fine to throw these away."

Brandon helped Kate to the shower to begin cleaning her up while I tackled cleaning the bathroom.

"It's like she caught the stomach bug all over again," I bemoaned to Brandon as we cleaned. "It usually takes forty-eight hours for a virus to settle in." I began mentally counting back two days from the onset of the second round of the virus and my mouth suddenly fell open. "Do you think she picked up a second stomach bug at the emergency room last week?"

Brandon thought for a moment. "That could very well be the case."

The more I thought about it, the more I became certain that was what had happened. We'd had to share a bathroom with all the other kids in the emergency room and I'd seen a few throwing up in the lobby on our way in. Kate had felt fine the following day, but then had started not feeling well again the next day—forty-eight hours later. And now, after a few days of throwing up, the bug was making its way out again.

Or could it be that her leukemia had…no. I immediately pushed the thought from my mind.

It took about an hour for us to clean up Kate and the bathroom and the three of us went back to bed. Kate eventually fell asleep, but Brandon and I did not. Every half hour or so, I would lift my head up to peek at him. His eyes would meet mine in the dark as if to say, *Yes, I'm still awake, too.*

312

It wasn't long before sunlight glowed outside our window, the new day greeting us after a mostly sleepless night. Brandon was scheduled to fly out that afternoon for a business trip and asked hesitantly before he left for work that morning, "Are you sure it's okay for me to go?"

I shrugged. "I don't know. Let me think on it, okay? Let's wait and see what they say at the clinic today."

He kissed me goodbye and left and I lay back down next to Kate, watching her sleep. Kate's appointment at the clinic was not until lunchtime, so she had the morning to catch up on some sleep.

Shortly after Brandon left, I heard Jenna scratchily calling me from her room. When I went into her room, she greeted me with a croupy cough. I wanted to throw my hands in the air in exasperation. I couldn't take much more.

"Morning, baby," I murmured. "Are you feeling okay?"

Jenna shook her head no. "I have a bad cough," she replied and then dramatically demonstrated the cough.

The wheels of my brain were turning. I knew Kate could not get sick with anything else and definitely did not need to be around Jenna. It was time to call for reinforcements.

My parents had been on vacation in New England for the past two weeks, but were scheduled to fly home that day. They had felt so helpless being so far away, but I assured them that we would not have let them help even if they were in town. We didn't want anyone else getting what Kate had.

Now, however, we needed to get Jenna out of the house to protect Kate. I called Grammy in Florence to ask her if she could meet me halfway in an hour to keep Jenna for a few days until her cough settled down. She immediately agreed and I rushed to get the kids ready.

I texted Brandon to let him know what was going on, hurriedly fed Jenna and Elijah a banana and some cereal, then rushed to get myself ready. My mind felt numb as I threw some things in a bag for Jenna. I was too tired to think straight, but managed to pack a decent bag for her.

Kate woke up a few minutes before we needed to leave, had no interest in eating, but I filled a cup of water for her to sip on as we drove to meet Grammy in Athens.

I firmly instructed Jenna and Kate not to touch each other in the van and warned Jenna to make sure she turned her head away from Kate when she coughed. We met Grammy and I transferred Jenna over to her car, giving instructions as I loaded.

How it hurt my heart not to be able to take care of my sick baby myself! I wanted to be the one to hold my Jenna when she cried. I wanted to be the one to dote on her while she didn't feel well. Cancer had robbed me of this too.

After bidding farewell to Jenna and Grammy, I called Brandon at work as we drove back to Huntsville for clinic.

"Hey," he greeted me when he answered the phone.

"Hey," I replied. "I just dropped Jenna off with your mom. I have a question. How big of a deal is it to cancel your business trip?"

He immediately answered, "It is not a big deal at all."

I sighed in relief. "Good. I just don't have a very good feeling in my stomach right now. And I want you home."

When we arrived at the clinic, the isolation room was already taken by another sick patient and we had to stay in the exam room. I stood in the doorway while Kate's nurse Jessica checked her over. Jessica was asking me questions about her vomiting and diarrhea and making notes.

"Kate was in a lot of pain last night at bedtime, so we let her sleep in the bed with us. She woke up around one thirty in the morning and couldn't even make it to the bathroom…" My voice broke as I started sobbing. "I'm so sorry," I told Jessica before I walked away from the door, out of Kate's view. I wept there in the hall for a minute and then struggled to calm down.

"Mommy, why are you crying?" Kate asked when I came back into view again.

I tried to smile through my tears. "Mommy is just sad that you've been sick for so long." I calmed down enough to finish answering Jessica's questions and then settled down in the chair in Kate's room with Elijah in my lap.

The isolation room we were usually put in was small enough as it was, but the exam room was just big enough for two people and no more. After Kate was accessed and her blood had been drawn, I once again called Brandon at work.

"Can you come get Elijah?" I asked. "We are in the exam room for the day and I just don't think I can manage him in here."

Brandon immediately agreed and offered to bring me some lunch as well. I accepted his offer and held down the fort until reinforcements arrived. One of the nurses found a portable DVD player for Kate and she settled in bed to watch movies for the afternoon. While she watched, she nibbled on crackers and graham crackers and my heart was encouraged that she was wanting to eat.

Brandon arrived a little later with lunch for me. I ate while we visited for a few minutes and then he took Elijah home for his nap.

"Keep me posted," were his final words as he left.

"I will," I assured him as I finished the last bite of my sandwich. I wadded up the trash and threw it in the garbage can. I checked the clock on the wall. Kate's counts should be coming back soon. Most of the patients had left for the day, so I ventured to the nurses' station to see if Kate's counts were back yet. Jessica was sitting at the computer, clicking away.

"Are Kate's counts back yet?" I asked, peeking my head in the door.

Jessica slowly nodded her head. "The top half of her counts are back. Her white blood cell count is 0.8, platelets are 90, and hemoglobin is 9.6."

I struggled to process what Jessica had just told me. "Her white blood cell count is *what*?"

"0.8," Jessica answered, carefully watching my face.

"That's 800," I repeated dumbly and she nodded her head in affirmation. "Her counts haven't been that low since she was on heavy chemo back at the beginning of treatment." My hands flew up to my face. "I'm so scared, Jessica. I think I'm going to be sick."

My greatest fear was coming true. Kate's leukemia had returned. She had relapsed. That's why she had not been able to get past this stomach bug. This was my worst nightmare.

Jessica came over to put her arm around me. "I know you're scared. But let's wait and see what the rest of her blood chemistry looks like once the bottom half of her report comes in."

I slowly nodded, but my mind was already whirling again in another direction.

"I want to be sent to Memphis," I declared suddenly. "I want for Dr. Pui to see her and get to the bottom of this."

Jessica nodded. "I will check on that for you. Can I get you anything?" she offered.

I numbly shook my head no. I went into the nearest bathroom and stood at the sink, holding on to it for support. I gasped for breath as my emotions overwhelmed me.

"You said You would save her," I whispered to God. My whisper turned into a silent angry shout as I shook my fist at the ceiling. "You told me from the beginning You would fight for her! You said You would save her!" Silent sobs engulfed me as I covered my face with my hands.

I felt betrayed. I felt robbed. I felt a fear unlike anything I'd felt before. The words of Shadrach, Meshach, and Abednego suddenly flashed in my mind—*if He does not*. I crumbled.

I began shaking uncontrollably just as Mom had shaken before her surgery—a trembling of nervous anticipation of what was to come.

I stayed in the bathroom until my wave of grief had subsided and then wandered back to Kate's room. I slipped back inside the room, but Kate was engrossed in a movie and hardly acknowledged that I'd reentered. She probably didn't even realize I'd left.

316

Once I was back in the exam room with Kate, Heidi came in and announced the rest of Kate's counts had come in. She relayed the news that Dr. Pui did want to see us. We would leave for Memphis that night and Kate would meet with her doctor in the morning. Before we left, though, Dr. Cox wanted us to get some antibiotics from the pharmacy at the hospital for Kate.

It was time to call Brandon. He was very calm, as always. I asked if he could get his parents to keep Elijah and we could drop him off on our way to Memphis. I also asked him to pack our bags as we would leave soon after we got home.

We waited almost two more hours in that tiny room for the pharmacy to get Kate's meds ready. Dr. Cox met with me before we left with some instructions. "Dr. Pui wants Kate fasting, so I'm assuming she will have a bone marrow aspiration in the morning. They have already made arrangements for you at Tri Delta Place for tonight, so check in there once you arrive. Everything is ready for you." She followed up with some brief instructions on Kate's antibiotics, and then we gathered our belongings to leave.

When we opened the door to Kate's exam room, the staff had lined the hall to hug us.

"We'll see you when you get back," they whispered to Kate, and I fought back tears with each hug. "We love you." All I wanted to do was run away screaming and bawling; it took every fiber of my being to make it out that door without doing so.

Kate and I arrived home and I packed a few more things while Brandon fed Elijah some dinner. The rest of us were not hungry. We drove to Florence and dropped Elijah off with Brandon's parents. Kate fell asleep soon after we left and slept the rest of the way. We arrived at the hospital around eleven that night but were sent to a local hotel to stay the night as the Tri Delta Place was booked.

Brandon and I gave Kate her antibiotics, settled her into bed, and climbed into bed ourselves. I had thought I wouldn't be able to sleep a wink that night, but we had both been up since the wee hours of the morning and were completely drained by such an emotional day. We soon fell asleep for a few hours before our alarm went off to begin our day.

Kate's first appointment was in assessment triage, and when she weighed in the nurse said slowly, "Okay, Mom. She's lost eight pounds since her last visit here. That's about twenty percent of her body weight."

"That's why we're here," I replied with a sad smile.

Kate's port was accessed, and after her blood was drawn we went to the A Clinic lobby to wait to meet with Dr. Pui. It wasn't long before we were called back.

We met Justine with anxious looks on our faces. She handed us the paper with Kate's counts listed and they were the same as the day before.

Dr. Pui arrived a minute later. I had held on to the hope that he would walk in, all smiles, and wave off my fears with a few words, but Dr. Pui's face was very grim.

"Her blood is showing that something is wrong. Whether it is virus or that her leukemia has returned, I do not know. It is 50/50. If it is virus, we will determine what it is and help her get better. And if it is leukemia, we will start over again with chemo."

His words were like a knife in my heart. Brandon and I nodded our heads slowly and Brandon found his voice.

"Are you going to do a bone marrow aspiration today to determine if her leukemia has returned?" he asked.

Dr. Pui shook his head. "Her leukemia is T-cell. Because it is T-cell, we can just look at her blood and tell. If leukemia cells are in her bone marrow, they will also be in her blood." He reached for the phone on the wall and made a quick call.

After mumbling a few questions into the phone, he hung up and turned to us. "The lab says they will have her blood chemistries ready in three to four hours. We will know then."

We took some deep breaths and began gathering our belongings in the room. On the way out, I turned to Dr. Pui. "Can Kate eat something?" I asked. He looked confused. "You wanted her fasting this morning. If she wants to eat, may we give her something?"

He gave his consent, so the three of us walked to the cafeteria in search of breakfast. Kate was surprisingly very hungry and eagerly pointed at a few things we passed. We were very hesitant as to what to feed her. She had not thrown up in two days, but after the past three weeks, we were scared to try anything other than applesauce and crackers.

I agreed that Kate could have a breakfast bar and some cereal and grabbed a cup of steaming oatmeal for myself. I wasn't really hungry, but neither Brandon nor I had eaten since lunch the day before and we knew it would be good to eat.

The oatmeal was delicious and its warmth spread through my body. Kate eagerly ate her breakfast, but began slowing down as she neared her last few bites. She stopped eating and sat with an uncertain look on her face.

"Are you okay?" Brandon asked.

She nodded slowly and after we cleaned up the table, we loaded Kate into her wagon and headed to play at the area outside the pharmacy. Kate listlessly played with the train table for a few minutes until she suddenly clutched her stomach. "I'm about to throw up!" she cried. I grabbed an emesis bag and we ran into the bathroom just a few feet away. Everything Kate had eaten at breakfast came right back up. After Kate finished, we washed up and headed back out again. She was still not feeling a lot better, so she lay back down in the wagon and we went to A Clinic to rest and wait.

Kate lay in her wagon for a while until our friends, the Molloys, stopped by to sit with us while we waited. I was grateful for a distraction and for the company, although I wasn't much of a conversationalist at the moment. Kate played with Zoe while Beverly chatted with Brandon and me.

Three hours went by. Justine came out of clinic and apologized that we were still waiting for news. "Dr. Pui is in a meeting right now and I keep on calling him, telling him he's got to give me something! You all are just sitting here waiting. He told me he is checking in every few minutes with the lab to see if her bloodwork is ready. I will let you know as soon as he knows something, okay?"

We nodded and resumed our waiting. Another hour went by. It was well past lunch by this time. Beverly offered to go get us a sandwich, but we didn't feel like eating. We urged Beverly to go eat, but she refused to leave our side.

A few minutes later, Justine came out into the lobby again and sat beside Brandon and me on the couch. Beverly slipped over to entertain Kate while we talked with Justine. "I just got off the phone with Dr. Pui," she began. "He is still in his meeting, but most of Kate's labs have come back. He said that Huntsville had reported Kate's myelocytes as being at six, but our lab here is reporting at one. This number alone is making him lean toward this just being a stomach bug. But he does want to get the rest of her labs back before being certain."

My spirits rose and hope flamed in my heart. I didn't want to celebrate just yet until we had met with Dr. Pui, but I knew they wouldn't give us false hope. Hesitant smiles spread across Brandon's face and mine. "So we can breathe a little bit?" Brandon asked.

Justine smiled. "Yes. I will call you back as soon as he gets out of his meeting and the rest of Kate's labs are back." She gave us quick hugs and went back inside clinic.

Beverly eased back over with a questioning look on her face and praised God when I told her the news. It wasn't much longer before we heard Kate's name being paged to report to A Clinic. Beverly hugged us and we gathered our things to meet with Dr. Pui.

We settled into the room and waited on Dr. Pui to join us. Just a few minutes later, he entered the room with a huge smile on his face and a slight bounce to his step. Any lingering fears in my heart were immediately washed away.

"It's just a virus!" he announced, beaming. "There was no trace of leukemia cells in her blood."

Brandon and I smiled in relief and inwardly thanked God. While joy filled our hearts at this news, we couldn't fully celebrate. We still had to figure out what was going on with Kate. Dr. Pui immediately sat down and began throwing out orders to Justine, who was hurriedly jotting down his instructions. He wanted to alter Kate's antibiotics and wanted more blood drawn to begin running tests to determine what was plaguing Kate. Dr. Pui also wanted to push back Kate's end of treatment visit to Memphis to allow her an extra couple of weeks to get over this virus, regain her strength, and give her counts a chance to rise. Our minds were whirling at the new information and Justine promised to type everything out for us, once Dr. Pui finalized everything.

After Dr. Pui finished with Kate, we began to file out of the room. I stopped at the door, turned around, and walked back to Dr. Pui, who was still sitting at the computer.

I leaned over and hugged him from the side. "Thank you for taking such good care of our daughter, Dr. Pui."

He never made eye contact with me and abruptly replied, "Okay, okay, okay."

But he had a small smile on his face.

Brandon, Kate, and I first went back to assessment triage for Kate to have more blood drawn. After Kate's labs were drawn, we waited on her new medicines in the pharmacy. While we waited, I texted our family and friends the good news.

It was six o'clock in the evening before her meds were ready and we finally made our way back over to the hotel. Kate had been saying she was hungry again, but I firmly decided I would only let her have applesauce and crackers until she went at least two days without throwing up. She begged for everything under the sun—potato soup, tacos, chicken nuggets—but I stood my ground. My goal was for her to keep her food down for the next two days. We all snacked on some crackers before going to bed.

Physically and emotionally drained, we slept well that night and woke early to report back to the hospital that morning. While Brandon and I got ready, Kate watched a show about African animals on television. We scrambled about, packing up the room, and flipped off the television once we were ready to go, not paying a lot of attention to what was playing on the television. We paused, though, as we noticed Kate sitting on the bed, her bottom lip trembling.

Brandon knelt down beside the bed next to her. "Kate, are you okay?" he asked.

Kate tried to say something and bit her lip as she tried not to cry. She suddenly broke down and sobbed a pitiful heartbreaking cry. Brandon pulled her into his lap and sat on the edge of the bed as she cried onto his shoulder, tears streaming down his face now too.

I sat on the bed next to them, rubbing Kate's back, as my tears flowed as well. *She finally understands what all has been going on the past couple of days*, I thought, and my heart hurt for our little girl who'd had to grow up way too fast.

"Do you want to talk about it?" I asked Kate gently.

Kate's sobs gradually began to slow down as she stumbled through her words. "The horse died." Uttering those words caused a new wave of sobs.

I was confused. "The horse?"

Understanding dawned on Brandon's face. "The show she had been watching at first went off and the next show was an animal rescue show. I caught a glimpse of a horse that was lying down, but didn't think anything about it."

We both gave sad smiles at each other over Kate's shoulder and our hearts softened. No, she didn't understand what had transpired over the past twenty-four hours. Instead her little tender heart grieved for the horse she had seen on the television.

We headed to A Clinic once again that morning. There was no news from Kate's bloodwork the day before, but Justine said they would call us if they determined the cause of Kate's illness. We met briefly with a nutritionist to come up with ideas of foods that would be easy on Kate's stomach and then went home.

Jenna was still under the weather in Florence with Grammy and Papa Don and Elijah had joined her in running a low grade fever. We stopped by to check on them, being sure to keep Kate away from them because her counts were still low. Grammy and Papa Don were going to the beach the next day and planned to drop Jenna and Elijah off at my parents' house in

Birmingham on the way down, so Brandon, Kate, and I headed home to rest and recuperate.

After a couple of days of keeping her food down, we slowly let Kate branch out to foods other than crackers and applesauce. We tried a new food group each day and breathed a sigh of relief when she kept them down. The stomach bug had officially and finally made its way out of Kate.

As you ran around outside playing one morning a couple of days after we came home, I was amazed at the difference between that day and just two days earlier. Forty-eight hours earlier, we had been in such a dark place—with doubt and fear overpowering our hearts. Forty-eight hours earlier, we thought your cancer had returned and that we were about to begin our journey all over again. Forty-eight hours earlier, we had been robbed of our joy.

As I said before, the Devil is awfully good at what he does—sowing seeds of doubt and stealing joy. As you remained sick for so long with the stomach bug, the Devil sprinkled his seeds into our hearts. We doubted if God had really healed you and our faith wavered. We doubted God's promise of saving you. Maybe His plan of salvation for you was not a physical one and His plan for you was not our plan.

And our joy was gone. At a time when we should have been exuberantly counting down the last few weeks of treatment, we were worried sick about a stomach bug that was ravaging your body. At a time when we should have been shouting for joy at the words "no more chemo," we were terrified of that horrible word "relapse." This was not the way our journey was supposed to end.

But God would not let the Devil claim victory. God chose you, Kate, to display all His glorious majesty. All these years, all the thousands of prayers uttered for you, all the sweet children who prayed for you every night—these souls would see the power of God to heal.

And this last huge trial was one more display of how God hears and answers our prayers. Your myelocyte level at Huntsville Hospital was at six percent, a strong indicator that cancer cells were once again present in your blood. However, the very next day at St. Jude, your myelocytes were reported at one percent.

That is the power of prayer. That is the power and glory and magnificence of our God!

And our joy comes from Him!

Love,
Mommy

"The Lord is my rock and my fortress and my deliverer, my God, my rock, in whom I take refuge, my shield, and the horn of my salvation, my stronghold and my refuge, my savior; you save me from violence. I call upon the Lord, who is worthy to be praised, and I am saved from my enemies" (2 Samuel 22:2-4).

"The Lord will fulfill his purpose for me; your steadfast love, O Lord, endures forever. Do not forsake the work of your hands" (Psalms 138:8).

"But when Jesus heard it he said, 'This illness does not lead to death. It is for the glory of God, so that the Son of God may be glorified through it'" (John 11:4).

Chapter 19: A New Land

November 7, 2015

Dear Kate,

Everyone has a scar or two from their childhood. And each and every scar has a story behind it.

There was a time when an outsider could look at you and take a guess at what you were going through. The bald head, the bruised arms from busted veins, the "moon face" from steroids, the lump on your chest where your port lay hidden—all were telltale signs of something bigger.

At the close of your journey, all that will remain as a reminder of your journey is a scar.

But what a story that little scar will have!

That scar will represent two years and seven months—145 infusions of chemotherapy, 555 doses of steroids, 531 doses of oral chemotherapy, seventeen blood transfusions, ten platelet transfusions, and countless rounds of antibiotics and other infusions.

That scar will say that you are a fighter! You have had to battle a monster that no child should ever have to face. You are a survivor!

But most of all, that scar will tell that God is mighty and faithful. It will shout that God heard our prayers and smiled down on you. It will say that you were healed by our Creator and Maker. That will be your scar's greatest story!

We reported to the Affiliate Clinic in Huntsville the following Tuesday for a count check, and Kate's counts were completely normal again. I was amazed at the drastic difference from that visit to the visit we had made just a week before.

As we left the clinic, we scheduled Kate's No Mo' Chemo party for the following Tuesday, right before we would leave for Memphis for her end-of-treatment appointments. We had postponed and rescheduled and postponed it long enough! I was so glad our time for celebrating was almost here!

The next week, we loaded the car for Memphis but first went to the Affiliate Clinic for Kate's party. Nonna, P-Daddy, and Grammy met us in the parking lot and we all went in together as a family to close this chapter of Kate's life.

Kate and I passed out gift bags to all the staff when we arrived. Each bag contained a photograph of Kate with the staff member, a picture Kate had drawn, and a card from me. There were about twenty staff members in all, and she and I had been working for months on those gift bags!

Krysee, the music therapist, was in charge of Kate's party and the back of clinic was decked out with a congratulatory banner signed by the clinic staff as well as colorful streamers and balloons. The table was adorned with a cake and presents galore. Brandon and I provided lunch for the clinic that day, so a local restaurant had set up a taco bar in the back as well. It was very festive, just as it should have been! We were celebrating something huge!

Our family stood together as everyone else at clinic—nurses, doctors, patients, and their family members—gathered around opposite us to sing farewell to Kate. With Krysee leading on guitar, they launched into the traditional No Mo' Chemo farewell song. We had waited two years and seven months to hear this song being sung to us. It felt surreal for it to finally be our turn, and my smile was so big I was sure my face was going to break. I held Kate in my arms while Brandon held us from behind and we soaked up the moment as everyone sang farewell.

I held it together as the song came to a close, but suddenly, as the last note was sung, everyone pulled out a toy dinosaur from behind their backs and roared at Kate. This roar had been Kate's trademark at the clinic as she greeted her nurses and other patients every week with a mighty dinosaur roar.

And suddenly, the tears poured.

Caroline, Kate's nurse, had been missing during the song and found Kate afterward. She scooped Kate up in her arms and they stood chatting in the corner of the room. Tears were flowing from Caroline's eyes.

"I'm going to miss you very much, my sweet Kate," she said, hugging Kate close.

Kate was very serious. "I'm going to miss you too, Caroline. I will try every Tuesday from now on to think of you."

My heart warmed as I witnessed this special bond between a patient and her nurse.

Along Kate's journey, we met some amazing people who wear the seemingly simple title "nurse." These amazing women—and a few men—have made this trial so much easier to bear with their joyful attitudes, loving hearts, encouraging spirits, and tireless devotion to so many.

A nurse isn't just someone who gives medicines and shots, takes vitals, and records numbers. Being a nurse goes far beyond this typical job description. Kate's nurses have fetched blankets and pillows for Jenna, grabbed drinks and food for me, and changed Elijah's diaper. They have called to check on Kate and have stayed late for long chemotherapy days. Her nurses have danced with our girls, rocked a crying baby boy in their arms, hugged me when I was at my lowest, and been genuine and honest every step of the way.

They did these things not because it was required of them, but because it was in their hearts to care for us like that. The nature of a nurse is to be a servant to others, and their care goes far beyond medicine and needles.

From the beginning, I thought that I would be crying at Kate's No Mo' Chemo party because I would be so happy to be done. Now that the end was here, my tears were bittersweet. Obviously, I was overjoyed to move on from this trial. But rivaling the joy was the heartache of missing these dear nurses whom we had come to love so much.

They had not just become our friends. They had become our *family.*

Kate and Caroline hugged and chatted for a few more minutes as we began cleaning up. It was nearly time to leave for Memphis. We hugged everyone as we left, but knew we would be back soon for a count check. I hugged Caroline especially hard as we left and smiled through teary eyes at this dear nurse whose exuberance and charm had won our hearts from the beginning.

In the parking lot, we said goodbye to our parents. Nonna and P-Daddy would be joining us in Memphis the following day, so we told them we'd see them soon and then headed west for the last time with a chemo patient!

The next morning started off with an appointment with our social worker at St. Jude, followed by lunch and a visit with a psychologist. The psychology appointment was conducted to determine if Kate's cognitive development had been affected by the years of chemotherapy. Brandon had taken Jenna and Elijah back to the Tri Delta Place for a nap, so I took Kate for her appointment. I sat in the waiting room until Kate was done and it wasn't much longer before the psychologist escorted Kate to the waiting room.

"She did fine," the psychologist offered as Kate sat down beside me on the bench. "I don't see any areas of concern. In fact, she performed very well in reading and spelling!"

As her mother—and her kindergarten teacher—I felt very proud!

"Thank you," I replied and Kate and I waved goodbye as we left.

Nonna and P-Daddy had arrived at the Tri Delta Place during Kate's appointment, so we were happy to see them for our big celebration the following morning.

The next day was a huge day for Kate! While this visit would not include Kate's last round of chemo as originally planned, she still had numerous tests and appointments scheduled for the day as well as her last round of pentamidine, the antibiotic to prevent pneumonia.

Brandon took a fasting Kate to assessment triage early that morning to be accessed and have blood drawn. The appointment went quickly, and he and Kate headed straight for her next appointment to have a CT scan.

I stayed behind to get Jenna and Elijah fed and dressed. As we sat in the breakfast area of Tri Delta Place, I reflected a moment on the very beginning of our journey. I had sat in this same room on our third day at St. Jude and overheard a grandmother talking to her granddaughter on the phone and congratulating her on her last day of chemo. And I had cried because that day seemed so far away for us. Well, today it was our turn to celebrate the end of our journey.

Jenna, Elijah, and I joined Brandon and Kate at the hospital and went to A Clinic to meet with Dr. Pui for the last time under therapy. He was happy for us and we thanked him once again for taking such good care of Kate. Kate's nurses gathered to sing her No Mo' Chemo song and throw confetti on everyone, and once again we reveled in the moment. Kate lifted her face and hands in sheer joy and triumph as the confetti rained down on us. Our celebration came to an end when Dr. Pui (with a smile) hollered at the nurses, "Now get back to work!"

After the song, we passed out gift bags to Dr. Pui and Kate's regular nurses and distributed cupcakes to the nurses in assessment triage, A Clinic, procedures, and the medicine room.

Then we went to the Chili's Care Center to wait for Kate to be called back for her MRI and bone marrow aspiration. She was still fasting, and as it was nearing noon she was starving. Nonna and P-Daddy joined us and were a nice distraction for about a minute before Kate resumed complaining of how hungry she was.

"Just remember," I told her, "this is the last time you ever have to do this!"

"She has to have her port out in a few weeks and she will have to fast for that," Brandon reminded me.

"This is the *next* to last time you ever have to do this!" I corrected myself with a peppy smile.

Kate was not amused.

Kate and I planned her menu for what she wanted to eat when she woke up and the first thing on her list was a turkey sandwich with cheese and tomatoes. I assured her I would have a turkey sandwich waiting for her when she woke up.

Finally, around one o'clock, Kate was called back. Only one parent was allowed to go back, so Brandon went to be by her side. The rest of us ate lunch and returned to Tri Delta Place. Nonna and P-Daddy took Jenna to the playground while I settled Elijah down for a nap. Brandon joined us an hour or so later after Kate's procedure had begun. The nurse said she would call us when Kate was done.

About an hour later, Brandon's phone rang and he and I went back to the hospital while Nonna and P-Daddy kept Jenna and Elijah. We planned to meet them at the cafeteria for dinner once Kate had finished with her last appointment in the medicine room.

Kate was still sound asleep when we arrived at recovery at the Chili's Care Center, so Brandon and I sat by her bedside, chatting with her nurse and doctor while we patiently waited for her to wake up.

Ten minutes went by before Kate stirred. Without even opening her eyes, Kate mumbled, "Where's my turkey sandwich?"

Brandon and I both laughed and I quickly reached in my bag and pulled out her turkey sandwich. "Right here!" I announced.

Kate sleepily opened her eyes and reached for it. She began munching on it as her nurse checked her vitals. Everything looked great and she unhooked Kate, declaring she was ready to go! I carted her over to the medicine room for her final infusion of pentamidine while Brandon went to meet everyone else for dinner in the cafeteria.

330

The nurse got Kate hooked up immediately and I put in a movie for Kate to watch as she finished her turkey sandwich. The pentamidine ran for an hour and then she was done.

Done!

Done!

As her nurse unhooked her from her line and de-accessed her port, I told Kate, "That was it! You are done!"

Her nurse paused. "Done? As in completely done?"

I smiled with tears in my eyes. "As in completely done!"

She smiled back. "Well, congratulations!" she told Kate.

While we didn't get to savor the moment of Kate's final round of chemo, I was cherishing this moment of the final infusion and the final de-accessing! Joy filled my soul!

I put Kate into her wagon and she lay down as I pulled her out of the medicine room. It was around six in the evening by this point, and the halls of the hospital were quiet and empty. I felt a little dazed as I pulled Kate down the hall to the cafeteria. This was the last time we would walk the halls of St. Jude as a cancer family. This was the last time I would pull my daughter in a wagon, sleepy from her anesthesia, down these halls. This was the last day of a very long and grueling trial. The moment seemed surreal once again.

The dazed feeling left as soon as we found the rest of our family waiting for us in the cafeteria. They had mostly finished eating, and I ate Jenna's leftovers while Kate rested in her wagon. After we cleaned up our area, we returned to our rooms for a good night's sleep. It had been a long day, but to say it had been a good one would be an understatement.

The next morning, my parents and some of the moms and kids from Bartlett Church of Christ came to the Tri Delta Place to celebrate no more chemo for Kate. We celebrated with some sweet tea and cupcakes, per Kate's request, and enjoyed visiting with everyone. After a little while, everyone packed up to go their different ways and we walked upstairs to dress the kids for Halloween. It was Halloween Eve and St. Jude was legendary for trick-or-treating!

Every department at St. Jude, totaling about sixty, had selected a theme for their trick-or-treating booths. These themes ranged from princesses to the circus to mythical creatures and more. Every booth was intent on handing out more candy than the booth next to them. The kids, Nonna and P-Daddy, Brandon, and I filed in line, weaving our way around to each booth. We had only made it about halfway through and the kids had already collected more candy than they could eat in a lifetime! We began politely refusing any more candy and just told everyone we wanted to see their booths and costumes!

By the time we'd made it through all sixty booths, the kids were hungry and worn out. We stopped at a local restaurant on the way out of town for a quick lunch and all three kids fell asleep for the rest of the way home.

During the ride home, I received a call from Martha May.

"Erin?" she asked when I answered the phone. "It's Martha. Are you on your way home?"

"We are," I replied, holding my breath for her next words. Brandon glanced at me with a questioning look on his face.

"Well, I'm calling with good news from Kate's bone marrow aspiration yesterday. Her MRD was negative, meaning she is still in remission!"

I gave Brandon a thumbs-up and smiled. "I wasn't expecting anything different," I told her, "but that is still nice to hear!"

"I have the report from her bone density scan as well," she informed me. "Her bones are showing weakness from the years of chemotherapy. However, her levels are not low enough that she will need medication. Just focus on a calcium-enriched diet to help boost her calcium and vitamin D levels."

We talked briefly about the next few appointments coming up for Kate. Kate would have her port removed in Huntsville in the next few weeks, we would report to the Affiliate Clinic in Huntsville after the Christmas holidays for a count check, and we would return to Memphis to see Dr. Pui in February. I wasn't sure what I would do with myself if I did not have to haul three kids to the clinic every Tuesday!

After we arrived at home later that afternoon, we got the kids settled in bed for the night. As I unpacked, I pulled out the Ziploc gallon storage bag containing Kate's medications and began unloading its contents one at a time—dexamethasone, oxycodone, diphenhydramine, ranitidine, 6mp, ondansetron, nexium, gabapentin, and more. I pulled out the single bottle of acetaminophen I had brought, just in case, for Jenna and Elijah. I took one look at that single bottle for our two youngest children and then looked at the cluster of medications for Kate.

I turned to Brandon, who was reading through our mail on the kitchen counter behind me.

"I'm ready to cry now," I whispered to him.

"Huh?" he asked, not having heard me.

"I'm ready to cry now," I repeated. I held out my arms for him as my face crumpled.

Brandon's expression softened as he gathered me into his arms. We stood there in our kitchen for some time and Brandon held me while I cried. My tears were slow and purposeful—each one significant and each one symbolic. I shed a tear for each chemo Kate received, a tear for every milliliter of every dose of steroids Kate received, a tear for every scream of pain uttered by our child, a tear for each and every worry-filled day, a tear for every ounce of fear that filled my heart. The flow seemed never-ending.

But finally, the last tear fell—the most special tear of all. This tear represented our new normal of life after cancer.

The next week, we geared up for Kate's final No Mo' Chemo party and fundraiser for St. Jude with all our family and friends. Brandon and I had reserved our neighborhood's clubhouse for this special occasion. I had a friend put together a photo and video montage to show too. We'd also asked local restaurants and a local florist for donations to help keep our costs minimal. The bouquets were to present to Kate's doctors and nurses. A couple of restaurants even donated gift certificates for our parents as a thank you for all they had done.

We also had two big reveals we planned to share!

It had been a lot of hard work over the past few months to coordinate the party, but I knew the celebration would be worth every ounce of effort I had put in to it.

The long awaited day finally arrived! The clubhouse looked beautiful, thanks to the help of some of my friends the night before. These sweet friends had stayed late, helping string hundreds of cards from the ceiling. Kate had received all of them over the past two and a half years. The cards lined the walls all the way around the clubhouse—and we still had hundreds left over! We had also hung pink and orange pom-poms, laid pink and orange tablecloths, and hung banners around the room that some teenagers from church had made. It was perfect.

The party was "come and go" with a special presentation before lunch, and guests began to trickle in at ten that morning. We had set up a table outside where guests could sign scrapbook pages for Kate, purchase a T-shirt, and make a donation to St. Jude in lieu of gifts. (We ended up raising $5,000 for St. Jude that day!)

We enjoyed visiting with our friends and family, some who'd driven for a few hours to share our special occasion, and before I knew it, it was time to begin our presentation.

Brandon and I went to the hearth around the stone fireplace where we'd set up a speaker and microphone, and I nervously handed Brandon his script. I pulled Kate up beside the hearth with us as Brandon got everyone's attention. Kate froze when she realized everyone was beginning to look at her and ducked behind me, her thumb going immediately in her mouth. I motioned for Jenna to come up and join us, but she shook her head no and sat in the floor in front of us with her buddies. Elijah was hanging out in the crowd with a friend.

Once everyone had gathered into the clubhouse and gotten quiet, Brandon began our speech.

L. Erin Miller

"Our daughter, Elizabeth Kate Miller, was diagnosed with Acute Lymphoblastic Leukemia on March 26, 2013. She was three years old. At diagnosis, Kate's white blood cell count was 539,000, more than one hundred times that of a normal person, and her platelets and hemoglobin had reached critical levels. She was sent to ICU at St. Jude in Memphis and placed in the care of Dr. Ching-Hon Pui, a world-renowned specialist in childhood leukemia.

"Within just a day or two of being at St. Jude, we knew it would always have a place in our hearts. St. Jude has covered every medical expense we've incurred for the past two and a half years. St. Jude also covered all expenses during our stays in Memphis, including shelter, food, and reimbursement for gas. We have never been given a bill from St. Jude. Not one.

"St. Jude is the only pediatric cancer research hospital where families never pay for treatment not covered by insurance. No child is ever denied treatment because of the family's inability to pay. Thirty percent of St. Jude's revenue comes from insurance and the other seventy percent comes from donations. It costs over two million dollars a day to make St. Jude run! Kate's first phase of treatment, induction, lasted six weeks during which she achieved remission. Her second phase of treatment, consolidation, lasted eight weeks, and the final phase of treatment, continuation, lasted 120 weeks.

"During Kate's treatment for cancer, she had seventeen blood transfusions; ten platelet transfusions; twenty-eight lumbar punctures; 531 doses of 6mp, her oral chemo; and 555 doses of steroids. Through her port, Kate received fifty infusions of methotrexate, four twenty-four hour infusions of high dose methotrexate, five infusions of doxorubicin, two infusions of daunorubicin, thirty-three infusions of vincristine, thirteen of cyclophosphamide, seventeen infusions of cytarabine, four of high dose cytarabine, and seventeen infusions of pegaspargase. This totals to 145 infusions of chemotherapy!

"Though there were tough times, Kate always bounced back. She has a zeal for life, is kind and compassionate toward others, and has quite a sense of humor. She is brave. And now, after two and a half years, Kate gets No Mo' Chemo!"

A cheer erupted from the crowd and I hugged our little hero standing beside me, her face still buried against me.

Brandon continued, sharing our first big announcement.

"In honor of Kate's fight and the fight of so many other children battling cancer, we have established Fighting for Kate, a non-profit organization, to fundraise for St. Jude Children's Research Hospital and for children battling cancer. The goals of Fighting for Kate are to raise awareness of childhood cancer; to educate on the extensive treatment plan for leukemia; to fundraise for St. Jude and children undergoing treatment for cancer; to recognize and honor the doctors, nurses, and staff in pediatric oncology; and to celebrate God's power to heal!

"Today, through our T-shirt sale and your donations, marks the first official fundraiser held by Fighting for Kate…with more to come! Our next endeavor will be to form a team to run the St. Jude Rock N Roll Marathon and Half Marathon in Nashville at the end of April.

"We'd like to take a minute to recognize some special people who have seen us through the past two and a half years."

Brandon paused as I motioned for our parents to join us. I grabbed a pair of envelopes from off the fireplace as he began to read.

"We first want to recognize our parents, Kate's grandparents. It is a terrible thing to watch your child suffer, but our parents had a double blow as they not only had to watch their children suffering, but their granddaughter as well. Our parents dropped everything to help us out after Kate was diagnosed. When we came home from Memphis the first time, our house had been cleaned from top to bottom, even our carpets had been steam cleaned. They took care of Jenna whenever necessary and came to visit us at the Ronald McDonald House during our extended stays there. We are so thankful for their encouragement and support, even during their own battles with cancer, over the past two and a half years."

L. Erin Miller

There was a round of applause as I handed each set of grandparents an envelope containing a gift certificate for a night out to dinner. We hugged them and they snuck hugs from Kate, who was still clutching my leg with one hand and sucking her thumb with the other.

"We also want to recognize our youngest two children—Jenna and Elijah." Brandon scanned the crowd for our kids. "They're out there somewhere." A friend from church waved Elijah's hand in the air and I pointed out Jenna to Brandon.

"They say when a family member is diagnosed with cancer, the whole family is diagnosed. That statement could not be truer. While Kate has had the much more difficult journey of enduring chemotherapy, steroids, and more, it is not just us as her parents who are walking her journey with her. It is her siblings, too.

"Jenna and Elijah went to Memphis with Kate. They went to the clinic every Tuesday with Kate and spent most of the day there. They ate hospital food, took naps in darkened exam rooms, played with medical toys, lived in isolation when Kate did, suffered the backlash from Kate's steroid mood swings, and they loved Kate's nurses as their best friends just as Kate did. Kate is not the only courageous child we have. Jenna and Elijah have been there to see her through it all. So let's hear it for Jenna and Elijah!"

Everyone cheered and clapped once again. When the applause died down, Brandon added, "Sorry Jenna and Elijah. We don't have any gifts for you. You are spoiled enough anyway!"

The crowd laughed and Brandon continued, "Next, we would like to recognize the St. Jude Affiliate Clinic staff. When most hear of St. Jude, they think of the main hospital in Memphis, Tennessee. Many do not know that there are eight St. Jude Affiliate Clinics, one of which is located here in Huntsville." A dozen or so of Kate's doctors and nurses came to stand at our side and Kate, who was gradually beginning to overcome her stage fright, smiled at them.

"Over the past two and a half years, these people standing before you have become a part of our family, and the clinic became our home away from home. These wonderful doctors, nurses, and staff have seen us at our lowest of lows and at our highest of highs. They have supported us through difficult times and cheered us on to the finish line."

Brandon turned to look at the faces of these ladies we had grown to love so much.

"We can't thank you enough for taking such wonderful care of Kate, but thank you most of all for loving her." Each member of the staff came forward and Kate presented each one with a long-stemmed red rose and a big hug.

After all the staff had been presented a rose, Brandon turned to the crowd in front of us.

"We also want to thank all of you for your support. Every note written, every prayer offered, every meal brought, every word of encouragement helped renew our strength to make it through each hurdle. It is such an amazing privilege and blessing to be a part of the family of Christ."

Brandon paused for a moment before wrapping up his presentation. "This journey we have made has obviously, hands down, been the hardest thing we have ever faced in our lives. There were tears, there was anger, there was frustration, there was despair. We never could have borne this burden alone. God, through His Word, the Bible, through His servants, and through the avenue of prayer, gave us enough strength to muddle through. He took the rest of the burden Himself. Time and time again, God answered our prayers. He, through Kate, displayed all His glory, power, and majesty. So may every breath Kate takes remind you of the power of prayer and of just how much we are loved by our Father in heaven. Every time you look at Kate, may you always remember that she was healed by the great I AM! Praise God from whom all blessings flow!"

A hearty "Amen" resounded from the crowd and Brandon took a moment to compose himself before he let a special guest take over. "Now we have a surprise for Kate and our family today!"

Brandon handed the microphone to two volunteers from Make-A-Wish—our second big announcement! After introducing themselves, one volunteer shared that Kate had requested to meet a unicorn for her wish.

Suddenly, the crowd parted and a couple of friends brought out a giant stuffed unicorn for Kate. It was almost as tall as she was! We laughed and the smile that lit up Kate's face was priceless.

The other volunteer spoke up as Kate hugged her unicorn tight. "Kate also had a wish to go to the Walt Disney World Resort. Well, guess what? The Millers are going!"

Everyone cheered and once they quieted down, Brandon began the photo and video montage that our friend had put together for us. As I watched it, Kate in my lap, Jenna by my side, Elijah chattering somewhere behind us, and Brandon's hand in mine, I thought my heart would burst. We had waited so long for our joy to come. We had waited through sleepless nights of worry. We had waited through blazing fits from steroids. We had waited through hundreds upon hundreds of hours in hospitals. We had waited through countless needles. We had waited through heartache and pain.

But in the end, God, in His great faithfulness, saw us through it all. He, in His abundant mercy, allowed our little girl to be healed.

All along, He was fighting for Kate.

And He saved her.

I read Deuteronomy 8:2-10 just a few weeks before you finished chemo, Kate. I pray that as we resume a normal life and time goes by, we will never forget how God has seen us through the wilderness during the past two and a half years.

Bless the Lord, oh my soul, for bringing us into a new land of life after cancer!

Love,

Mommy

"And you shall remember the whole way that the Lord your God has led you these forty years in the wilderness, that he might humble you, testing you to know what was in your heart, whether you would keep his commandments or not. And he humbled you and let you hunger and fed you with manna, which you did not know, nor did your fathers know, that he might make you know that man does not live by bread alone, but man lives by every word that comes from the mouth of the Lord. Your clothing did not wear out on you and your foot did not swell these forty years. Know then in your heart that, as a man disciplines his son, the Lord your God disciplines you. So you shall keep the commandments of the Lord your God by walking in his ways and by fearing him. For the Lord your God is bringing you into a good land, a land of brooks of water, of fountains and springs, flowing out in valleys and hills, a land of wheat and barley, of vines and fig trees and pomegranates, a land of olive trees and honey, a land in which you will eat bread without scarcity, in which you will lack nothing, a land whose stones are iron, and out of whose hills you can dig copper. And you shall eat and be full, and you shall bless the Lord your God for the good land he has given you" (Deuteronomy 8:2-10).

"Bless the Lord, O my soul, and all that is within me, bless His holy name! Bless the Lord, O my soul, and forget not all his benefits, who forgives all your iniquity, who heals all your diseases, who redeems your life from the pit, who crowns you with steadfast love and mercy, who satisfies you with good so that your youth is renewed like the eagle's" (Psalms 103:1-5).

"O Lord my God, I cried to you for help, and you have healed me" (Psalms 30:2).

Epilogue

Kate had her port removed just a few days before Thanksgiving. It was an emotional day, knowing this was the final step in closing the door on her very long journey.

Our family was able to take Kate's Make-A-Wish trip to the Walt Disney World Resort in January of 2016. It was wonderful. We stayed at Give Kids the World and spent the week park hopping, riding roller coasters, meeting famous Disney characters, and eating delicious food. Give Kids the World even arranged for Kate to meet a "real" unicorn!

Our friend Darcy celebrated her thirteenth birthday in the spring of 2017, something doctors believed would never happen. Darcy battled many side effects as her tumors progressed, and she passed away in October of 2017. Her hometown was covered with pink balloons and bows for her "celebration of life."

My mom enjoyed remission for two years before relapsing. She began a clinical trial and, after another year of chemotherapy, was determined to be in remission once again.

Our nonprofit organization "Fighting for Kate" has been very active and has been our way to give back. We have held a couple of fundraisers for St. Jude and have helped some other St. Jude families through difficult times. We pray that the families we help can see the love of Christ and the power of God to see them through their journey, just as He did for us.

Kate has had a few follow-up visits with Dr. Pui in Memphis since finishing treatment.

She is still in remission.

And God is still good.

And always will be.

> *"Then our mouth was filled with laughter, and our tongue with shouts of joy; then they said among the nations, 'The Lord has done great things for them.' The Lord has done great things for us; we are glad"* (Psalms 126:2-3).

Definition of Terms

A-Clinic—the clinic for leukemia patients at St. Jude Children's Research Hospital.

Absolute Neutrophil Count (ANC)—The ANC is a measure of the number of neutrophils in the blood. Neutrophils are a type of white blood cell responsible for fighting infection. A normal ANC ranges from 1,500 to 8,000. An ANC below 500 is considered neutropenia.

Acute Lymphoblastic Leukemia (ALL)—A cancer of the white blood cells characterized by an overproduction of immature white blood cells known as lymphoblasts. This overproduction inhibits the production of normal blood cells in the bone marrow such as normal white blood cells, hemoglobin, and platelets. ALL is most common in children ages two to five years old.

Assessment triage—The first stop at St. Jude Children's Research Hospital is at assessment triage. Here the nurse took Kate's vitals, measured her weight and height, and accessed her port. From the port, the nurse drew vials of blood to check her blood counts and blood chemistries.

Bone marrow aspiration—A procedure that involves a sample being taken from the soft tissue of the bone. While the patient is under general anesthesia, a needle is inserted into the spine. The sample is examined to determine if cancer cells are present.

Chili's Care Center—Located at St. Jude Children's Research Hospital, this building houses laboratories, inpatient rooms and clinics, as well as outpatient clinics.

Consolidation—The second phase of Kate's treatment, after induction. This phase is designed to further reduce the number of cancer cells and increase the likelihood of complete remission. Kate received four rounds of high dose methotrexate over the course of two months during this phase.

Continuation (or maintenance)—The third and final phase of Kate's treatment, after induction and consolidation. Kate received one or more chemotherapies every week for 120 weeks during continuation.

CT scan—A series of X-ray images taken at different angles. Kate had a few CT scans to check her bones and lungs.

Cyclophosphamide—A chemotherapy used to treat leukemia. Kate received thirteen infusions of cyclophosphamide, as well as hours of fluids before and after to flush this chemo out of her bladder. Side effects include infertility, secondary cancers, and ulcers in the bladder. It is considered a "count dropper" chemo.

Cytarabine (Ara-C)—A chemotherapy used to treat leukemia. Kate received seventeen infusions of cytarabine and four infusions of high dose cytarabine. Cytarabine is considered a "count dropper" chemo.

Daunorubicin—A chemotherapy used to treat leukemia. Kate received two infusions of daunorubicin. Common side effects include hair loss and vomiting. It is considered a "count dropper" chemo.

Dexamethasone (DEX)—A steroid used during continuation. Kate took this steroid three times a day for five days every four weeks. She had 555 doses of DEX. Common side effects are upset stomach, mood swings, and increased appetite.

Diphenhydramine (Benadryl)—This medicine was used as a third-tier anti-nausea medicine. We learned that Kate absolutely had to be premedicated with both ondansetron and diphenhydramine before anesthesia in procedures to prevent vomiting when she woke up.

Doxorubicin—A chemotherapy used to treat leukemia. Kate received five infusions of doxorubicin. Another name for this chemo is "red devil" or "red death" due to its dangerous side effects and red color. Side effects include hair loss, bone marrow suppression, heart damage, and secondary cancers.

Eclipse—An intravenous medicine ball for Kate's prophylactic antibiotics.

Gabapentin—Nerve pain medication to offset the effects of the chemo vincristine.

Grizzlies/Tri Delta Place—Short-term housing for up to one week stays on the St. Jude Children's Research Hospital campus.

Hemoglobin—A red protein responsible for carrying oxygen in the blood. A normal hemoglobin for children ranges 11-13. A blood transfusion is needed when the hemoglobin drops below 7-8.

Intravenous Immunoglobulin (IVIg)—Immunoglobulins are part of your blood's plasma that fight germs or disease. Because Kate's treatment for leukemia was prolonged, her immunoglobulins were wiped out, causing her to get sick more often. She received an IVIg every four weeks to help boost her body's ability to fight off germs.

Induction—The first phase of treatment for leukemia. The goal of induction is to achieve remission, although millions of leukemia cells can still remain. (Hence the need for consolidation and continuation.) Kate achieved remission on day forty-two of induction.

Intensive Care Unit (ICU)—A special department of a hospital that provides intensive treatment. Kate spent her first week after diagnosis in the ICU at St. Jude Children's Research Hospital and spent many weeks due to fevers and pneumonia in PICU at our local hospital throughout her treatment.

Leucovorin—A medication given eighteen and twenty-four hours after Kate's high dose methotrexate to prevent it from damaging her kidneys.

Low bacteria diet—A diet Kate adhered to when her immune system was suppressed. Kate had to avoid raw fruits and vegetables, leftovers, any food or drink that had been sitting out for more than an hour, tea, raw honey, soft cheeses, and more. The goal was to keep her body free of bacteria that may be present on these foods and beverages.

Lumbar puncture with intrathecal chemotherapy (LPIT or spinal tap)—Because leukemia cells were found in Kate's spinal fluid, she received twenty-eight rounds of intrathecal chemotherapy. Kate was put to sleep in procedures at St. Jude Children's Research Hospital and had three rounds of chemo—hydrocortisone, Ara-C, and methotrexate—sent to her brain to kill any leukemia cells.

Medicine room—The medicine room located at St. Jude Children's Research Hospital is open twenty-four hours a day, seven days a week, including holidays. Patients receive chemotherapy, blood products, and other medicines in this area. It also operates as an after-hours clinic.

Mercaptopurine (6mp)—An oral chemotherapy taken for leukemia. For most of Kate's treatment, 6mp had to be refrigerated and taken at night after fasting for two hours. Kate took 531 doses of 6mp. She never missed a scheduled dose of 6mp.

Methotrexate—A chemotherapy used for treatment for leukemia. Kate received fifty infusions of methotrexate and four infusions of high dose methotrexate. Common side effects are vomiting, hair loss, and liver problems.

Minimal Residual Disease (MRD)—The name given to cancer cells in the bone marrow. A negative MRD means the patient has achieved remission.

Monocytes—A type of white blood cell that wards off disease and infection.

Montelukast sodium—An allergy medication.

Myelocytes—An immature white blood cell found in the bone marrow. An increased percentage of myelocytes may indicate the presence of cancer cells.

Neutropenia—A low count of neutrophils, raising the risk of infection.

NPO (nil per os)—A Latin phrase meaning "nothing through the mouth." Kate was NPO for eight hours prior to anesthesia for every LPIT.

Ondansetron (Zofran)—A medicine to prevent nausea and vomiting.

Oxycodone—A narcotic used to treat moderate to severe pain. Kate took oxycodone to offset the pain caused by her chemotherapies and steroids.

Pegaspargase—A chemotherapy used to treat leukemia. Kate received seventeen infusions of it. Common side effects are nausea and weakness.

Pentamidine—An infusion to prevent pneumonia. Kate switched from the antibiotics trimethoprim and sulfamethoxazole to the infusion pentamidine once a month during her treatment.

Platelets—A blood cell that helps the body form clots to stop bleeding. A normal platelet count is between 150,000 and 300,000. A critical platelet count is under 25,000 and a transfusion is necessary.

Prednisone—A steroid used during induction. Kate took prednisone three times a day for forty days. Common side effects are mood swings, depression, and weight gain.

Procedures—An area at St. Jude Children's Research Hospital where Kate was put to sleep for her LPITs.

Prophylactic antibiotics—Antibiotics used to prevent infections. When Kate's ANC and white blood cell counts were critical for prolonged times, she was put on up to three prophylactic antibiotics to prevent infections.

Ranitidine—An antacid used to offset the side effects of steroids. Whenever Kate was on steroids, she also took ranitidine.

Red blood cells—A type of blood cell responsible for oxygen delivery to the body's tissues.

Re-induction—Re-induction one (weeks seven to nine of continuation) and re-induction two (weeks seventeen to nineteen of continuation) during which Kate received harsher chemotherapies in order to continue to wipe out any lingering leukemia cells.

Ronald McDonald House—Housing provided for families for average length stays (weeks up to several months) at St. Jude Children's Research Hospital. Although minimal, St. Jude covers the cost for families.

Subcutaneous port—A small metal chamber with a rubber top and a flexible tube. It is placed completely under the skin on the chest of the patient and the tube is threaded into the heart. IV medicines and treatments can be given directly into the bloodstream through the port after a needle is inserted through the skin and into the rubber top of the port.

Target House—Long-term housing assigned to St. Jude patients who are expected to be outpatients for a few months to a year.

Trimethoprim and sulfamethoxazole (Septra)—Antibiotics to prevent pneumonia. Kate initially took these three times a day on Mondays, Tuesdays, and Wednesdays for the first year of treatment. Because trimethoprim and sulfamethoxazole can also suppress blood cell counts and Kate's counts were lower than desired, Kate eventually switched to pentamidine.

Vincristine—A chemotherapy used to treat leukemia. Kate received thirty-three infusions of vincristine. Common side effects are nerve damage, difficulty walking, and hair loss.

White blood cells—A type of blood cell involved in protecting the body against disease and bacteria. A normal white blood cell count ranges from 5,000 to 10,000. A critical white blood cell count is less than 500.

Treatment Plan for Acute Lymphoblastic Leukemia

(ALL), Standard/High Risk

Induction

(Patient also takes prednisone three times a day for days 1-40.)

Day	Treatment
1	LPIT, vincristine, daunorubicin
2	leucovorin
3	pegaspargase
4	LPIT
5	leucovorin
8	LPIT, vincristine, daunorubicin
9	leucovorin
11	LPIT
12	leucovorin
15	LPIT with bone marrow aspiration, vincristine, pegaspargase
16	leucovorin
22	LPIT, vincristine, cyclophosphamide, 6mp
23	cytarabine, 6mp
24	cytarabine, 6mp
25	cytarabine, 6mp
26	cytarabine, 6mp
27	6mp
28	6mp
29	6mp
30	cytarabine, 6mp
31	cytarabine, 6mp
32	cytarabine, 6mp

33	cytarabine, 6mp
34	6mp
35	6mp
42	bone marrow aspiration

Consolidation

Patient takes oral chemo 6mp daily, if blood counts are acceptable. During consolidation, the patient has four rounds of high dose methotrexate, infused every two weeks, if blood counts are acceptable.

Continuation

Week	Treatment
1	dexamethasone, doxorubicin, vincristine, pegaspargase, 6mp
2	6mp
3	LPIT, pegaspargase, 6mp
4	dexamethasone, doxorubicin, vincristine, 6mp
5	pegaspargase, 6mp
6	6mp
7	re-induction I: LPIT, dexamethasone, doxorubicin, vincristine, pegaspargase
8	re-induction I: doxorubicin, vincristine
9	re-induction I: dexamethasone, vincristine, pegaspargase
10	6mp
11	doxorubicin, vincristine, pegaspargase, 6mp
12	LPIT, 6mp
13	pegaspargase, 6mp

14	dexamethasone, doxorubicin, vincristine, 6mp
15	pegaspargase, 6mp
16	6mp
17	re-induction II: LPIT, dexamethasone, vincristine, pegaspargase
18	re-induction II: vincristine
19	re-induction II: dexamethasone, vincristine, high dose cytarabine, pegaspargase
20	-
21	pegaspargase, 6mp
22	6mp
23	pegaspargase, 6mp
24	cyclophosphamide, cytarabine
25	LPIT, dexamethasone, vincristine, pegaspargase
26	6mp
27	pegaspargase, 6mp
28	cyclophosphamide, cytarabine
29	LPIT, dexamethasone, vincristine, pegaspargase
30	methotrexate, 6mp
31	methotrexate, 6mp
32	cyclophosphamide, cytarabine
33	LPIT, dexamethasone, vincristine
34	methotrexate, 6mp
35	methotrexate, 6mp
36	cyclophosphamide, cytarabine
37	LPIT, dexamethasone, vincristine
38	methotrexate, 6mp
39	methotrexate, 6mp
40	cyclophosphamide, cytarabine
41	LPIT, dexamethasone, vincristine
42	methotrexate, 6mp

43	methotrexate, 6mp
44	cyclophosphamide, cytarabine
45	LPIT, dexamethasone, vincristine
46	methotrexate, 6mp
47	methotrexate, 6mp
48	cyclophosphamide, cytarabine
49	LPIT, dexamethasone, vincristine
50	methotrexate, 6mp
51	methotrexate, 6mp
52	cyclophosphamide, cytarabine
53	LPIT, dexamethasone, vincristine
54	methotrexate, 6mp
55	methotrexate, 6mp
56	cyclophosphamide, cytarabine
57	LPIT, dexamethasone, vincristine
58	methotrexate, 6mp
59	methotrexate, 6mp
60	cyclophosphamide, cytarabine
61	dexamethasone, vincristine
62	methotrexate, 6mp
63	methotrexate, 6mp
64	cyclophosphamide, cytarabine
65	LPIT, dexamethasone, vincristine
66	methotrexate, 6mp
67	methotrexate, 6mp
68	cyclophosphamide, cytarabine
69	dexamethasone, vincristine
70	methotrexate, 6mp
71	methotrexate, 6mp
72	methotrexate, 6mp

73	LPIT, dexamethasone, vincristine
74	methotrexate, 6mp
75	methotrexate, 6mp
76	methotrexate, 6mp
77	dexamethasone, vincristine
78	methotrexate, 6mp
79	methotrexate, 6mp
80	methotrexate, 6mp
81	LPIT, dexamethasone, vincristine
82	methotrexate, 6mp
83	methotrexate, 6mp
84	methotrexate, 6mp
85	dexamethasone, vincristine
86	methotrexate, 6mp
87	methotrexate, 6mp
88	methotrexate, 6mp
89	LPIT, dexamethasone, vincristine
90	methotrexate, 6mp
91	methotrexate, 6mp
92	methotrexate, 6mp
93	dexamethasone, vincristine
94	methotrexate, 6mp
95	methotrexate, 6mp
96	methotrexate, 6mp
97	LPIT, dexamethasone, vincristine
98	methotrexate, 6mp
99	methotrexate, 6mp
100	methotrexate, 6mp
101	dexamethasone, vincristine
102	methotrexate, 6mp

103	methotrexate, 6mp
104	methotrexate, 6mp
105	methotrexate, 6mp
106	methotrexate, 6mp
107	methotrexate, 6mp
108	methotrexate, 6mp
109	methotrexate, 6mp
110	methotrexate, 6mp
111	methotrexate, 6mp
112	methotrexate, 6mp
113	methotrexate, 6mp
114	methotrexate, 6mp
115	methotrexate, 6mp
116	methotrexate, 6mp
117	methotrexate, 6mp
118	methotrexate, 6mp
119	methotrexate, 6mp
120	methotrexate, 6mp

About the Author

L. Erin Miller is a graduate of Auburn University in elementary education and taught school for six years before choosing to become a stay-at-home mom. She is a member of the Family Advisory Council for St. Jude Children's Research Hospital and is the founder and president of the nonprofit organization Fighting For Kate. Erin resides in Madison, Alabama with her husband and three children.

Erin can be reached at l.erin.miller.author@gmail.com.

Or write to her at:

> L. Erin Miller
> P.O. Box 2255
> Madison, AL 35758

Be sure to like her Facebook page and visit her website at www.lerinmiller.com.

Watch for the Companion Study Guide

Fighting for Kate

Keeping the Faith Through Trials

COMING IN 2018

We are a Christian-based publishing company that was founded in 2009. Our primary focus has been to establish authors.

"5 Fold Media was the launching partner that I needed to bring *The Transformed Life* into reality. This team worked diligently and with integrity to help me bring my words and vision into manifestation through a book that I am proud of and continues to help people and churches around the world. None of this would have been possible without the partnership and education I received from 5 Fold Media."

- Pastor John Carter, Lead Pastor of Abundant Life Christian Center, Syracuse, NY, Author and Fox News Contributor

*The Transformed Life is foreworded by Pastor A.R. Bernard, received endorsements from best-selling authors Phil Cooke, Rick Renner, and Tony Cooke, and has been featured on television shows such as TBN and local networks.

5 Fold Media
5701 E. Circle Dr. #338, Cicero, NY 13039
manuscript@5foldmedia.com

Find us on Facebook, Twitter, and YouTube.

Discover more at www.5FoldMedia.com.

CPSIA information can be obtained
at www.ICGtesting.com
Printed in the USA
LVHW01s0128120118
562777LV00003B/4/P